Tabloid From Hell

Tabloid From Hell

❖

The Rise & Fall of a Beloved Newspaper
2nd Edition

Michael A. Raffaele

Writers Club Press
San Jose New York Lincoln Shanghai

Tabloid From Hell
The Rise & Fall of a Beloved Newspaper

All Rights Reserved © 2002 by Michael A. Raffaele

No part of this book may be reproduced or transmitted in any form or by any means, graphic, electronic, or mechanical, including photocopying, recording, taping, or by any information storage retrieval system, without the permission in writing from the publisher.

Writers Club Press
an imprint of iUniverse, Inc.

For information address:
iUniverse, Inc.
5220 S. 16th St., Suite 200
Lincoln, NE 68512
www.iuniverse.com

ISBN: 0-595-22792-9

Printed in the United States of America

*To City Editor Paul Mickle & The Trentonian sports staff:
You have done a heroic job in miserable working conditions.
You are the heart and soul of the paper.
To Sam the Man, a real artist.*

Contents

Foreword ix
Introduction 1
CHAPTER 1   GLORY DAYS 5
CHAPTER 2   THE 'EVIL' EMPIRE TAKES OVER 159
CHAPTER 3   THE DARK AGES. 195
CHAPTER 4   RESTORE THE ROAR? 209
CHAPTER 5   THE STORY OF A LIFETIME. 231
CHAPTER 6   BLOODBATH. 257
Epilogue 267
Afterword 273
About the Author 299

Foreword

Andy Hussie was angry.

Usually, Hussie and "angry" aren't used in the same sentence.

Hussie and smooth. Hussie and bars. Hussie and drinking. Those are more common thoughts about The Trentonian's veteran copy editor.

But Hussie and "anger" are a rare combination.

It was the spring 1998, and Hussie was indeed angry—angry over the words uttered by Trentonian reporter Chris Dolmetsch.

"(The Trentonian) isn't a good read," Dolmetsch said, "not a good read at all. It's not worth 35 cents."

With his back turned on young cop reporter, Hussie whirled in his chair and said:

"*You got to be kidding me*," Hussie said. "This paper is a marvelous read.

"Think about all of the county rags out there, and this is so much better."

Hussie knew The Trentonian, a 60,000-circulation paper at the time was a cut about the rest—with its stories about grisly crimes, steamy sex, celebrities and sports.

The Trentonian was a cut above a lot of papers its size—and even the metropolitan papers.

The newspaper industry by nature is dull. The Trentonian featured compelling stories that Hussie would say had a "twist."

A "twist" is a bizarre angle and hook that will get people talking. For example, a person is murdered. Now, murders happen all the time. But if this person is slain over a card game, the motive provides the reader with a twist that makes this particular story unique.

Filled with stories with bizarre "twists," The Trentonian had a magical ability that most newspaper editors would cherish—it connected with its readership.

It was an unbelievable read.

Dolmetsch, a capable reporter, was dead wrong.

This book is a newspaper book—with a twist.

Today, most books have the same tired theme. Most authors on journalism claim newspapers must delve into the issues and provide more extensive enterprise pieces

Yes, I agree. The industry is in peril. Most newspapers are lifeless—filled with stories about meetings and political activity.

Newspapers fail to consistently generate anything readers really care about. A successful newspaper will be filled with stories that make people say "holy shit!"

Most newspapers are boring.

Stories about Scientology and the IRS don't make me say "holy shit."

I won't buy the paper.

I'm not the only one. Fewer and fewer people are reading newspapers than ever before. The presence of the Internet does curb sales somewhat, but the majority of the blame should be doled out to the newspapers and their editors.

Most newspapers *do not provide enough* stories about crime and entertainment. They don't generate stories that people are interested in, but instead peddle stories the editors think readers *should be* interested in.

This preachy approach usually leads to circulation slides at the newsstands.

A New York Times' story about Scientology doesn't connect with most readers. They don't care. Readers determine what's newsworthy, not a bunch of snobby editors.

Collectively, readers are a hell of a lot smarter than any mediocre editor, who thinks he knows it all.

How do you know what interests the readers? Just look at the circulation figures. A reader votes with his wallet. If sales go up because of a particular story, it indicates the readers believe the topic is important.

Circulation is the only objective method of circulation success.

But most editors don't pay much attention to the day-to-day sales figures. Television news is filled with crime, celebrities and entertainment because executives in the industry rely on ratings.

The ratings indicate that viewers are more interested in those types of stories.

Most journalism books do not delve into circulation figures. These journalistic eggheads hardly ever mention circulation when writing about the decline of the industry. They get wrapped in what they perceive lack of journalistic standards.

But most editors in this industry think the readers are dopes, and provide "snooze" stories that appeal to a very limited audience.

This book argues that if the readers want stories about crime, steamy sex, entertainment and celebrities, the editor must reflect that in the final product.

This book will stress the importance of letting the readers determine what's newsworthy.

◆ ◆ ◆

While researching this book and looking back on the Trentonians from 1997 and 1998, I realized that this 60,000-circulation paper had a wonderful voice.

I use excepts from a lot of the stories for this book. I believe the leads and writing style from The Trentonian during this period should be taught in classrooms.

The writing was impeccable—better than most newspapers.

The writing had a powerful voice.

Forceful.

Pulled no punches.

The writing appealed to a wide general audience.
That's all you can ask for in the writing.

◆   ◆   ◆

You won't be reading this in a textbook on journalism.
Because this is reality.
What has happened to The Trentonian in the last four years is typical in the industry as a whole.
The Trentonian was once beloved by its readers as a pull-no-punches, tell-it-like-it-is newspaper. It delivered what the readers really wanted.
It was "No.1 in the hearts of the people."
When a new publisher arrived in 1998, the newspaper feebly attempted to become a mainstream publication. It didn't to appeal to its core, blue-collar readers.
The publisher targeted a more sophisticated audience. It became a typical newspaper.
Unfortunately, most newspapers today are bad.
The Trentonian had a winning formula and discarded it.
This book chronicles the paper's rise and very tragic fall.

Mike Raffaele
May 2002

Acknowledgements

Reporter Eric Ladley helped me research and write portions of the book about The Trentonian.

Ladley is more than a reporter who has an uncanny ability to get pictures of sexy babes.

He is one great newsman.

◆　　◆　　◆

Researching this book made me appreciate how special The Trentonian's editorial staff in 1997-98 really was.

It reflected in the daily product with its hard-hitting writing, sensational headlines and dazzling designs.

It was a paper people really cared about.

We had a common bond, and sadly, we will never work at a place like the Trentonian again.

The staff was like family to me. The Trentonian had stronger staffs in previous years, especially in 1993-1997, but this was the most treasured group I've managed.

Writers like Dom Yanchunas, Jon Blackwell, Chris Wilson, Chris Dolmetsch, Molly Davis, Barri Orlow, Tony Wilson, George O'Gorman, Jim Davis, Rich Timlen, Scott Esposito, Chris Collins, Chris Baud, Linda Dougherty, Sherry Sylvester and Dave Sommers.

We had editors who knew what type of stories that connected with readers. They were advisers any editor would cherish: Erik Lukens, Bob Shields, Storm Gifford, Todd Venezia, Mike Regan, Andy Hussie, Rick Methot, Bob Zecker Jay Dunn, Jim Fitzsimmons, Eric Barrow, Ted Holmlund and of course, Paul Mickle.

Photographers Leslie Barbaro, Jeff Zelevansky, Gregg Slaboda, Chris Barth and Bob Castelli kept their patience—despite some the wacky photo assignments.

Sam Guerrero and Cindy Manion are graphic designers who knew how to produce a dramatic front page. The artistic talents helped the paper grow during its glory days.

Of course, the team was a reflection of its leader: H.L. "Sandy" Schwartz III.

As the paper declines, Schwartz's legend grows.

This was a special team and the bond will never be broken—even after The Trentonian goes out of business.

Without their hard work, this book would not have been possible.

Thank you all.

Introduction

It was Aug. 6, 1998.

Summer was mild. The temperatures weren't as searing as the previous summers in the Northeast. Actually, there was a chill in the air. There was a feeling of fall.

My phone rang. I wasn't sure whether to answer it or not. Calls from work came in frequently and were much more annoying in the last 30 days.

I had been editor of The Trentonian for nearly a year and a half. News breaks and I have to be ready to receive a call from the office at all times.

Thank God, I had caller ID.

The call was coming from a pay phone.

It was Trentonian reporter Dom Yanchunas. He seemed worried.

Yanchunas is a reporter who connects with the community. He has a good nose for news. He also knows when trouble's brewing in the workplace.

Dom and I have worked together before. At The Delaware State News in Dover, Del., he was a reporter and I held the position of copy desk chief. That paper produced a lot of scars for both of us.

Its mediocrity proved the most disconcerting. The State News, located in Delaware's capital city, was irrelevant—a so-called community newspaper out of touch. The newspaper's bigwigs thought it was great.

But its news columns showcased a lot of town meetings, sewer stories and fluff pieces. Its circulation was 23,000, and dropping.

No one cared about the paper.

But now we were a part of a winning organization. A newspaper with swagger. The Trentonian was a feisty 60,000-circulation newspaper that connected with its community. The atmosphere in the newsroom was almost like family. Days were action-packed. For both of us, it was a dream job.

I hired Yanchunas in August 1997. For a year, he covered murders, scandals, Major League Baseball, NBA, fires, deaths of fellow employees and education. Name it. Yanchunas covered it for The Trentonian.

The paper never pulled any punches.

But Yanchunas on the phone seemed dazed like he was just walloped by a haymaker. He had been dining at Marsilio's—a popular Italian restaurant right in the heart of the Chambersburg section of Trenton.

"I just talked to two waitresses," he said. "They said the publisher of The Trentonian was (at the restaurant) bashing the paper. He said he was going to make this paper respectable and there was going to be two respectable newspapers in Trenton."

A month ago, the Journal Register Company, the parent company of The Trentonian, hired a new publisher.

Robert Jelenic, the president and CEO of the Journal Register Company, appointed David Bonfield, a former advertising executive for the company in the early 1990s, to become the seventh publisher of 58-year-old tabloid newspaper.

Bonfield replaced revered and fiery publisher H.L. "Sandy" Schwartz III, who retired in May.

When Schwartz took over in April 1989, The Trentonian was on brink of extinction. By the time he retired, the paper turned into the most talked about 60,000-circulation publication in the country.

Schwartz, who had an extensive editorial background, put zeal and fire into the paper. Most importantly, the readers relished the final product.

Now, he was gone, replaced by a lightweight ad executive who seemingly like a little kid wanted to be liked by everybody.

One month into his tenure, Bonfield made marketing-driven decisions that softened the paper and circulation dropped nearly 2,000 papers as a result. He declawed The Trentonian.

Even though the circulation dropped significantly, reporters like Yanchunas were unaware of the looming changes.

He was now.

The publisher was ripping The Trentonian in public. Yanchunas knew the honeymoon was over. Bonfield was ridiculing what made The Trentonian great. He was prepared to demolish the foundation.

We both knew we were going to shopping our resumes soon.

Yanchunas was puzzled. Why would anybody want to change the course of this newspaper?

Bonfield was brought into the paper as an advertising and marketing expert. The paper wasn't generating enough advertising. In Bonfield's mind, the paper had to appeal to another audience. Instead of the typical city resident, the publisher apparently wanted to lure the so-called intellectual residents in nearby Princeton.

This book will chronicle my experiences at The Trentonian, a once-powerful paper now struggling.

Find out how Jelenic and the Journal Register Company used knee-jerk decisions to weaken a solid franchise, transforming a must-read paper into an irrelevant one.

I worked at the Trentonian from March 1997 to October 1998 and then from September 2001 to December 2001.

When David Bonfield took over the Trentonian in 1998, the circulation was 59,000 to 60,000. By September 2001, it was 48,500, losing about one-sixth of its papers sold.

Circulation is the only objective method of measuring success in the newspaper industry. Editors and publishers will try put the emphasis on readership studies and editorial awards. The Trentonian ditched the readers it once revered.

Circulation holds the truth.

Unfortunately, most newspaper executives come up with excuses—like the recession, population decline or the explosion of other forms of media. They try to find a silver lining with bogus readership studies.

If a paper is compelling, people will buy it. It won't matter what the financial climate is. Under Bonfield, the paper wasn't compelling anymore. It was a tiger without its teeth.

The Trentonian's fall is typical of most newspapers. Corporations come up with grandiose plans to boost readership, but ultimately, all of the ideas fall flat. They simply don't have the stories people want to read.

Bonfield and Jelenic were quick to pin blame on the sports, news and circulation departments. Jelenic, in my opinion, believed people in those departments were sabotaging the operation in spite of him.

Bonfield usually agreed.

Now here is a tale of a paper on the decline.

1

GLORY DAYS

Trenton, N.J., is filled with history—even though it is hard to find in the late 20th century. But it held a key part in the birth of our nation.

Then it was a giant in the industrial world. In fact, the bridge connecting the city to Pennsylvania has a sign, "TRENTON MAKES THE WORLD TAKES."

Now, it's a skeleton of its illustrious past—it makes little and takes a lot more.

Just outside the area people never admit they are from Trenton. They say they live near Princeton, but never Trenton.

There is a gritty, lovable quality to this area. It's an underdog and proud of it.

In fact, the city of Trenton is the smallest city in the country to have two daily newspapers: The Trentonian and the Times of Trenton.

The circulation area for both newspapers covered Mercer County (featuring Princeton, Hamilton, Lawrence and Lawrenceville), Burlington County and Bucks County, Pa.

Through the years, the Times of Trenton focused on the suburbs—mainly Princeton. In fact, the flag of the Times doesn't even mention Trenton.

Trenton, you see, has a negative reputation. If you want to appeal to Princeton, don't dare mention Trenton. The Times always neglected Trenton. The people in Trenton are considered poor. They don't buy cars and serious goods and services. Advertisers don't want to appeal to poor people.

The Times of Trenton neglected the Trenton reader and was proud of it.

The Trentonian, however, always related to the city—a feisty, never-say-die attitude. It was a paper for the working man, and was proud of it.

"No. 1 in the hearts of the people," was The Trentonian's slogan. Those people were the hard-working residents of Trenton.

The Trentonian's rebellious attitude stems from its history. The Trentonian had originally formed in 1945 as a strike paper from the Trenton Times. It developed as an on-the-record paper and waged an intense battle against the more established and better financed Times.

In 1974, Editor Gil Spencer won the Pulitzer Prize for editorial writing. The Trentonian still boasts that it is the city's only Pulitzer Prize-winning paper.

Awards in this industry don't matter—it's how many people who buy your paper.

The battle for newspaper supremacy in the market went back and forth for nearly 40 years—until the Washington Post bought the Trenton Times in 1974. At the time, the Times held a 72,665 to 59,077 circulation advantage over The Trenton.

The Times became a smaller-sized version of the Washington Post with the focus on international and national news.

Forget local.

The Trentonian under the leadership of Editor Emil Slaboda turned to basics to bounce the powerful Post out of Trenton.

Slaboda focused on local news. Pet stories, crime and bake sales. If it happened in Trenton, it was in The Trentonian.

The paper ran the underworld's lottery numbers. It was a gambling town, and The Trentonian was rolling lucky "sevens" with the readers.

It drastically cut the Times' circulation advantage to 66,370 to 65,838.

Katherine Graham, the famed publisher of the Post, called Trenton her "Vietnam."

It was a victory for Trenton's gritty and blue-collar population.

The Post bailed in 1981.

Eventually in 1986, Advance Publications purchased the Times, and its deep pockets started to punish The Trentonian. The Times went local, and it had much larger resources than The Trentonian.

The Trentonian covered all the meetings, and was a paper of record. But the Times had a deeper staff, and The Trentonian couldn't play its game.

It was getting crushed. The paper was hemorrhaging financially and circulation was sliding. The Times held a 74,958 to 67,293 lead in circulation.

It could not match the Times local story for local story anymore. The Times had greater depth.

The end was near for the feisty Trentonian.

Enter H.L. "Sandy" Schwartz III.

◆ ◆ ◆

H.L. "Sandy" Schwartz III replaced Ed Hoffman in 1989, and the Trentonian immediately became a tabloid in the real sense: Sensational.

Schwartz had an incredible flair for tabloids and the ability to cut right through the bullshit to get to the heart of a story.

The approach was not to cover all of the meetings in the community. Just select the stories that people will talk about. The stories must generate an emotional reaction—good or bad.

The stories must make people say "holy shit."

Forget about changing the world. Just run stories that make people run the gamut of emotions: laugh, cry and most importantly, get them mad as hell.

The irony is that Schwartz covered Watergate for the Associated Press. I've always believed Watergate has triggered the downfall of journalism—creating a new brand of journalist that believes a newspaper should change the world.

After Watergate, newspapers weren't producing stories the readers want, but instead these new editors ran stories that they believe readers *should* be interested in.

These journalists were the antithesis of Schwartz's approach.

A native of New York, Schwartz had been a newspaper publisher since 1979, working at The Pottstown Mercury and Delaware County Times in Media, Pa., and the Orange Coast Pilot in Costa Mesa, Calif. The Mercury was strong and won a Pulitzer for editorial writing just after Schwartz left.

Schwartz started his career as a reporter in Wilmington, N.C., after serving three years in the Marine Corps. He spent 12 years with the Associated Press in Philadelphia, Pittsburgh, Detroit and Washington bureaus.

In 1968, as a Michigan news executive, Schwartz led a team of nearly 24 AP personnel in coverage of the Detroit riot that claimed 44 lives.

In 1972, Schwartz and another AP reporter were cited by the Columbia Journalism Review for what the magazine called the "largely uncredited achievement of exclusively disclosing the link between the Watergate burglars and the Committee to Re-Election Nixon."

He made Nixon's enemies' list.

Schwartz showed the staff "there's a new sheriff in town" on his first day at The Trentonian.

A severed head was found on a golf course in Mercer County. The paper's reporter was reluctant to cover it.

Most newspapers wouldn't make a big deal about it—a head being found on a golf course.

Unfortunately, it normally would be a brief or a short story in the paper.

But not with Schwartz.

"SEVERED HEAD IN HOPEWELL" was the paper's lead story. The lead, which obviously had Schwartz influence, went like this: "HOPEWELL TWP. —A golfer braving yesterday's rain to play a round at a Hopewell club hooked a shot out of bounds and discovered a woman's severed head on the banks of the Stony Brook while seeking his lost ball, authorities said."

It was a brilliant, hard-hitting lead. According to Trentonian legend, the reporter who wrote it resigned in disgust in the paper's sudden change in direction.

The headline hit home. Staffers were frustrated and furious.

That was only the beginning.

Two weeks later, The Trentonian ran the following headline: "HEAD HAD AIDS"

It was—and still is—the most famous headline in The Trentonian's history. Mention The Trentonian, "HEAD HAD AIDS" will be mentioned.

The lead paragraph also jarred readers:

"A woman decapitated by a frenzied killer might have avenged her own death if the murderer was splashed by her spurting blood, authorities said yesterday in disclosing the victim had AIDS."

The powerful headlines and the punchy, no-nonsense approach in the writing elevated the paper.

Schwartz came in and shook things up. Many of the old, established reporters bailed—mainly in disgust over the changes. If they didn't leave, he and his new editor, Gale Baldwin, hounded them to the point where they were so miserable they left anyway.

Schwartz hired fearless young go-getters in their place. These people weren't afraid to stick their neck out for a story.

They realized that the front page of the tabloid, with its big letters and the possibility of gruesome photos, could evoke powerful emotions. People bought the paper on impulse at the newsstands because these crazy stories drew them in.

The lead story, often called the "line" or the "wood," became the most important element of the paper.

News meetings would be devoted to getting that one good story and coming up the proper wording to put on the front-page headline to compel people buy it.

Schwartz also exploited the male desire for female flesh.

On Page 6 of the paper, he put pictures of sexy, young women in bikinis. He had taken a page out of the British tabloids, which have topless women gracing Page 3 of their papers. These were just attractive locals girls, scantily clad, appearing in our paper. Some people were outraged, but the paper experienced a 3,000-reader bump.

Along with the Page 6 girls came the Monday poster girl, which consistently made that day's paper the best sale of the week, attracting at least 1,000 readers above the paper's average weekly. For the first time since the Revolutionary War, Trenton had something with a British quality to it.

The Trentonian grabbed a great deal of publicity and was featured in The New York Times, New York Newsday, The Maury Povich Show and Hard Copy. Most importantly, the paper was stirring the pot. People were used to staid, boring papers, but now they were getting their money's worth. Women's groups hated it, but readers loved it.

With the readers firmly on their side, there was a colossal upswing in readership. The peak came in 1993, at 82,044, when The Trentonian's whipping boy, Democratic Gov. Jim Florio, was defeated by Republican Christie Whitman by 31,000 votes. Everything looked good for Sandy in the early 1990s. The Trentonian was advertised as "Jersey's Fastest Growing A.M. Paper."

It had become one of the most controversial publications in the country.

In 1996, officials the Journal Register Company, the parent company of The Trentonian, decided to raise the price of the paper from

25 to 35 cents. The Times remained priced at 25 cents. JRC was asking people to pay more for a tabloid than a broadsheet.

It's a rule in the newspaper world: Hike the price and watch the circulation sink. Most newspaper executives raise the price to bring in more revenue. In a newspaper battle in a small market like Trenton, N.J., such a price increase could be fatal—especially for a tabloid that relies on single-copy sales.

Readers apparently feel ripped off when a price is raised; loyalty to a publication is tested. Usually, it fails—no matter how good the newspaper is. Just imagine what happens to newspapers that stink. Most newspapers today do stink.

At that time, the Philadelphia Daily News' circulation lost about 30,000 off its circulation for raising the price from 50 to 60 cents.

The Trentonian—even under Schwartz's leadership—was unable to buck the trend. The paper's circulation plunged from 75,000 to slightly below 60,000—in only 11 months.

Troubles loomed in The Trentonian's editorial department. Editor Gale Baldwin was promoted to became publisher at Journal Register Company's newspaper in Alton, Ill. Baldwin was terminated at the Alton paper just three months later.

Mark Waligore, a Rider College graduate who joined the paper as a cop reporter in the late 1980s and became the managing editor of the paper at age 23 in the early 1990s, was named The Trentonian's new editor.

Waligore was filled with energy, but was inconsistent in providing the paper with a direction. At times, he wanted the paper to be sophisticated—a New York Times. He detested the Page 6 girl, and even convinced Schwartz to get rid of the centerfold girl on Mondays.

That was a bad move.

Circulation dropped on Mondays—once the best day of the week—to nearly 57,000 because of Waligore.

There were days Waligore seemed like a tabloid king. He couldn't maintain a consistency to be successful.

Waligore would have one of the shortest reigns as editor. Thanks mainly to Journal Register Company President and CEO Robert Jelenic.

♦ ♦ ♦

"I could put the word 'FUCK' as big as you can on the front page," Waligore would say. "And nobody would care."

Jelenic, who lives in nearby West Windsor, loved local sports.

He believed that local sports would save the paper.

"It's the franchise," he would say.

Jelenic from his Trenton offices would create a reign of terror for Waligore and whoever the sports editor was at the time—finding mistakes in box scores and agate.

The CEO of a company that owned more than 23 daily newspapers at the time, who believed mistakes in box scores loses readers.

Mistakes in box scores may lead to termination.

Jelenic may have had other motives.

Jelenic's son, Lee, played ice hockey for West Windsor-Plainsboro High School. He was a high school hockey expert. He devoured all of the local sports copy. Make the slightest mistake, and you're the jerk.

One day, Waligore was the jerk.

Waligore had a late night—TWA Flight 800 went down off of Long Island. With blockbuster news like that, a real editor would work until early in the morning until the paper went to bed.

Waligore was an aggressive editor. A damn good one.

He left the office at about 3 a.m.

At 9 a.m., he was in the office. He was a jerk.

The sports "on the air" agate, the sports television schedule, had a mistake in it—the same item appeared twice.

The CEO of the company proclaimed Waligore a failure.

All because there was a mistake in a piece of agate.

Waligore—only 28—knew he had to go.

Normally, editors don't get posts at such an early age. Waligore was special. Usually, 28-year-old editors don't normally look to leave newspapers after only seven months on the job.

But those 9 a.m. phone calls were hellish.

Those Jelenic calls can trigger madness. How can a CEO of a company what owns more than 23 newspapers be so anal?

Jelenic used to pound Schwartz with calls filled with obscenities.

It didn't matter if the word "FUCK" appeared on Page 1.

It was because of all of those sports mistakes.

◆ ◆ ◆

By December 1996, Waligore was gone. He accepted an assistant metro editor position at the Pittsburgh Post-Gazette.

Hours before he was offered the Pittsburgh position, he hired me as sports editor.

Being named sports editor at The Trentonian sports editor—thanks to Jelenic—was like getting like getting a red suit on the U.S.S. Enterprise.

It was a death wish.

In the past five years, the Trentonian went through six sports editors. I was No. 7.

I was 27 years old at the time; I had worked at the Trentonian before as the assistant news editor from October 1994 to April 1996. I worked at the New York Post briefly before accepting the sports editor position.

During my first stint at The Trentonian, Schwartz "thought (I) was an asshole."

"You would not stand in the fucking corner," Schwartz said. "Not say a word with your shirt hanging out."

"I would say to Waligore, 'who the fuck is that guy?'" Schwartz said. "But he would say nice things about you."

But now, I was the guy in the red suit waiting to get zapped—the sports editor.

I knew the deal. On paper, the sports editor position at The Trentonian is great.

The paper covers both New York and Philadelphia professional sports teams, and at the same time, has a large local market for high school sports. You have large, hard-working staff already in place; it just needed the proper guidance.

I looked at the position as opportunity. In this chain, if I was a successful sports editor, it would open doors.

In 1996, the sports department was struggling. It was a major mistake that got me offered the job in the first place.

In November 1996, Evander Holyfield stunned the boxing world—beating champ Mike Tyson in an 11th-round TKO.

A shocker. A type of story the Trentonian would lead Page 1 with. But on this day, news judgment became typical of the industry: bad.

Really bad.

Linda Dougherty, a feisty horse-racing writer whom Schwartz hired, was working the copy desk that night. She was keeping track of the fight.

Dougherty was a typical horse racing writer—she relished boxing. Most racing writers also cover boxing because both sports have a sleazy underbelly.

But Dougherty knew a big story when she saw one.

Chris Collins also knew a good story when he sees one. He knows the simple rule: if story makes you say "what the fuck!" then you run it.

Both had solid newspaper judgment, but their voices of reason—no matter how loud it was that night—went unheard.

It's because Laura Eckert—the sports editor at the time—didn't have a clue.

It cost her the position.

Firstly, she was a "stone tablet" editor; once a section was put into place, you don't change it—no matter what the story.

The "stone tablet" is destroying the newspaper industry. For some reason, most newspapers cannot adjust to breaking news.

It's because most editors are lazy and don't want to change the game plan.

And that's one of the numerous reasons why the newspaper industry is dying.

Eckert thought the Tyson defeat wasn't newsworthy. It wasn't as compelling as the high school football game that graced the front page of the sports section.

Despite the pleas from Collins and Dougherty, Eckert ran the story on page A15 with a file photo of Holyfield during the weigh-in.

That was a disgrace for any newspaper executive.

Like any true newsman, Schwartz was furious. This was the story everybody was talking about. Tyson stories were easy; everybody had an opinion of the boxer.

Schwartz wanted to change the sports department.

My phone rang two days later.

"The fucking asshole" was back with the paper. Two months later, Eckert found a job at the Morris County (N.J.) Daily Record.

The sports department made blunders just like the Holyfield-Tyson fight all the time. It put too much emphasis on local sports.

Local sports, especially in a market that appeals to both New York and Philly sports fans, appeal to only a small readership segment.

The readers were craving for a section that was more hard-hitting—like the news section. They got it.

♦ ♦ ♦

On the day I was introduced as sports editor, I met Scott Esposito.

Esposito, who previously worked as a part-timer at the New Haven Register in Connecticut, was just named sports columnist of the paper. He was the shining star. Jelenic loved him.

He covered high school hockey exceptionally well.

A columnist provides a voice the public can connect with. A personality with a strong voice can lure readers to the paper.

Television is filled with personalities. People relate to them. Every day a weatherman comes into people's homes. He's like a part of the family.

I wanted Esposito to have a strong voice with personality.

In my first week as sports editor, I ordered him to write a column explaining why the woeful, 1-13 Jets would beat the playoff-bound Eagles.

The back page read:
WHY JETS WOULD BEAT BIRDS!

That started a stream of success for the sports department. I put a great deal of emphasis on national sports, columns and extensive packages.

I used the news section as a blueprint.

Sex and crime are two important elements in the news section, can also be applied to sports. Not only did I start playing up national sports, I started focusing on the sexier sports stories. The best sports story we ever led with was when an Eagles practice player, Chris Buckhalter, was accused of raping a hooker the night before a 1996 playoff game with the San Francisco 49ers. An Eagles source close to our part-time reporter Al Thompson gave us all the juicy details. This also was the same day Cowboys star receiver Michael Irvin was charged with rape.

The Trentonian led with the front page:
NFL SEX SCANDALS!

Sex and the NFL—especially a local team like the Eagles—are a winning combination for any newspaper.

A couple of days later, I had Esposito write a column on why this Eagles sex scandal shouldn't be scoffed at because he is merely a practice player. Buckhalter is a representative of the Eagles. It was a hard-hitting column that struck a chord.

The column led the front page: SHAME ON EAGLES

On Jan. 3, 1997, Schwartz decided to give Jelenic a call. How about that sports section, now? But on that day, the features department made a dreaded mistake.

A high school hockey picture accompanied a story about ice skating in Mercer County. The caption read: "Lee Jelenic skates during a game at Mercer County Park."

Problem was, it wasn't Lee Jelenic.

In fact, it was Bryan Bowser of Notre Dame High School in Lawrenceville—arguably the best player in the county. He was Lee's arch-nemesis on the ice.

The features department screwed up. Jelenic went on one of his typical tirades.

This time, he was justified.

Schwartz was red-faced, and the news and features departments were under siege.

The sports department was rocking; in a matter of weeks, we were the paper's only strength. We had produced nine lead stories for the front page in one month; we were better at covering news than the news department.

The back page was sexier than the front.

That's a bad sign for the entire paper.

◆ ◆ ◆

Despite Jelenic's insistence of local sports being the franchise, news is what generated the paper's sales. The Trentonian's glory days in circulation were linked to the news department.

Local sports had little bearing on the sales.

Waligore's departure left a large void at the paper. No one in the building stood out as an heir apparent.

An editor must always groom somebody to succeed him. With every person he hires, an editor must think: "Can this person become editor of the paper?"

It helps elevate the talent at the organization and increases depth.

With the editor position, The Trentonian had a depth problem.

The one person who could have been successful—News Editor Bob Shields—didn't want the post.

Schwartz had nothing

In a desperate move, he elevated reporter Anne Karolyi to managing editor. She was a friendly, clear writer, but she had no tabloid savvy.

She'd let stories slip right through her fingers that she should've sown up. The Times started beating us on tabloid-type stories they had no business beating us on. The paper lost its hard edge and grasp on the issues. When you have a weak editor, the reporters become lazy. They don't want to work. In fact, in this instance, they all started sending resumes out. The reporters were miserable.

Nobody was talking about the Trentonian anymore.

Schwartz needed another change. By March 1997, he made the following moves:

He made cop reporter Paul Mickle the city editor

He made me the executive editor.

I then appointed Bob Shields as managing editor.

Karolyi and her husband photographer Mike Orazzi were transferred to two Journal Register papers in Connecticut.

A month later, people were talking about The Trentonian again.

◆ ◆ ◆

"Restore the roar" was my motto.

The Trentonian had to find the right note to connect like it did when the circulation was 75,000 in 1993.

In March 1997, it was 58,000 and sliding. The Times were selling 78,000 papers daily.

The Trentonian had been soft since Waligore's departure. It was time to go back to the basics: cover hard-hitting news and personalize politics.

The Trentonian had to take a page from television news

Newspaper editors today scoff at TV news—considering it thin, flimsy and too dramatic.

The TV news is still the No. 1 source for getting news.

Why? Two reason why. Firstly, it's more immediate than newspapers. Secondly, the TV news executives use ratings as a guide to what the public wants. That's the reason why TV news leads with crime daily. People want it. The people determine what's newsworthy.

Television news has better news judgment.

The newspaper industry claims to be objective, but fails to rely on the only objective method to discovering its success: circulation.

Our circulation figures would indicate our readers loved reading about crime.

◆ ◆ ◆

However, in my first move, I wanted to find another foil for the Trentonian. Another politician like Gov. Florio. A person The Trentonian can bash to bring home sales.

U.S. Sen. Robert Torricelli became locked in my crosshairs.

The rookie Democratic senator was unabashedly liberal and had a knack for putting his foot in his mouth. "Torri" was pompous and a jerk.

Following legislation is boring. I wanted to capture the essence of Torricelli, his stupid comments, and, most importantly, what made him act as he did. The Trentonian was going to stay away from being policy wonks. We weren't just mindlessly following the path of legislation.

State workers were our target audience. There were so many of them, and they were constantly taking smoke breaks and gossiping about work. The paper was a must-read with this audience during the Florio years.

On my first day as editor, we led with a Torricelli blunder. At least it would be considered a mistake with a blue-collar, conservative audience.

The man who is nicknamed "The Torch" by friends—and enemies—gave family leave to homosexual staffers.

Erik Lukens, a hard-hitting editorial writer, wrote the headline:
TORRI'S GIFT TO GAYS

For an extra touch, Bob Shields used a lavender background on Page 1.

In my opinion, the front page was old-school Trentonian, the type that would draw emotions from the readers.

The type of front page everybody talked about. I made sure we followed the story. At the end of the week, our editorial writer, Mark Stradling, ripped Torricelli in his Geek of the Week feature, an editorial column devoted to attacking local politicians or knuckleheads who screwed up.

We named Torricelli and his homosexual staffers as the biggest geeks that week. My strategy was running on all cylinders.

The readers got six front pages leading with Torricelli in the next 10 days.

The Torch was on fire.

The sales, however, were cold.

The circulation numbers arrived and indicated the sales actually slipped further in my first 10 days. Oh boy.

Circulation numbers make the world go around.

My world had stopped.

◆ ◆ ◆

Readers vote with their wallets.

If they like newspaper, they will buy it. If they don't like it, they don't buy it.

It's so easy, but today's newspaper editors don't understand that concept.

Today, newspaper executives turn to polling and readership studies for their answers.

This is a synopsis of what these studies usually discover:

Newspapers should have more good news; there's too much crime, more local issue stories, and more board meetings and high school sports.

All lies.

And circulation usually reflects that with sagging sales.

Editors want to sound important and for some reason, it's bad to run stories with the sole purpose of selling newspapers.

Most editors want to run relevant stories. They want to change the world and people's lives. For some reason, they think some stories—especially those involving sex—are irrelevant.

An unread newspaper is irrelevant.

With that point, a well-read newspaper is relevant.

Simple points for such a simple industry.

But newspaper executives want to appear intellectual. They believe they know what's newsworthy. They think they are smarter than their readers.

Wrong.

The readers collectively are a lot smarter than editors. It's a mismatch. The readers can detect bullshit, boring stories. The readers can determine the newsworthiness of a story. Self-absorbed editors don't.

The newspaper industry is crumbling because editors don't pay attention to readers.

They don't know what the readers want; therefore, the editor has lackluster news judgment. From there it's a domino effect.

With lackluster news judgment comes a decline in sales. Readers will not buy newspapers filled with stories they find boring.

With the decline in sales, advertising revenue loses steam. Businesses are always looking for maximum bang for their bucks. They will not sink their money into a shrinking newspaper.

With declining ad revenues, newspapers are forced to cut back and eventually will lead to closings.

With cutbacks, newspaper editors have a convenient excuse why their papers stink. They claim they don't have the resources. If they had the resources, they could sell papers.

That is a world-class cop out.

If an editor connects with the readers, it won't matter how many people he has on staff. Usually, editors with unlimited resources produce papers filled with crummy, boring stories. More resources create more of the same. More stimulating stories on sewers, wastewater and issues.

Sometimes it's better for newspapers to have limited resources.

The editor must have a solid relationship with the circulation director.

Who knows how to sell the paper better than the circulation director?

The circulation director should attend the daily news meeting—and his input must be cherished.

The sole goal for the circulation director is to sell papers.

He will know what works. He will tell you when the paper stinks at the newsstand.

Unfortunately, more circulation directors are fired than editors.

Editors must look at the circulation numbers as their win-loss record. If the circulation doesn't improve the editor must be fired.

But most editors are entrenched, cranking out mediocre products and watching the industry die.

Schwartz expected to see improvement in the sales of the paper or I would be out of a job. He knew the standards for editors.

As an editor, I constantly consulted our circulation director at that time—Jim Farrell.

Farrell, a veteran circulation man, had strong feelings about the Torricelli stories.

He said they stunk.

The readers were [weren't?] buying the junk we were putting out. Since the readers didn't like it, we had to make adjustments.

Get off of Torricelli.

I don't think the readers rejected the stories because Torricelli is a great man. It's because he doesn't make a direct impact on our lives.

When a governor like Florio is incompetent, it hurts the readers. It hits them in the wallet; his arrogance made them pay more tax dollars.

Whenever readers are hit in the wallet, they are enraged.

Enraged readers buy newspapers.

Senators' moves never affect the constituents directly as a governor would. Torricelli is just one of 100 U.S. senators. A governor is just one man, who is considered the guardian of state government.

With Torricelli off the hook, what now?

How about City Hall?

◆ ◆ ◆

The Trentonian was always a watchdog over the city of Trenton. It's a city that has crackpot characters and colorful personalities.

When I became editor of The Trentonian, the City Hall coverage was nonexistent.

The problem was, the City Hall reporter was beloved.

Bad City Hall reporters are beloved ones.

There is a tendency in the newspaper business to strive to be liked. But newspapers should want to be respected.

The politicians of the city liked our City Hall reporter because he printed what they wanted. He never hit them hard.

He wasn't respected.

If he were respected, some pols would have hated him. That's because there would have been negative stories in the paper.

At his going away party, the entire Trenton City Council and Mayor Doug Palmer attended.

They all loved him. He printed what they wanted.

The Trentonian led with a story from this City Hall reporter only once: A story about bad cabbies.

The headline read: HACKS FROM HELL.

Everybody hates cabbies. The pols, more importantly, were unscathed.

So I needed a City Hall reporter. I needed a person who didn't crave to be liked.

He demanded respect.

Jon Blackwell fit the bill.

Blackwell, an Albany State graduate who worked at the Cortland Standard and the Oneonta Daily Star, was just fired by the Times Herald-Record.

I worked at the Times Herald-Record and was familiar with the snobs who ran the paper.

Anybody who they didn't like was good for me.

The Times Herald-Record is typical of newspapers in the business. Its news department is filled with so-called intellectuals who want to change the world, instead of selling newspapers.

Based in Orange County, N.Y. (about 50 miles north of New York City), the Times Herald-Record was a tabloid that acted like a broadsheet. Its market was booming. But sales weren't.

Self-absorbed intellectuals who thought they knew better than the readers ran the paper. It had a liberal voice in a very conservative market. It pressed environmental issues while the readers craved crime.

The Record's strength is its sports department. The department is filled with solid, down-to-earth editors, who know what the readers want. But a sports department cannot carry the newspaper by itself.

The population was exploding with former New York City residents. Those readers yearn for papers like the New York Post and the New York Daily News.

What they got was a paper that was like New York Newsday, a paper that won three Pulitzer Prizes and was out of business. Lots of wastewater issues that wasted the readers' time. They were above covering crime hard.

It would be easy to assume a paper would grow the same as the population. It didn't. The circulation dropped nearly 10,000 from 1993 to 1997.

A losing organization.

So Jon Blackwell was fired by the news editors at the Times Herald-Record. That should be a badge of honor. A day after his termination in Middletown, N.Y., I hired Blackwell.

"He's crazy," Schwartz said after meeting Blackwell.

That's a compliment in our world.

Being crazy usually means a reporter would do whatever it takes to nail down a story. Blackwell was a perfect fit for The Trentonian.

City Hall returned to Page 1.

Blackwell had the honor of covering the mayoral election of 1998. Mayor Doug Palmer faced a challenge from two kooky contenders: Pat Daddio and Kim Rogers.

Pat Daddio was a junkman—like Red Foxx's legendary TV character Fred Sanford from "Sanford and Son."

Unfortunately, Sanford was a lot smarter.

Daddio, who was white, but he looked black, made a splash when he announced his candidacy in January 1998 He dressed in an African kufi cap and a down jacket, and he did a rap at City Hall when he filed his candidacy. He compared himself to Rocky, and he called Palmer Apollo Creed.

"I'm trying to appeal to dark complected broads," he explained.

We ran the text of Daddio's rap:

"This year's election is gonna be fun.

"It reminds me of Rocky One.

"Where the odds against me are a million to one.

"It's the Italian Stallion against Apollo Creed.

"It's give me your votes, that's-a what I need.

"Six months have passed since I declared.

"I think I'm getting you very scared.

"My signs are going up and some are coming down.

"What are you gonna do when they're all over town.

"You're a flamboyant mayor; and sometimes polite.

"But that's gonna change on election night."

Daddio was typical of Trenton. The Times—filled with snobbery—didn't match the color of the story Blackwell captured.

Daddio admitted he stopped reading The Trentonian in 1968 because of its stance for desegregation. That's something you wouldn't want to say in the city of Trenton.

"Daddio may be a 15-watt bulb in a 100-watt world," said our editorial after his announcement.

But Daddio was a stronger candidate than Kim Rogers.

Rogers, the daughter of legendary Councilman "Bo" Robinson, had the name recognition, but was a rotten candidate.

Blackwell uncovered that she was once a go-go dancer. In Trenton, this can actually help a candidate. While asking her about her go-go dancing past, her husband interrupted and wondered why the paper didn't have a story about Palmer being a "drug-addicted faggot."

Rogers stood by her husband's claim.

We ran those comments.

On the front page, the headline read:

MAYORAL CANDIDATE WAS A GO-GO DANCER

Underneath, we had...

PLUS: Check out what they said about Doug

The husband of a mayoral candidate is calling the mayor a "drug-addicted faggot" and the candidate stood by those remarks.

That's a major story.

The mayor then sued the couple.

That's news. We exploited it.

The next day we led the paper with Palmer filing a lawsuit against the couple.

Blackwell wrote this lead:

"'Branded a 'drug-addicted faggot' by one of his leading opponents, an incensed Trenton Mayor Doug Palmer fought back yesterday by filing a slander lawsuit."

Two years later, Blackwell interviewed for a job at one of the bureaus at the Associated Press. He used this story as one of the examples of his good work.

The news editor called it "irresponsible" and never in his wildest dreams would have run such a story.

That editor is a man with no guts. Most editors—and most reporters—would have agreed with the AP editor. That's the problem. The industry doesn't have much guts anymore.

I consider this a community service. Would you want to know that the mayoral candidate's husband called the mayor a "drug-addicted faggot," and the candidate then never disputed those claims?

Would the voters want to know about this?

Blackwell's guts were perfect for The Trentonian.

Doug Palmer did win the election in May 1998—garnering 87 percent of the vote. Daddio, the junkman, finished second with 7 percent.

But we had solid sales from the crazy chronicles of that election. We wouldn't have gotten that bounce without Blackwell.

My favorite City Hall front page he produced was a story about all of the numerous blunders by the Trenton City Council.

The overline read:

Nobody's laughing at...

COUNCIL CLOWNS!

In the story, Blackwell wrote:

"As they approach the May 12 election, City Council members are struggling to overcome a reputation for incessant power struggles, bizarre behavior, sexist taunts and missed meetings.

"The councilmen up for re-election would like Trenton voters to see them as a statesmanlike partner to the popular Mayor Doug Palmer—matching him every step of the way in fighting crime, building new houses and revitalizing the battered Capital City.

"But a slew of buffoonish incidents have tarnished nearly every one of the seven incumbents during their four-year terms, providing heavy ammunition for a large slate of challengers:

"—In 1995, Council President Bill Young tussled with a meter maid who ticketed his car. A few months later, his Stuyvesant Avenue house was shot up in a bizarre attack that remains unsolved.

"—At-large Councilman Paul M. Pintella admitted forging young baseball players' signatures on a sign-up form in 1995. He was investigated by the prosecutor's office but not charged, and ignored the calls of two fellow councilmen who urged him to resign.

"—The South Ward's John Ungrady shouted 'f——whores' in 1995 at a pair of female reporters when they failed to leave a council executive session. Last year, asked what he was doing at an Atlantic City conference, he joked he was 'learning to roll dice.'

"—North Ward Councilwoman Jane Robinson declared virtual war on Palmer last month by likening his administration to 'Mr. Magoo.' She has also been late or tardy for more than quarter of all meetings.

"And one male councilman—who has never stepped forward to identify himself—anonymously disparaged women in government in '95 by telling a Trentonian reporter, 'You know how women get at that time of month.'

"The sexist insults infuriated some female voters, who had to respond in kind by ousting male incumbents."

Blackwell, who didn't want to make any friends in City Council, had a temper. He was notorious for slamming phones—he's busted them. One time, he threw a chair at my office door.

That's wonderful. He has passion for his work.

Newspapers are too bland today—usually that's a direct link to the personality of the newsroom.

A newsroom should have personality with colorful characters.

The Trentonian had lots of it.

The most colorful of them all was City Editor Paul Mickle.

♦   ♦   ♦

Mickle, a veteran of the business for 20-plus years, came from the old school. He just did whatever it took to get a story.

With Mickle, you don't want to know how he got the story. It's a "don't ask, don't tell" policy.

Mickle worked for a wide variety of newspapers including the Philadelphia Bulletin and the Burlington County Times.

After leaving the Burlco Times, Mickle went to Trenton Times for the job. In fact, he walked right into the editor's office.

"How did you get in this building?" the editor asked.

"I'm a reporter," Mickle said. "I'm supposed to do those things."

The editor threw him out of the building.

Hours later, he was hired by The Trentonian.

There are legendary stories about this legendary newsman. Mickle, according to legend, broke into the Trenton Times' composing room and stole a photo of a crime victim off of their page. The photo then appeared in The Trentonian.

Mickle denies this story.

Anybody who knows Mickle could see the story possibly being true.

At one murder site, Mickle was seen looking through a Dumpster, hunting for the murder weapon.

"We looked for murder weapons those days," Mickle said.

Mickle wasn't a exactly cuddly type—even though you could hear him saying "baby sweetheart" or "little guy" to his children on the phone.

This guy was a pitbull.

He was an old-fashioned newsman. The type that are becoming extinct in this age of advocacy journalism. Those papers as Mickle would claim "are being edited for boredom."

One time, he told a doctor who was facing legal trouble that "the jig was up."

"You might as well talk to us," Mickle told the doc. "You are in enough trouble already."

According to one legend, Mickle called the family of a victim who was burned to death.

"You didn't know he died," Mickle said. "I'm sorry. He was torched, burned up to a crisp, just like that."

Once again, this story is a legend, but with Mickle, it's possible.

Mickle had one train of thought: Get the story at all costs.

Like a pitbull, he would never let go—even when the story wasn't there.

When he assigned a story to a reporter, a phrase like "if you look into it, you will find…" would always be a part of it.

Mickle was always skeptical, never trusted the establishment, which are perfect traits for a city editor.

A city editor will never believe a story is dead and will question everything.

But Mickle energized the newsroom. He was the driving personality.

Today's newsrooms are too sterile. It shows in the final product.

Newspapers are too lame.

The Trentonian under Schwartz could never be lame.

The Trentonian's atmosphere was lively and candid with each other. When something sucks, say, "it sucks."

One time Schwartz, according to legend, told a buxom reporter she should use her assets. This dominated the paper.

Fights are good. Newsmen should be brawling. They should be drinking, and they should care about the type of stories that is running in the paper.

Chairs should fly. Voices raised. Phones slamming. Profanities ringing through the air.

Now that's newspapering.

A solid newspaper staff is one that drinks together. A worker can drink in the office—as long as he doesn't get caught.

The Trentonian did have its drinkers. Heck, some of them obviously had a few before they came to work.

Andrew Francis Hussie didn't drink before he came into the office, but he organized a nightly gathering at the watering hole. He was the paper's social director and one hell of a copy editor.

Hussie works at one speed, slow. In fact, he operates more efficiently at the bars. He has little regard for his health. He smokes cigarettes and eats all the wrong foods. His face is beet-red and he can often be seen holding a coffee in one hand, a cigarette in the other and complaining about how he doesn't get any women.

As copy editor, he, at times, couldn't catch a cold. He detested editors. His favorite times at The Trentonian are when the editor position is vacant.

That means, nobody will be there to pressure him, ride him and put his life through misery with standards. He goes in, smoothly does his job and hits the bar at 12:45 a.m.

Some called him, "the Dean of the Copy Desk."

No, that's "the Dean *Martin* of the Copy Desk."

Now, how can a guy be slow and hate his bosses, yet be an effective copy editor?

Hussie has great news judgment.

He knows what sells the paper.

He can find the unique twist buried in the story that could be elevated into the lead story.

He's the man.

But he had a personality that helped shape the newsroom. He was one of the wild cast of characters. I did catch the copy desk boozing in the newsroom after deadline. A copy desk that can drink together can work together.

A perfect combination.

The newsroom was filled with colorful personalities, and it reflected in the paper.

The Trentonian was colorful—no one could question it.

Journalists today take themselves too seriously. They think the world hinges on their work.

The Trentonian at its peak had a special bond with its readers, and that's better than most staid papers can claim today.

◆ ◆ ◆

Our world depended on sales, and for the first 10 days, our world was collapsing.

Sen. Torricelli wasn't catching fire. Not even the slightest spark.

I would be feeling the heat if we didn't improve. Soon.

The 10th day of the Raffaele regime was the most pivotal; it shaped the entire era. We were slumping, and after that day, we broke out of it. Big time.

Reporters Chris Wilson and Mark O'Reilly were the catalysts.

Wilson with his dogged reporting was able to turn a fatal shooting into a dramatic reflection of your society. Most editors frown on shootings in the city. In their snobby worlds, it is not news for shootings to occur in the inner city.

But if a shooting occurs in the suburbs, it's a blockbuster story. Middle America is under fire. Every breaking story must be attacked by a reporter—no matter where it is.

This story happened in the heart of Trenton's inner city.

Wilson got word that a drug dealer was gunned down in Trenton. A mundane story for most papers, which are inherently racist and don't care about so-called "bottomfeeder" drug dealers, especially ones in the inner city.

The neighborhood reaction to the fatal shooting struck me. Kids, instead of wiping tears from their eyes, started looting the man, taking drugs and guns off his person. At our news meeting that day, we all knew this was the lead story.

We just couldn't frame it properly for a top-selling headline. An unclear headline that makes little to no sense won't produce any cents for the paper.

It takes about 10 seconds for readers to decide if they are going to buy a paper. Cloudy headlines mean trouble. The head must be dramatic, hitting the reader right between the eyes.

KIDS SWIPE GUNS FROM CORPSE kept running through our heads, but that was just clunky. It had to be more aggressive, straightforward.

We were stumped. Another bad day in a hideous slump was looming.

An unlikely source bailed us out. Jeff Zelevansky, a photographer, was not a tabloid guy. He was laid back, a 23-year-old who looks 28. But his work was tremendous. He just blurted out, "KIDS MUG CORPSE."

Zelevansky hit the home run.

We went with it.

The story read like this:

"A mob of looters led by an 11-year-old boy swarmed over a city murder scene in the minutes before cops arrived last weekend, stealing guns, cash and even bullets right from a dead man's pocket, police said.

"The scavengers set upon the drug dealer's corpse as he lay sprawled in a pool of blood on a Hills Place stoop after a shootout Sunday afternoon.

"The gang also barged into the nearby drug den where the dealer was shot, stripping the place clean of weapons, drugs and loot even though the man who allegedly shot the dealer lay wounded inside.

"'If he were there another five minutes, he would have been naked,' Deputy Chief Joe Constance said, calling the crime scene bandits "jackals who took advantage of a dead man's body.'"

This story, and the headline, captured the grittiness of the urban landscape, its endemic problems and its bizarre cultural norms in a way that a supposed "issue story" never could.

It was the best sale of the week.

It set the standard for stories from then on.

"What we need right now is a story like KIDS MUG CORPSE," Mickle would constantly say when the news was dreadfully slow.

◆ ◆ ◆

KIDS MUG CORPSE did open our eyes. A simple crime story was by far our best-selling product.

That's what the readers of Trenton wanted. That's what they would get.

We followed with a plethora of simple, straightforward crime lines:

VICIOUS STABBING

DR. DEATH HELPS BUCKS FOOTBALL STAR DIE

MASS SUICIDE AT MANSION

MINISTER WANTED ME TO DRESS LIKE HOOKER

Simple, straightforward, crime-oriented front pages were delighting readers. That coupled with a BINGO! game promotion, put the Trentonian past the 60,000 mark in circulation. Actually the circulation was closer to 61,000. The good, old days were back.

◆ ◆ ◆

For Bob Jelenic, it didn't matter how good the front pages sold.

We stunk.

Because we continued to make, in his mind, "end the world" mistakes in the sports. A high school baseball box score didn't add up? Let the firings begin.

In the last weekend of March 1997, Scott Esposito, in Jelenic's mind went from a heavenly writer to one that will go directly to hell.

One weekend, and Esposito would face eternal damnation. JRC style.

The high school hockey all-Colonial Valley Conference teams were announced with the player of the year and all-county teams.

It was a blockbuster high school hockey package.

Firstly, before we came out with the player of the year, we wanted permission to name Bryan Bowser—not Lee Jelenic—as the region's top player.

In 1996, Jelenic was named player of the year—despite Bowser having better statistics and a much better team.

That year, Bowser's Notre Dame team trounced Lee's West Windsor-Plainsboro team 11-2.

Trentonian hockey writer Brian Dohn still went with Jelenic as the top player—basically saying he was hands down the most complete player.

The Times properly named Bowser player of the year.

The high school hockey community—even though it was microscopic in size—knew the deal: Lee's father owned the Trentonian. It was a complete joke in the high school sporting world. We covered high school hockey more extensively than boys' basketball. Regular season high school games involving West Windsor graced lead position of the back page constantly.

When Lee played Little League, his team made the front page—even a rain out story.

The favoritism was painfully obvious and our sports writers were the butt of many jokes. According to office legend, one high school baseball player hit a home run. As he rounded third base he said his "name will finally get in the paper, but wait my name isn't Lee Jelenic, so it won't get in."

A couple of months after naming Lee Jelenic player of the year in 1996, Brian Dohn was offered a position with the New Haven Register—the largest paper of the Journal Register Company chain.

Esposito was in Dohn's league. Then objectivity got in the way.

Esposito wanted to name Bowser player of the year in 1997. Bowser was the all-time scoring leader in the CVC—so it would be ridiculous for the paper not naming the most prolific scorer in CVC history on the league's best team.

We asked Schwartz to run it by Jelenic.

Jelenic approved it, but he said "we won't be hearing much from Bowser after this."

Bowser, you see, was going to be attending Division III Geneseo State while Lee was headed for Division I Yale.

Schwartz wanted to make sure Jelenic was on the first team. Now, I assumed he was referring to CVC, the league. Lee made it to the first team CVC. He deserved it. He was the second-best player in the CVC.

But underneath the all-CVC team, Esposito announced the all-county team, which included prep powerhouse Lawrenceville. It ran in 6-point agate type.

It might as well appeared in 500-point.

Lawrenceville is the best team in New Jersey, and objectively speaking, its top 10 players are better than any of the CVC players, including Bowser.

So the first-team, all-county squad had nothing but Lawrenceville players.

Lee Jelenic and Bryan Bowser made the second team.

The offices of the Journal Register Company on 50 State Street, Trenton, figuratively exploded.

Jelenic took the move as a slap in the face by Esposito. How can Lee not be on the first-team, all-county team?

Funny thing, Esposito was right, but it didn't matter.

Jelenic promptly ripped Schwartz, who then buried me.

It was rolling downhill.

Esposito wasn't the shining star anymore, and this team would haunt him for the next five years.

He was lucky to have a job.

♦ ♦ ♦

Sandy Schwartz was angry.

Angry at the front page that led with the headline SOUR NOTES, which was supposed to reflect how the Democratic candidates for governor were "Johnny One-Notes." In their race against Republican Gov. Christie Whitman, the Dems couldn't find a single message that struck a chord with voters.

"Who the fuck wrote the front page headline?" Schwartz said.

"I did," I meekly replied.

"Let me tell you something," Schwartz grumbled. "If I left this fuckin' place for two weeks—*two weeks*—this place would turn into the fuckin' Philadelphia Daily News."

Schwartz detested the Philly Daily News. In his view, that tabloid paper led with numerous convoluted headlines that made no sense. He constantly ripped the news judgment of the paper, calling it "soft" and a "bunch of crap."

SOUR NOTES stunk.

SOUR NOTES was one of the worst front pages I've produced. Schwartz was right—it made no sense.

I shouldn't have led the paper with political writer Sherry Sylvester's package. I picked SOUR NOTES over Tiger Woods record-breaking victory at the 1997 Masters. Most of the papers led with that story. For one day, I was a "Johnny One-Note" myself.

It was bad job by me.

The bug called bad news judgment can bite anybody.

♦ ♦ ♦

Most newspapers refrain from using the word "HOOKER" in headlines.

The editors at those publications believe it is in bad taste. Inappropriate for a paper that is delivered to families.

I embrace hookers—in headlines.

Headlines must be clear and comprehendible, and HOOKER is a shorter, punchier word than prostitute.

Cowardly newspapers shy away from the word.

My favorite hooker head at the Trentonian was: MINISTER WANTED ME TO DRESS LIKE HOOKER.

This came just one month after KIDS MUG CORPSE. We ran the picture of the seemingly pleasant minister.

It worked.

Chris Wilson pieced together this prose:

"PEMBERTON TWP. —A prominent Lutheran minister has been indicted on a slew of shocking sex charges after a 14-year-old girl claimed he sexually molested her over two nightmarish years, The Trentonian has learned.

"The Rev. Robert Wilms of Browns Mills fondled the girl, spanked her and showered her with X-rated undergarments in a twisted bid to turn her into his private pre-teen call girl, the victim's outraged mom told The Trentonian."

Because the story involved a minister, it prevented it from becoming what Schwartz would classify as "Today's Molester."

Every day, our daily news budget, produced by Mickle, was filled with stories about molesters—men fondling young girls and boys.

It became so frequent—that Schwartz would label it "Today's Molester."

"Wouldn't it be great," Schwartz once mused, "if we can create a 'Today's Molester' logo with a pair of hands."

We never went that far, but molesting stories are becoming as frequent as parking violations with nothing outstanding to report. Most of the molester stories appeared in the paper as briefs.

But those involving priests or ministers warranted front-page coverage.

GLORY DAYS   39

♦   ♦   ♦

Bob Shields and I were desperately searching for a headline.

A headline that could serve as a follow-up to the massive suicide that mansion the day before.

On March 26, 1998, 39 people were found dead in a San Diego mansion. It was a mass suicide.

On March 27, 1998, The Trentonian hit the stands with MASS SUICIDE AT MANSION.

We needed something dramatic—especially after it was discovered these people were Internet geeks who committed suicide because they wanted to hop on the Hale-Bopp Comet as it was passing Earth.

Now, these people were world-class weirdoes.

We needed a headline to capture the essence of the story. A headline that would advance the story to a new level.

Shields sat my desk in my office. With feet propped up on the desk, an idea lit up his brain.

"Internuts," he said.

"That's it," I said. "That's the lead headline. INTERNUTS."

Schwartz loved the headline and approved it to lead the paper.

But he wanted more in our package.

In the news meeting, Schwartz said nobody but perverts probed the 'Net.

Mark Stradling said he gets information for his editorials on the Internet all the time.

"OK, let me see," Schwartz said. "Let's say that about 15 million people go on this Internet. About 200,000 go on it just like Stradling, just to get information.

"The rest of them go on it are perverts and weirdoes."

Todd Venezia interrupted, "I go on the Internet all the time."

"*That's* exactly my point," Schwartz said.

Chris Wilson was summoned into the news meeting. He had to do a story about how the majority of Internet users were perverts and weirdoes.

Wilson was floored. How could he write story like this? Wilson uses the Internet, but if he mentioned it to Schwartz, he would have undoubtedly gotten the same response Venezia received. Like Mickle, Schwartz gets one train of thought, and he cannot be derailed.

Somehow Wilson mustered his resources together.

With the headline "Experts: 'Net is balm for bozos," Wilson reported:

"Space-age suicide cultists Higher Source sought refuge in the same high-tech hideouts of the Internet that lure some many other cybermisfits away from the outside world, experts said.

"The far-out death group—whose members earned a lucrative living designing Web pages—broadcast their bizarre philosophies online and probably felt most at peace surfing the 'Net before ending it all.

"'Because the Internet and computers are so isolating, their urge to become a family style cult became even stronger,' said pop psychologist Dr. Joyce Brothers.

"'After a while, they all convinced each other that what the cult leader believed was true, and looked for a better life in the hereafter.'

"Brothers said the computer cultists may have felt validated by the instant legitimacy of the Internet when they tapped out strange predictions, peppered with talk of comets, UFOs and the afterlife."

Maybe it was a short of proclaiming all Internet users are nuts, but it was close enough.

A day later, it was revealed that one of the victims was the brother of "Star Trek" star Nichelle Nichols.

For the front page, we ran the picture of BEAM HIM UP with a sexy picture of Nichols' character Lt. Uhura.

◆ ◆ ◆

Todd Venezia and Chris Wilson are typical journalists.

They spend the night at the bars—kicking back a couple of brews.

Journalists live a night-owl life. A great number of those in the newspaper industry are helplessly single or divorced. They drown their sorrows in brew.

Venezia and Wilson are single and always on the prowl to have a good time.

On the early morning of April 3, 1997, Wilson and Venezia were kicking back at Joe's Mill Hill Saloon at North Broad and Market streets.

This duo—two of the best reporters in Trentonian history—were unaware of what happened in the parking lot while they were pounding some beers.

Nancy Houtz reported:

"A Ewing man just four days away from marriage stumbled into a nightmare yesterday when a small-time drug dealer struck him with a single punch and left him brain dead on the pavement outside a Trenton bar."

The victim, 27-year-old Dennis Hunter, was the son of a popular restaurateur Larry Peroni. The son of a prominent businessman left brain dead days before his wedding.

That's big news.

Houtz was in her first week as a reporter at the paper. Houtz was hired by Anne Karolyi right before Schwartz elevated me, and to Houtz's dismay, she had a new boss when she arrived.

It could be unsettling for a new reporter. Thoughts of "would this guy have hired me?" must have been running through her head.

Houtz, however, made a lasting impression when she sneaked into Hunter's hospital room. And she came back with a dramatic, tearful tale.

However, she relished the exhilaration of the moment—of a reporter getting the job done to add details to the story. She was like a little kid that just hit a home run in the bottom of the ninth inning to win a Little League game. Her eyes lit up when she told Mickle, Schwartz and I the tale of her getting into the hospital.

She seemed like the "Daughter of Mickle."

"She's great," Schwartz said.

As one of the sidebars to the package, Houtz reported on her findings in a hospital room where a beloved son was brain dead.

"In a cold, sterile section of Helene Fuld Medical Center the only things tying Dennis Hunter to life were the thin tubes and wires hooked to life support machines.

"As the equipment forced Hunter's chest to rise and fall, his parents were huddled in a small room down the hall, discussing his fate with doctors.

"With little more to offer than their sympathy and the tragic truth, doctors explained that Hunter was brain dead and there was no hope.

In an open corner of the ICU, Michele Vannozzi didn't seem to notice the tubes that pumped life into her fiancé's body. Tears streamed down her face as she stroked his hair and whispered secrets that he would never hear.

"'They were going to fly to Lake Tahoe this weekend to get married. They were so much in love and ready to start their life together,' said an emotional Mary Striker, Hunter's aunt. 'How can something so senseless send it all?'

Shocked relatives and friends, who extended from the foot of Hunter's bed out through the lobby, sobbed for their loss.

"'There is no hope," said one relative. 'But what do you do? It just isn't that easy.'

But the boy's mother and stepfather, Gloria and Larry Peroni, there was only the awful decision to be made—when should they remove Dennis from the artificial life support?

"'This is very serious,' said Larry Peroni.

Late last night, however, an improvement in Dennis' blood pressure gave the family a small window of hope that he yet may recover.

"So they flew him to Thomas Jefferson Hospital in Philadelphia for special treatment.

"'She's going to marry him,' said Vannozzi's sister, Kelly, last night. 'If Dennis comes out of this, she's going to marry him.'"

The next day, we led with BRAIN DEAD AFTER SUCKER PUNCH as the wood.

Days later, the Peronis gave up hope and removed Dennis Hunter off of life support.

◆ ◆ ◆

Rich Timlen was my henchman in the sports department. I tell him to do it, and he does it.

No matter how crazy the story is.

Good soldiers follow the orders to a "T."

One of our kooky sources told us that legendary coach Lou Holtz was forced out of Notre Dame.

Three months earlier, Holtz resigned saying it was the "right thing to do" at the time.

Now, we have a guy who is fairly close to Holtz saying he was pushed out.

Most reporters would be reluctant to write this story—because the source might be considered "thin." Some reporters in the building thought the source was a crackpot.

Not Timlen.

He tackled the story with zeal:

"Lou Holtz was pressured into resigning as head football coach at the University of Notre Dame, The Trentonian has learned.

"A source close to the university told The Trentonian that there was no "chemistry" between Holtz and Athletic Director Mike Wadsworth and that Wadsworth approached Holtz saying 'we are thinking about making a move.'

"'There was enough ill will for Lou Holtz to step down from the job he cherished,' the source said. 'Wadsworth was concerned with some of the recruiting and they lost some games they shouldn't have. Lou felt he didn't have 100 percent support from this guy.'

"One of those games was a 20-17 overtime home loss to Air Force, which was a considerable underdog to the Irish.

"'That was the straw that broke the camel's back,' the source said. 'That was too big of an upset from home."

South Bend, Ind., is 706 miles away from Trenton, but Notre Dame is America's Team.

They were like the Trentonian. People loved them or hated them. We led the back page with the headline, WHY LOU LEFT.

This story was a good talker, and too many editors would have talked themselves out of it because it was either too thin or it wasn't in their circulation area.

Editors must lower the bar in running stories. We had a source close to Lou Holtz say he was forced out so we went with it.

Editors will hide behind the cloud of "responsible journalism." Instead they are scared of rocking the boat and being bold.

And we were bold.

◆ ◆ ◆

Sex and The Trentonian go hand in hand.

Mention The Trentonian, people immediately mention the Page 6 girl. The Trentonian is the only paper in the county to feature models. It had a cult following. The readers loved the girls—especially those who were local.

Readers don't want to admit it, but sex sells.

Put the word "sex" in the headline, and the circulation will soar. Use that picture with a beautiful woman and you have a complete winner.

Readers won't admit they buy a paper for sex. It's frowned upon in our society. You wouldn't be considered intellectual if you merely bought a paper just for the sex.

One time, Schwartz was dispatched to St. Louis by Ralph Ingersoll to offer guidance for the struggling tabloid—the St. Louis Sun.

After browsing through the paper, Schwartz asked "where are the girls?"

Actually, it took a tragedy to initially convince me that sex connected with the Trenton reader.

We had a story about a coed (which is an automatic seller of a word) who collapsed on a treadmill and went into a coma. We didn't have a picture of this woman. The story sold all right—better than most political stories. However, there was a perception that this woman was fat. And if she were in shape, it wouldn't have happened in the first place.

A month later, I assigned Barri Orlow, a reporter in the features department, to follow the story—basically to find out the coed's status.

Orlow did one step better—she got a picture.

This girl in a coma was attractive with a girl-next-door look.

When Barri showed me the picture, the headline was a lock: SLEEPING BEAUTY.

This story sold about 2,000 more copies than the original story—all because we had a picture that revealed her stunning looks.

Readers are sometimes cruel. They felt sorry for her only because she was good-looking, but the approach worked for us.

We sold papers. That's all that mattered.

Another sex saga was the clincher.

For me, this "discovery" came in May 1997 when The Trentonian led with "TEACH, TEEN HAD SEX IN SCHOOL."

The teacher was suspended after the mom found tales of love in the young girl's diary. It was unreal. Our photographer, Leslie Barbaro, got pictures of where the sexual experience occurred—in the school's auditorium.

The Trenton Times—our rival newspaper—brushed it off and they couldn't dare to run a spicy story involving sex between the teacher and a student.

With soaring sales, we plowed on. You see, hot sales gave us the mandate to continue to press a story. There was a reader demand. I'm a whore when it comes to readers. Their wish is my command.

Two days later, we led with STUDENT BRAGGED ABOUT SEX WITH TEACH. This story, which we broke, we didn't let up on. It was just too crazy of a story. We couldn't just break out developing aspects of this story. We wanted to keep the story in the news; we need an enterprise piece on a day when there was no news.

Publisher Sandy Schwartz came up with one.

"Aren't these teachers vulnerable to these hot little girls in skimpy outfits?" Schwartz asked. "We gotta do a story about how these sex kittens in the classroom prey on these lonely old men."

We assigned Nancy Houtz to do the story, and photographer Chris Barth had to go out to a local high school to find some attractive female students. It was a week before we got to run the lead SEX KITTENS IN THE CLASSROOM, because Barth had a tough time shooting pictures of girls at these suburban schools.

He couldn't find any hot-looking woman.

Armed with his camera, he sat in his car outside an area high school—waiting for the girls to come out of class. Barth felt like a prowler—a sex fiend of sorts. On paper, a guy waiting outside and looking for good looking girls to come out of class would be considered a predator.

But Barth was on the job; we ordered him to do this.

He failed on his mission.

The girls he shot fell woefully short of being considered sex kittens, who lure the poor male teachers.

We didn't have the story. You can't run a story without a picture. The story was an excuse to running a hot picture.

Schwartz hounded me

"Where's the fucking sex kittens?" he said.

I explained to him our situation. He understood. He knew the importance of the picture.

It was time to take matters into my own hands.

It was time to turn to our resident sex kitten—Molly Davis.

Molly Davis, a Rider graduate who lived in Bucks County, Pa., was a reporter who attracted the attention most of the males in the building.

Including Schwartz.

"What a body!" he proclaimed after she walked by his office. "If I was a little younger…"

Davis was a solid reporter, but her body was needed to save the day.

She was going to be a model for a photo illustration.

Jeff Zelevansky, fresh off his KIDS MUG CORPSE fame, was ordered to take a picture of Davis in front of the pressmen's lockers. Davis wore a short skirt—one that Catholic schoolgirls would wear—and used a belt to serve as a bookbag. We cut off the top of her head. So the image was just her legs, skirt and blouse.

It was a sexy picture—taken years before Britney Spears' famous video.

So we had the picture with the headline, SEX KITTENS IN THE CLASSROOM on the front page.

Nancy Houtz, with help from Venezia, hit a home run with a sizzling lead:

"To a 16-year-old boy, the sight of a short skirt, a tight shirt and the big young eyes of a 16-year-old girl stirs feelings that are new and hard to resist.

"Sneaking peeks at bare legs, flirting in gym shorts and stealing kisses and touches in the back of the school bus can become a way of life and a way to learn important things that books don't teach.

"And when that boy grows up, becomes mature and is charged with teaching the young himself, those feelings—no longer as new—are still firmly in place.

"That's why all too many men and girls put in close contact find each other irresistible and break one of the strongest of society's taboos—student-teacher sex."

Now, *that's* enterprise reporting.

The weather on the day when the SEX KITTENS paper hit the stands was miserable. It was steady downpour. Usually, that spells doom for circulation. Bad weather and missed deadlines will curb a sale no matter what is on the front page.

Farrell initially said the sales were slow. Nobody was buying from the paper boxes because of the rain.

But when he gathered all of the data, the sales in the stores boomed—our best in months. If it wasn't for the rain, it likely would have been the top-selling issue of the year.

SEX KITTENS went "purrfectly" well with our readers.

Photo illustrations with stories about sex wasn't uncommon. One of Davis' friends, who needed the money, posed for a picture for a story concerning phone sex. We had pictures of her talking on the phone—in a bikini.

We paid Davis' buddy $75; I felt like a pimp.

But those sales were hot.

A month later, SEX IN THE MORTUARY hit the stands. A story most newspapers would have blown off.

A story developed when Mickle got a tip about a lawsuit. It had been filed two years before, but it was never reported.

A woman who used to work for a funeral parlor accused her boss of having sex with her in their workplace. The woman claims she was fired, because something went wrong in their relationship. Chris Barth got a picture of the woman, but unfortunately she wasn't good looking. She was chunky and in her 40s. A picture like that never works unless the woman is totally hot. We ended up getting a picture of the casket on Page 1 instead.

Before the story went to press, everybody was talking about this story.

Irene Bagley, our beloved chain-smoking obituary writer, couldn't believe this funeral director had actually been up to such naughty deeds when she heard about the story. "But he's such a nice guy," she said. "He would never do anything like this."

Also inside that issue was the "Down the Shore" section. Most papers would fill the section with stories with what to do on the Jersey Shore. It was an excuse to run pictures of hot women frolicking around the beach in bikinis. About 10 percent of the section had information—the rest was devoted to the sexy pictures.

Combine SEX IN THE MORTUARY with the "Down the Shore" section, it was our best sale of 1997. Hands down.

Under the page 3 headline, INTERCORPSE, Chris Dolmetsch reported:

"BORDENTOWN—A prominent funeral director turned his mortuary into a cadaver-packed bordello—making love with an intern on the embalming room floor, cavorting around in a towel and demonstrating sex sessions inside a coffin, the woman is charging in a lawsuit.

"This shocking suit claims William L. Huber, the owner of Huber Funeral Home and Burlington County's chief medical investigator, also demanded sex in other bizarre situations—during autopsies, as an intern embalmed the corpse of an AIDS victim, and as they left a funeral at a veteran's cemetery.

"The papers, filed in 1995 in Burlington County court and only revealed this week, also claimed the respected mortician masturbated in front of her as she worked on cadavers, urinated in a utility sink and walked around the funeral home only in a towel.

"After intern Dorothyann Forman refused the mortician's increasingly ghoulish sexual brainstorms, Huber turned 'hostile and angry' and stopped having sex with her in September 1994, the suit claims."

Bob Jelenic wasn't happy with the story. He thought that because the story was two years old; it should have been buried. It wasn't worthy of the read.

He said the paper should lead with Tiger Woods that weekend if he wins the U.S. Open. Woods was fresh off his record-breaking victory at the Masters. If not the golf, lead with the Bulls winning the NBA title.

"It would attract our black readers," he said.

SEX IN THE MORTUARY attracted all: blacks, whites, yellow, purple and red.

Instead of being bothered by Jelenic's complaints. I found it refreshing; it was the first time he ever complained about the news section—even though the issue was the best-selling paper of the year.

The results were in: Sex was working at the Trentonian. Bolstered by the success of the SEX IN THE MORTUARY and SEX KITTENS IN THE CLASSROOM, we brought the Monday poster back—calling it "THE GIRLS OF SUMMER."

Every Monday, we would run a large picture of a beauty down the side of Page 1, and run a two-page centerfold inside.

The Trenton readers welcomed it with open wallets.

♦ ♦ ♦

Finding and taking pictures of beauties seems like a ideal job for male photographers. They were getting paid to talk to heart-stopping babes.

We would dispatch our lensmen out to the beach and try to convince women to pose for the paper. We offered $50 for a photo to appear on Page 6, and an additional $100 was awarded if they were picked for a Monday poster.

But this dream job turned into a nightmare for the photographers.

Zelevansky and Barth were miserable. They would often get rejected. Good-looking girls were tough to find. They felt like weirdoes, going up to women all day and asking to take their pictures. Sometimes the girls would threaten to call the police.

Girls would often call and cancel appointments. If the photo was taken, they would constantly call about their check.

"It was so frustrating," Zelevansky said. "It's like getting rejected for a date a hundred times during the day."

Zelevansky left the paper because he hated Page 6 so much.

It just got worse after Princess Diana's death that September, because women were more wary of photographers and journalists than ever before.

Page 6 girls drove Barth to bail from the paper.

Put the readers wanted it, so we delivered girls. Local girls.

Newspaper editors today chuckle at how pathetic The Trentonian was in running Page 6. Whenever I talked to others in the industry, I would hear wisecracks about the "Page 6 slut."

Meanwhile, those same editors are touting stories about open space in New Jersey and the startling new development in wastewater management.

Those editors were losing readers.

The snobby newspaper industry mocked The Trentonian's recipe for success. The Trentonian survived as a tabloid in the smallest two-newspaper market in the country. It found the right combination to connect with its readers.

Most so-called "respected" newspapers would have gone out of business in a similar setting. The combination of hard-hitting, local news, sex, Page 6 and hard-hitting sports was working. Extremely well.

We didn't care what other snobs in the industry said about it.

◆ ◆ ◆

With my promotion to executive editor, the sports editor position was vacant. I held both positions.

Nobody was racing to become sports editor. Nobody wanted to wear the bulls'-eye.

Who would blame them? Taking a sports editor position was like wearing a "KICK ME" sign on your back. Take the promotion and get ready to be fired. With Jelenic's ridiculous ranting and standards, nobody was masochistic enough to take the position.

I offered the position to several people. Fat chance, they said. Jelenic made it so unbearable that no qualified individual would even join the department—don't even consider the sports editor spot.

People in that department avoided me like the plague.

I made a split-second decision.

I appointed Rich Timlen as sports editor with George O' Gorman the scholastic sports editor.

A masterful stroke of genius? Well, it looked good on paper.

Timlen worked with Esposito on the high school hockey beat. He was my first hire as sports editor.

In December 1996, the department had troubles—especially with placement of stories and design.

We had this sports writer position, and the staff overwhelmingly backed a part-time sports writer, who had a passionate attitude toward his work.

I snubbed him.

I had to go with someone else to change the department's image. The part-timer also showed up in sweat pants when I interviewed him for the job.

Timlen, on the other hand, came in and interviewed well. A Rider graduate, Timlen applied for a news job, but I convinced the managing editor at the time for Timlen to be hired in sports.

Timlen was a safe bet: he was an outsider loyal to me, not to the staff.

The department was furious over Timlen's hiring. The part-timer did pay his dues. But if I hired him, I'd be sending a message to the rest of the department that what they were doing was acceptable, and that's not the impression I wanted to relay.

At the time, the sports section had to change its ways.

The first hire is the most important; it puts your imprint on the staff. It helps you mold the personnel.

Problem was, Timlen received considerable backlash.

Some of the staffers thought Timlen was lazy. He worked eight hours and went home. He was efficient, and did a solid job on high school hockey with Esposito. Anybody who does well on the high school hockey beat deserves a promotion at this place.

The Timlen hiring and promotion antagonized the sports department that was constantly bombarded with troubles from corporate.

The O'Gorman promotion was based on ability, and it was a political masterpiece.

George O'Gorman is the ideal sports writer.

With a larger-than-life personality, O'Gorman, who worked for The Trentonian since the late 1970s after a stint with the Trenton Times, is a versatile reporter connected to the community.

He knows what a good news story is.

Usually, sports writers are knuckleheaded and only focused on results. Who cares about the war in Afghanistan? The Sixers play the Nuggets tonight.

Only concerned about sports, nothing else. These types couldn't find a decent news story—even if it was slammed in their face.

For example, Rick Fortenbaugh, a wrestling writer for the Trentonian for nearly 20 years, ignored a story about an one-legged Trenton wrestler who was unbeaten.

Undefeated—with one leg.

Fortenbaugh didn't think it was a story—because the kid hadn't beaten any quality opponents.

This kid was unbeaten on one leg, an obvious human-interest story. No question, a lead story for the front page.

The wrestler's competition wasn't stiff enough for Fortenbaugh to write a feature story.

O'Gorman, however, is a true newsman, and man born and bred in Trenton.

He is Trenton.

A complete workhorse, O'Gorman worked two full-time jobs and covered the New York Giants, high school girls soccer, girls basketball, cross country, indoor track, high school baseball, recreation soccer....

The list goes on and on.

If he wanted, he would be a tremendous news reporter. He gave us tips for at least five lead stories. He heard that Sammy "The Bull" Gravano admitted to making hits on two Trenton residents. He got it confirmed and we had a solid front page featuring, the BULL'S TRENTON HITS.

O'Gorman just wanted us to be the best paper the state, and cared about every page.

That's all you can ask from a sports writer. If every newspaper had an O'Gorman, the industry would be saved.

But O'Gorman was linked to the high school sports world, and he dealt with Jelenic at sporting events.

Jelenic's daughter, Laine, at the time was an up-and-coming high school soccer, basketball and softball player. O'Gorman would see Jelenic at events and give him grief.

O'Gorman always spoke his mind—no matter how "important" the person was.

The Trentonian, since it's a newspaper in the smallest two daily newspaper market in the country, was always surrounded by rumors of closing. O'Gorman was aware of it and constantly asked Jelenic if the paper was closing.

O'Gorman complained to Jelenic about the shortage of employees in the department, "how can you expect us to compete in local sports, when you don't give us the same amount of bodies."

O'Gorman ripped him for getting on the department's case, "if you want us to get better, give us some reporters."

Vintage O'Gorman.

Jelenic seemingly liked O'Gorman's guts and personality. O'Gorman is indestructible, and won't get rattled by Jelenic's ranting. In fact, he would strike back.

Sports editors tend to get devastated by the CEO's complaints, and eventually bail.

O'Gorman wasn't going anywhere.

He's the rock.

If Jelenic called me to rip the section, I would tell him I would consult with O'Gorman.

O'Gorman's personality could protect everybody.

Timlen's time as sports editor was short-lived. It lasted three months, and it was a disaster. An editor has to be respected, and he wasn't—especially when at one time Timlen questioned O'Gorman's work ethic.

Never question Big George's work ethic.

At times, Timlen didn't follow my instructions. The staff didn't respect him. Jelenic was constantly calling. The end was near for Mr. Timlen.

The new sports personnel I hired—Ted Holmlund and Eric Barrow—weren't developing as quickly as I hoped. The duo, I considered the future of the sports department.

Holmlund came from the Poughkeepsie Journal in New York and was a solid wordsmith.

When Barrow arrived for his interview, he caught Mickle's eye:

"Who in the hell is that good-looking, black guy," Mickle said. "I'm sure he can get some news stories for us."

That was Barrow, a solid designer who worked in Japan and produced his own college sports publication in Madison, Wis.

Under Timlen, both newcomers struggled. We needed a change; somebody who would work for a couple of months and develop Barrow and Holmlund into sports editors.

I demoted Timlen in July.

He was relieved. The pressure was off. He was out of the crosshairs—for now. Getting demoted was never better.

Storm Gifford was summoned to my office.

◆ ◆ ◆

"You're going to take this job," I bellowed. "I need you to be sports editor, and you're going to do it."

Dealing with my hissy-fit was nothing new for Storm Gifford, a 26-year-old copy editor.

He was the "bartender" of the newsroom where everybody would vent and share their problems with him. Gifford, a professor at Mercer County Community College, was the pipeline for gossip—he knew everybody's problems.

He was a great listener.

He was a great healer.

I called him the "Gerald Ford of the newsroom." Ford, the 38th president of the United States, helped the nation heal after Richard Nixon's resignation from Watergate.

In some ways, Gifford's challenge with the sports department was just as stiff.

The sports staff resented being picked on by Jelenic, resented Timlen and hated me for putting Timlen in that spot.

Despite being a protector, O'Gorman couldn't maintain his duties as scholastic sports editor—there just weren't enough hours in a day for O'Gorman. He had too much on his plate.

I needed somebody who was respected, and more importantly, a person who agreed with my sports philosophy.

Gifford loved my philosophy.

◆ ◆ ◆

It was December 20, 1996.

I had been sports editor for a week. The department had been under my leadership for two weeks—I had made an impact.

The sports section had to become more like the news section in the past: a section that tried to appeal to the most readers and was talked about. Stories in the section must draw emotions: ranging from tears to wild fits of anger.

Our local sports coverage dealt mainly with game results.

It was dull and lifeless.

We started to run Esposito's columns and led the back page with them. We put much more emphasis on national sports.

O'Gorman and high school basketball reporter Jim Davis didn't like the trend. People buy the paper for local sports. Nothing else. If they want to read national sports, they would buy the New York Post or Philadelphia Daily News.

O'Gorman and Davis weren't afraid to pull any punches. Davis, who covered high school basketball since the late 1970s, was popular with our readers. These two reporters were icons.

Unhappy icons.

I was their target.

They cornered me into an office and closed the door.

It was the first day of high school basketball. The coverage traditionally transforms into one of the biggest spreads in the paper. Jim Davis and George O'Gorman were very concerned about this year's spread because of the paper's recent anti-local feel.

On this day, Rich Kotite, a former Eagles coach, resigned from the head coaching position with the Jets.

Big George and Jim Davis didn't care about national sports. Just local.

I was toast.

They asked me if I was anti-local. "I'm not anti-local," I told them. "I just want compelling stories that people will talk about."

"Will Kotite resigning as Jets coach or local basketball lead the back page?" they asked me.

"We will be leading with the Jets," I told them. "RICH WALKS will be the lead headline on the back."

They were outraged.

"People like to see pictures of their kids playing baseball in area gyms," Davis told me.

"If people want national sports, they can pick up the New York Post," George said.

But I used my mandate. We now had a guy, Chris Collins, to cover New York sports, and I wanted to use him to give national sports greater exposure. "I'm not anti-local. I'm not pro-national. I'm pro-story," I said.

"The best—the most talked about story—will be leading the back page."

Davis wasn't buying that line: "People in Trenton and Ewing actually care more about local sports," he said.

"What about people standing in line at a 7-Eleven?" I asked him. "What would they discuss?"

"People in Trenton and Ewing will talk about local basketball, not Kotite," he said.

My jaw dropped. People who follow local sports also follow national sports news. But a bulk of national fans couldn't care less about the local sports.

National sports appeal to a larger, general audience; therefore, more readers.

O'Gorman and Davis never accepted my arguments. They considered them lame.

I found the duo to be refreshing. You cannot go wrong with two workers who are passionate about their work.

They didn't hold back. Vocal personalities—even when they disagree with the paper—help elevate the quality of the product. It gives the newsroom personality. A lively newsroom equals a lively newspaper.

Lively newspapers sell.

Even though they disagreed with me, Davis and O'Gorman were making the paper with their passion.

The "national against local sports" has been a passionate argument in the sports editing world.

I have a simple rule.

If your circulation is less than 45 miles away from a professional sports team (that's not including minor-league squads), then you should emphasize professional sports. High schools fall through the cracks in professional markets because fans go to more professional games.

You must provide what the reader wants. High school fans more likely will follow professional sports. Professional sports fans may not be interested in their high school teams at all.

If you have a market that is more than 45 miles away, go with the local sports. In smaller markets, high school sports are a part of the fabric of the community. More people will attend games—because it's the only game in town.

Local sports do have to appear completely in the paper, but played down in larger markets.

Gifford was pro-national and he didn't hide it. He though local sports was crap. If there wasn't a clear-cut national lead, we led with columns.

Columns that would get people talking.

Columns that would enrage readers.

Sports had those columns.

We constantly led the sports section with "stir the pot" columns. The Trentonian covered New York and Philadelphia professional teams. Both cities are incredibly opinionated about their teams. Philly fans live for the Birds, Sixers, Phillies and Flyers, and these people are willing to go on a wild rampage for their teams.

So printing columns that spark rage from a Philly sports fans were sensational.

One column written by Rich Timlen was designed just to get Philly and New York fans to get into a fight. We ran pictures of bad boy Sixers Allen Iverson and Derrick Coleman; Flyers star Eric Lindros, and Eagle Ricky Waters with this headline:

THUG TOWN: Philly's top stars make New York's look like angels.

Inside, we called Philly the "City of Brotherly Shove."

Wonderful. And my phone rang constantly with irate Philly fans.

There should be a column played prominently in the sports section daily, and the Editor must get involved in the topics of the columns. Feel-good columns stink.

One time, to get fans ticked, I turned to Trenton Mayor Doug Palmer.

Palmer wasn't politically savvy when it came to picking his favorite sports teams; he was a die-hard Cowboys fan.

Palmer also knew how to stir up the Eagle fans. I had him write a column predicting that the Cowboys were going to beat the Eagles. A mayor in a city full of Giants and Eagles fans, and here he is rooting for the 'Boys. On the back page, he was wearing his Dallas Cowboys hat holding a pennant with the headline "RIDE 'EM COWBOYS!"

I knew this column would stir the pot with people, and Palmer got more feedback for his opinions on football than he did for running the city.

The idea was sparked after Palmer complained about a Timlen column criticizing Michael Irvin.

The day after the mayor's column, Storm Gifford wrote an opinion piece: NO WAY DOUG! BIRDS BEAT COWBOYS. We had a picture of running back Ricky Watters shaking his finger at a picture of the mayor.

The Eagles did win the game.

"Stirring the pot" was vital for the sports section—we wanted to develop strong reactions.

No one sparked more rage than Linda Dougherty.

♦ ♦ ♦

Dougherty, a feisty horse racing writer, had a pull-no-punches writing style that connected with the readers. Dougherty liked a good fight—as long as she wasn't a part of it.

Conversations with courageous columnist Linda Dougherty went like this.

"Hi, Linda."

"Mike," Linda would reply, "I guess you want a cookie-cutter."

"You bet."

"Cookie cutters" were columns—hard-hitting ones I needed to use on a slow sports day. Usually, these columns are the lead to the back page and have a strong voice. In these cases, I didn't have any significant local sports to lead with. I usually am reluctant to lead with regular-season snoozers.

Dougherty and Timlen were professional "cookie-cutter" columnists. These columns trigger a reader response.

On October 8, 1997, the New York Post reported that at least 10 Yankees partied at a bar—just hours after being eliminated from the playoffs by the Cleveland Indians.

Dougherty was ordered to bash the Bombers for showing that they didn't care about a devastating defeat for their fans.

On the back page, we ran the headline, SLIME OF THE YANKEES.

Underneath the inside headline, "Yanks for nothing," Dougherty dished out a doozy.

"The Yanks quickly forgot about their blown playoff series and focused their attention to a little action, with some of the players, according to the Post, leaving the Gaslight with some tantalizing buxom broads at 6 a.m.

"Meanwhile, across Gotham City, Yankee fans mourned. Those same fans that shelled out hard-earned cash for tickets, for expensive cable TV that showed the games, for overpriced Yankee merchandise.

"...Fans that worshipped guys like (Cecil) Fielder and (Bernie) William. And Cone, Jeter, Martinez, Wells, Hayes, Sanchez, Posada and Raines—the entire Gaslight Gang.

"It was, said some eyewitnesses, a shameful display straight out of Sodom and Gomorrah.

"...(After the final out), TV crews zeroed in on owner George Steinbrenner, who waved his hand in disgust and sneered.

"That gesture should be the one that Yankee fans give the horny Gaslight Group, for celebrating and fornicating on a night when the season stood still."

Dougherty managed to stir the pot—frequently and with staffers.

Copy editor Jay Dunn, a former baseball writer, and reporter Jim Davis urged Dougherty to stick to horse racing after reading the column.

I didn't care.

More people were talking about the column than any high school sporting event that day.

Dougherty's rise to fame—or infamy with some readers—started with a column I had her write about Mike Tyson taking part in WrestleMania XIV. Dougherty bashed Tyson's appearance by calling him a disgrace. She later launched a verbal assault on Dennis Rodman who wrestled in a WCW pay-per-view.

It drew fire from the readers.

Our readers—pro wrestling fans.

◆ ◆ ◆

Pro wrestling is the fabric of Trenton.

If somebody asked me about what would symbolize Trenton, I would say pro wrestling.

Reporter Dom Yanchunas found out the hard way.

Yanchunas was new in town and decided to stroll over to a local bar and watch a Phillies game.

One problem, it was Monday night—and pro wrestling dominates the television (programs with the WWF and WCW).

In a bar with at least 10 TVs, only one was devoted to the Phillies.

Pro wrestling was on the other nine.

Yanchunas noticed WWF owner Vince McMahon was getting arrested on TV.

Yanchunas remembered McMahon as good-guy announcer when he watched wrestling when he grew up.

McMahon was the bad guy now. The evil owner tries to hurt heroes like "Stone Cold" Steve Austin and The Rock.

McMahon's arrest was greeted by cheers in the bar.

When he asked why McMahon was headed to jail, a disgusted wrestling fan rolled his eyes and replied "it's because of his actions last week."

Yanchunas was a loser for not knowing.

As Yanchunas walked home, he noticed all of the apartments he strolled past had pro wrestling on the tube.

This is what this city is all about, he thought.

People in the office thought it was ridiculous that I was obsessed over pro wrestling. How can an editor constantly talk about this worthless junk?

The only reason I was obsessed about pro wrestling was our readers also were obsessed.

I was more obsessed in getting readers.

The Trentonian became the first newspaper in New Jersey to have a pro wrestling writer: The Trenton Strangler.

The Strangler's column quickly became most popular feature in the Sunday paper. He reported on rumors and possible developments in storylines.

Since pro wrestling consists of good guys and bad guys, the Strangler needed a foe, an enemy who threatens his existence.

That foe was Linda Dougherty.

Dougherty already received considerable heat for her Rodman and Tyson column. I ordered her to watch the Monday wrestling shows and write a column bashing them.

For Dougherty, it was easy—wrestling was a show for Neanderthals anyway.

Every week, she bashed the shows, and eventually started to write how lame the Strangler's column was.

Complaints were flooding in. Trenton loves pro wrestling, and Dougherty was annoying them. But they still had to read her column.

So it set up a storyline in the paper. Dougherty and the Strangler would fight over pro wrestling.

The storyline unfolded in her columns blasting wrestling.

One week, Dougherty wanted the Strangler canned. She arranged to have a meeting with me, and have the Strangler terminated.

In one column she complained about the "low IQs of both participants and fans."

"A friend who scalps tickets outside the CoreStates Spectrum, and has been doing so for many years, swears that pro wrestling fans have the lowest intelligence of any sports fan on earth," she wrote. "And he's right—they are on a par with recreational softball players. Instead of Dad 'tying one on' and cramming his beer gut inside a softball uniform (some are rumored to wear trusses) or dragging his children to a deplorable ECW match, he should be encouraging them to read, work and save money."

Dougherty took a pot shot at softball—because it is a pastime in the Trenton area. It riled readers. Like a true heel, she had no friends—she even attacked Little League and her own newspaper.

"Can someone explain to me why this newspaper devotes one or more pages of space a day to those absurd softball game results, or five pages to Little League while giving horse racing—a legitimate respectable sport with a long history and a guaranteed moneymaker for the glorious state of New Jersey—a half-page, at best?" she wrote.

"Jockeys are true athletes, not guys who are half shot in the 'can' as they swing at a little white ball, or 10-year-olds who have trouble remembering which is first base and which is second."

At this time, the Strangler started ripping Dougherty and her sport—horse racing.

"All of this war of words stemmed from sour grapes—a smell very familiar to anyone who has stood too close to (Dougherty) after a hard day at the empty stands of the track," the Strangler wrote. "You are just jealous that people don't take horse racing as seriously as you do.

"You are jealous, and you have allowed your extreme jealousy to gain control of your otherwise sleeper existence."

People started calling me; I shouldn't fire the Strangler.

"The Strangler was the only reason why I even buy your paper," I would hear.

But I was the boss. In wrestling, the boss is always the jerk.

Our opinion page, especially BackTalk (a call-in forum), was filled with complaints. It was the No.1 issue on our editorial pages—way ahead of a proposed gas tax.

Here's is a sampling of what appeared on our editorial pages:

—"I'd like to respond to Linda Dougherty's tirade about professional wrestling. She says you shouldn't waste your money on a $29.95 wrestling pay-per-view event, but that you should spend $35-$40 on a two-round Don King fight. I think this lady's crazy. And tell her to leave the poor Trenton Strangler alone."

—"This is a message for that sourpuss, Linda Dougherty. Quit picking on the Trenton Strangler and wrestling fans. Most fans already know that wrestling is fake. Why does everything have to be serious for you? Why don't you go back to your normal occupation of picking all of the losing horses."

—"Regarding the recent meeting between Linda Dougherty and the executive editor of your paper. I think he should can Linda Dougherty.

Nobody really cares about horse racing. And wrestling is entertaining. Keep the Strangler and get rid of Linda. She's a waste of time."

Dougherty did have some fans—sort of.

"I agree with Linda Dougherty, who says 'A mind is a terrible thing to waste especially on professional wrestling.' I believe that kids should be taught something that helps them build character, such as how to bet on horse races."

Playing the role of "evil boss," I stood by Dougherty, saying she was the voice of the paper, and I had little use for the Strangler. I said I was so sure horse racing was more popular than wrestling, I was going to prove it by having a reader poll.

If wrestling lost the poll, the Strangler would be fired. We, of course, made it a contest—one ballot would win $100.

We ran this ballot daily—we received nearly 1,000 coupons. Horse racing lost—by a landslide. The Strangler's job was saved.

A horseman at Philadelphia Park told Dougherty she didn't have a chance.

Not in Trenton.

Extreme Championship Wrestling, the third largest wrestling federation in the country at the time, wanted Dougherty to appear as a heel at one of its events.

The Strangler (I will never reveal his identity) became so popular he had requests to appear at numerous community events. He was in demand.

He was a celebrity.

Most newspaper executives would consider the pro wrestling feud cheap and mundane. Newspapers are supposed to change the world, not have stupid wrestling storylines in the paper, they would say.

That's why newspapers are sliding: out-of-touch editors who want to change the world. This was our most-talked about "issue" for nearly a month.

Newspapers should touch all emotions. Not making people "yawn" over open-space issues or high-occupancy vehicle lanes.

In Trenton, pro wrestling is relevant.
Fun.
And a big-seller.

◆　◆　◆

Paul Mickle is devoted to his work.
At times, Mickle developed an obsession with some stories.
Mickle couldn't let go of the case of Evalista "Flaca" Figueroa.
In 1996, Flaca, an 18-year-old sex kitten, helped murder her 41-year-old paramour, Trenton businessman Mohammed "Mike" Mahgoub.
Mickle was the night cops reporter at the time of Mahgoub's slaying. All of the neighbors mentioned how sexy this girl, Flaca, was.
Her stunning looks were legendary in Trenton.
Mickle, however, never tracked down a picture. Mickle, seemingly, always got the pictures victims and suspects. When dealing with Mickle, you never asked how he got the picture because he did whatever it took to get it. Sometimes, it is one of those things an editor shouldn't know. With Mickle, a "Don't Ask, Don't Tell" policy was necessary.
Tracking down headshots is one of Mickle's specialties.
In fact his desk has loads of pictures of most wanted criminals, victims—and his kids.
But somehow, Flaca's picture eluded Mickle's grasp. Mickle wrote an extensive weekend profile piece about Figueroa—providing extensive details of her physical appearance.
How would have Mickle known? He never saw a picture of the woman. He was relying on legendary accounts.
Adding to Mickle's frustration, the assignment editors in January 1997 screwed up on an opportunity to get a picture in court. When Figueroa made her court appearance, Anne Karolyi, the managing editor then, never sent a photographer to the courthouse.

The word "Flaca" appeared all over Mickle's notes. She was on his mind constantly. Mickle would doodle her name on notepads all the time. When bored, some people would doodle pictures of smiling faces or cars.

Not Mickle. He wrote the word "Flaca" down.

Flaca was the topic of one of the 15 best-selling front pages from 1997.

Mickle received word that a prison guard, Leonard Baum, was being investigated for having an alleged affair with her. Baum was fired a day later.

Mickle was in heaven.

Nancy Houtz was assigned the story and wrote it.

Mickle, however, did a large chunk of the reporting and constantly tossed Houtz information about it.

Houtz, who was frustrated with Mickle's meddling, wrote this lead:

"A guard at Mercer County's youth was fired yesterday, just 24 hours after The Trentonian launched a probe into allegations he staged an affair with a Trenton teen awaiting trial on murder charges."

A few paragraphs later, the story revealed the juicy details.

"The source described Flaca as a beguiling young temptress who enticed the muscular 30-something guard into an illicit cell-block romance.

"The source added that, as a supervisor Baum had the only keys to offices where he and Flaca were spotted together by shocked prison employees who spread the word that the pair were apparently engaged in a campaign of forbidden prison lovemaking.

"That, however, wasn't the only sexy big-house troublemaking the city teen allegedly had been engaging in.

"The source reported that Flaca ran afoul of guards by amassing a large collection of sexy Victoria's Secret lingerie, then prancing around in the little nighties in an apparent attempt to entice jailers."

The facts easily wrote the headline for us. Actually, this sounded eerily similar to SEX KITTENS IN THE CLASSROOM, which sparked red-hot sales at the newsstands.

Now, you can't go wrong with SEX KITTENS.

So we went with JAILHOUSE SEX KITTEN as our main headline.

After the booming success of the Flaca story, Mickle started to hunt for other SEX KITTEN headlines.

If he saw a good-looking woman working in the county building, he would try to come up with the story, SEX KITTENS IN THE COUNTY BUILDING.

Somehow, we never nailed down that story.

Mickle had to wait until mid-1999 to get a picture of Flaca. It was during her trial.

Nearly three years in the klink took its toll on the woman—she wasn't sexy after all.

But in Mickle's mind, the legend still lives.

◆ ◆ ◆

The news section was running smoothly.

Unlike most newspapers where editors chain reporters to their beats. Our staff relied on strictly general assignment reporting.

They covered breaking news. No beat was more important than that.

We didn't use enterprise reporting. Just breaking news.

We took a page from TV—as most papers should.

Most newspaper bigwigs frown on TV—considering the medium frivolous and flimsy. Mock them for more glitz than true substance.

But TV uses ratings as a guide to finding out what viewers want. Unfortunately, most newspapers don't use their guide—circulation.

Television covers breaking news extensively.

Why? The viewers want it.

I used more a television news approach for The Trentonian.

Breaking news—murders, fires and robberies—sold the paper. No beat was bigger than breaking news.

True to my new philosophy, I assigned Jon Blackwell not a City Hall but a crime story as his first assignment. He had to do a follow up on three kids who died in a fire.

The kids' mom was a prostitute, and she left them home with this drunk, while she went out and earned her money the hard way. It turned out that a candle tipped over, and there was no electricity.

The headline became one of our most famous:

MOM TURNS TRICKS AS TOTS BURN.

We had a picture of a relative crying, and of the three kids, Jennifer, 5, Angel, 6 and some other kid, 8.

Blackwell's lead read like this:

"A heroin-addicted hooker turned tricks on city streets as her three children perished in flames Sunday night in a Chambersburg house fire, cops said."

The headline—written by Night City Editor Todd Venezia—was sensational and effective.

Venezia was a natural tabloid genius; he knew what sold the paper. An editor needs to be surrounded by a staff that understands what sells the paper. That means the editor must disclose circulation numbers to the staff—good and bad. Most editors today keep the numbers a secret—probably trying to hide failure.

Venezia showed signs of being a tabloid phenomenon with a penchant for clandestine missions as soon as he was hired in 1995.

Venezia climbed the roof an area mall, after officials there claimed they'd removed tablets that caused pigeons to die if they ate them. Venezia discovered the pellets were still there and mall officials apologized.

His early success led to a promotion: night city editor. It was now his job to make stories punchy. We wanted The Trentonian to read like the New York Post or Star magazine. Why? Both papers are top notch when it comes to single-copy sales.

◆ ◆ ◆

"There is a bear in my tree," the caller said.

It was Gregg Slaboda, the son of legendary editor Emil, and a photographer on the staff.

"A bear is in the tree?" I said. "Get me a picture."

"I can't because the cops won't let me out of my house," Gregg said.

It was 1 a.m. on a Sunday morning. A bear trapped in a tree in Trenton is big news. I didn't have time to argue with Gregg.

We needed the story—and picture.

Pet stories are huge in the area.

One of Schwartz's favorite front pages was headlined:
SNAKES, RATS OVERRUN TRENTON

A bear stuck in a Trenton tree is a winner.

The only people around to get the story was veteran George O'Gorman and Matt Buzinski—an upstart clerk.

Buzinski, called a "newsman and a half" by Mickle, was a sports clerk who knew nothing about sports. But he was a solid administrator and he had a solid feel of the happenings of Hamilton Township—a critical circulation area.

Buzinski maybe was short on writing skills, but he relished breaking news.

"He'll be a publisher someday," Mickle said of Buzinski, who was 19 at the time.

O'Gorman and Buzinski failed to get the story in time. They missed deadline.

On Monday, Schwartz was ball of fire. Slaboda should have gotten the picture of the "fuckin' bear."

Slaboda was suspended a week because he failed to get the picture—during his time off.

The message was simple: the newspaper business is not a time-clock business. It is a passion. You live it 24 hours a day.

A major story was developing in Gregg's backyard; he didn't get it.

"The cops told me not to get out of my home," Gregg said. "What am I supposed to do?"

"GET ARRESTED!" Schwartz said. "You got to get the picture."

The union, with George O'Gorman the president, filed a grievance against the suspension. Schwartz fought it in principle, but he did not have much of a case and eventually backed down.

But it sent a clear message to the staff: Do whatever it takes to get the story.

Today's newspapers tend to back off after getting the basics. It's a lazy style of reporting. The industry must dig deeper in breaking stories—finding the human element that adds depth to the breaking story.

You must be relentless.

◆ ◆ ◆

Schwartz hammered home that point and we stressed to do whatever it took to get the story.

Todd Venezia climbed the top of a Macy's department store building.

Numerous reporters posed as strip club patrons. (Most of them didn't mind about that assignment).

Don't even ask Mickle how he got the story. We had a "Don't Ask, Don't Tell" policy with him.

I bilked a story—at the expense of my wife.

It was December 23, 1995, and I was watching the Giants play the Chargers in a game at the Meadowlands. New Jersey had a wild snowstorm just days before the game.

Martha was a reporter for the Princeton Packet, a twice-weekly 26,000-circulation newspaper.

Martha, who has no interest in football, watched a portion of the game, and pointed out "the acoustics won't be very good there."

"What?" I asked.

"The West Windsor-Plainsboro marching band will be performing at halftime," said Martha, who played clarinet in her high school's marching band. There are not many fans there so it will affect the acoustics, she said.

"Did you see my story in the paper?" she asked.

"Ahhh, of course," I said, shifting my eyes.

Shortly later, Martha had to go to the Laundromat and mayhem at the Giants game occurred.

Fans started to go bonkers and fire snowballs at anybody at the field. The game had to be stopped several times. For once, fans were going crazy—and they weren't from Philadelphia.

I added two-plus-two.

If these Giant maniacs threw snowballs at players, coaches and media, they would have definitely chucked some ice at those band nerds.

We would be able to scoop Martha's paper with that one. I wouldn't have even thought about it if she didn't tell me.

In this business, the ends justify the means. You rip a story off your mother if you had to.

I was assistant news editor at the time, and I mentioned it to Venezia, who was the weekend reporter that day.

Venezia found that yes, the WW-P band was pelted.

As he worked on this story, Venezia proclaimed, "These guys are geeks, man."

One band member said: "When you commit yourself to something like marching band, you're ready because anything can happen."

I would have fired an iceball at that clown.

Venezia got the story—and Editor Mark Waligore made it the line.

GIANT JERKS! was the headline.

Venezia wrote: "Rowdy and drunken football fans pelted a local high school band with hunks of snow and ice as they performed at halftime of yesterday's raucous Giants game."

It probably was the best Christmas Eve story in the paper's history—thanks to my wife.

The ends clearly justified the means.

◆   ◆   ◆

Trentonian City Editor Paul Mickle is a true newsman.

But even Mickle gets reeled into attending community meetings. Every editor must be involved in one way or another. Making public appearances is one of the major drawbacks of the job.

Mercer County sponsored a seminar in how to cover suicides. It was a community hearing to show journalists how cover suicides sensitively.

In Mickle's view, it was politicians telling the media how to do its job.

"This is horseshit," Mickle said. "This is a bunch of namby-pamby horseshit."

"Better you than me," I said pulling rank.

Mickle reluctantly attended the meeting. Meanwhile, a story about a man who put himself on fire had second thoughts and ran to the firehouse—a half-mile away. In fact, the torch was near The Trentonian offices.

Just image, people are walking down the street, then a human fireball runs by.

Now, that's a story.

But it's a suicide attempt. Most newsrooms will look for justification to not running this story. They would talk themselves out of running it. Usually, the guideline for suicide coverage is if it is public, it runs.

My guideline is broader: If it makes a good story, it runs.

Mickle is attending a seminar on suicides and we get a great story on a suicide attempt.

In fact, it's the lead story.

HUMAN TORCH RUNS TO FIREHOUSE
We didn't care what the people in the meeting thought.
The lead reflected it.
"A man distraught over his wife's infidelity soaked himself in lighter fluid and set himself on fire yesterday, then ran flaming down the street as scores of lookers watched in horror."

About a year later, a woman jumped off the Route 1 toll bridge—and survived.

The next day, Mickle and Eric Ladley sneaked into her hospital room. She tried to kill herself because she thought she was ugly.

Here's an excerpt from Mickle and Ladley's story:

"Trim with brown hair and a tattoo on her left shoulder, (the woman) confirmed word from the barside waitress that her jump was sparked by her visit to her husband's go-go bar.

"'All of the pretty girls were there, and I was tired of being so ugly. So I jumped off the big bridge,' she said breaking into tears. 'I want to be pretty again. I was pretty at one time.'"

"I WANT A NEW FACE" was a tease on the front page.

This was not cruel. This was reporting; this woman tried to jump off a major bridge in our area. She plunged 25 feet. She survived. Not every day you get a person who jumps off a bridge and lives.

That's news.

We wanted to know why she did it.

Most Editors whine about exploiting the victim. The man (the human torch) and woman (the bridge jumper) involved are mentality troubled. It is unethical to exploit them.

Who cares about ethics? Both stories made me say "holy shit."

The readers bought both papers. The readers could have rejected the paper, but they didn't. If the sales were slow, we would have probably never have done either story.

But these stories are in demand.

The Times, however, ran only briefs.

Guess so-called journalistic ethics prevailed in their newsroom.

◆ ◆ ◆

Auto insurance reform is a significant issue in New Jersey with drivers paying ridiculous amounts money for auto insurance.

In 1997, Leslie Hyatt proclaimed herself as an auto insurance reformer, fighting for reduced rates.

The Trentonian, however, proclaimed her a hypocrite.

Hyatt who organized a rally at the State House for auto insurance reform had a spotty driver's record. And that's putting it nicely.

In one of her last stories with The Trentonian before leaving for the Courier-Post in Cherry Hill, N.J., Kim Haban went out with a bang:

"Leslie Hyatt, the 26-year-old secretary who just last week staged a protest against New Jersey's sky-high car insurance, has a driving record that qualifies for the demolition derby.

"Since she got her license in 1988, the East Brunswick woman has been in four accidents, gotten three speeding tickets, blown at least one stop sign and faced fines for passing in a no-passing zone."

The front page captured the essence to the story: CRASH QUEEN.

We also had three bullet points:

- She's had 4 accidents
- She's had 3 speeding tix
- She's racked up 14 points in 9 years.

Of course, the editorial page duo of Lukens and Stradling piped in:

"Why is this woman being lionized and cheered," the editorial read. "She—and others like her—are a big part of the reason insurance rates in this state are sky high. Where does she get off making it seem that her $2,400-a-year premium is a plague visited upon her by evil gods of the insurance industry.

"…Well the fact remains that Hyatt is a bad driver who brought higher premiums on herself. The fact remains that her kind of driving affects the premiums of every other motorist in this state. And the fact remains that until something is done about that tiny faction of motorists who cause most of the problems, insurance rates aren't going to go down significantly for anyone anytime soon.

"If Hyatt and people like her really want to do something about insurance rates in this state, they could start by watching the road instead of shooting off their hypocritical mouths down at the State House."

After helping conceive the CRASH QUEEN front page, Erik Lukens was driving home and stumbled into another auto line for the next day, STATE BIG IS SPEED DEMON.

Lukens, while driving home on Route 1 in Princeton, noticed a state vehicle whiz by him. Lukens estimated he was going about 80 mph.

Lukens got the license plate number and tracked it down to the Human Services Commissioner of New Jersey.

Lukens produced this clever lead:

"If the wheels of state government turned half as fast as the ones on Department of Human Services Commissioner William Waldman's car, we'd all get our tax refunds by April 20."

"....Yesterday, Human Services spokesman John McKeegan confirmed that Waldman himself was behind the wheel of the car, a 1995 Mercury Sable owned by the state.

"'And yes,' McKeegan said, 'he was driving too fast.'

"He often does, if his driving record is any indication.

"According to the Department of Motor Vehicles, Waldman, 53, was ticketed for speeding in 1989 and in 1990. In 1991, he was cited for failing to observe a traffic control device. The 1989 infraction occurred while Waldman was behind the wheel of a state car."

◆ ◆ ◆

Combine your relentless nature with an innovative approach you can't lose.

The Trentonian was rolling.

We used wire stories to trigger ideas.

In 1998, the New England Journal of Medicine reported that 60 percent of Rutgers University coeds had venereal disease.

Now, Rutgers wasn't technically in our circulation area, but this story is a talker. And hell, we were in a slump. So, we had to make things happen. Usually when the news is slow, we will go out of the circulation area to get a story.

So I sent three women—reporters Molly Davis, Barri Orlow and photographer Leslie Barbaro—out to get this story nailed. First, sending women are better. Female students are more likely to tell women reporters about their sex lives and horrors over the VD scare.

Secondly, sending Barbaro as the photographer also was easy. Barbaro knew the unwritten rules: Get pictures hot women. An editor cannot order a staffer to just get pictures of hot women. Usually the instructions are followed with a wink and a nod. Barbaro read my mind and she was developing a scheme to get these babes.

Paul Mickle never was tactful with telling photographers to find hot women. One time, he wrote out a photo assignment for a story about the mild weather. "Get pictures of girls in short skirts," he wrote on the assignment slip, "maybe with the wind blowing them up."

Davis, Orlow and Barbaro came back with the story—and more importantly pictures of sizzling women.

The main headline read:

RUTGERS IN SHOCK OVER VD PLAGUE: Jaws drop over stunning statistic.

"Shock and fear spread across Rutgers University like a bad rash yesterday after the New England Journal of Medicine revealed 60 percent of the school's female students are infected with venereal disease," the lead read.

Not bad for a slow news day.

At The Trentonian, we managed to string together some breaking stories and developed a trend. A hot-selling trend. On one slow news day, we managed to connect four crime stories and developed an alarming trend.

It became a city issue.

We had a series of crimes:

- A boy exploded a bomb in a family basement
- A brother and sister mugged two people in the city of Trenton
- A couple of teens broke into the City Council president's home.
- A girl slugged a security guard in the mouth.

Most papers probably would have put of these items in the blotter or run in briefs package. For most Editors, the story involving a politician is the most interesting—because a politico is involved.

We found a common theme—of the incidents involved teen-agers. So we pieced a package together and ran the headline:

WILD TEENS RUN AMOK

Now, that is making something out of nothing; in fact, we created something that editors go bonkers about—an issue.

The next day, Mayor Doug Palmer called an emergency press conference to address the issue of teen terror.

We ran the next-day headline:

SAVAGE TEENS!

Newspaper Editors live for changing the community and the world. They usually make try to find a high-concept cause that draws little interest.

We did something: we covered the news. By simply covering the basic news, we made the community better. We addressed a problem that leaders had to address and improve.

More importantly, we also made something out of nothing.

Venezia, an innovative editor who has an aggressive personality, teamed with Mickle to coordinate the coverage of our one lead story, JOKE JAIL.

Under the bold face type we had three bullet points: "No Fence, No Guards, No Locks."

The lead read: "A private prison housing 300 criminals in Trenton has less security than a convenience store—the only thing standing between these prisoners and freedom is a piece of paper."

We credited this information to a Trentonian probe. This was an inside joke in the newsroom—ridiculing the pompous nature of our business. This probe lasted all of two days. It started on Friday night when Paul Mickle found out about it a convict walking away from jail and ended Saturday when Nancy Houtz did the story.

The Times did absolutely nothing. It took Mickle, an old-fashioned news hound, and the savvy Venezia to dig it up. The Times ran this story as brief.

Some guy just wanders out of a prison and most people wouldn't have cared. Mickle and Venezia turned this story into a legitimate, comprehensive piece.

Community journalists such as the ones who work at Times are the reason newspapers are dying. The mission of a newspaper should be to inform. If it helps the public in the process, a good thing has been done for the community. Just go out and report the news.

Because of The Trentonian, a fence was put up at the Bo Robinson House. Just following and reporting big news stories provides an informed public, not an ignorant one. Actually, ignoring stories like this is a community disservice.

◆   ◆   ◆

On slow news days, an editor must take gambles—willing to send reporters on "wild-goose" chases.

One Friday afternoon, a report of "a stabbing at a senior center" came over the police scanner. Typically, a solid police reporter would listen to the scanner to hear more developments. Trentonian cop reporter Chris Dolmetsch wanted to hear to more details.

Dolmetsch, a University of Delaware graduate who worked at the Daily Local in West Chester (Pa.), was right—he wanted to wait and see.

But we were desperate. I ordered him to leave right away. In this instance, there is a good possibility that a elderly person accidentally cut himself. This would be a waste of about an hour of reporter's time.

However, Dolmetsch and photographer Leslie Barbaro raced to the senior center hit paydirt. An elderly man stabbed another for arriving to lunch late.

We had the headline:
STABBED FOR BEING LATE TO LUNCH
The story was another winner at the newsstands for us, and a brief in the Trenton Times.

In essence, the editor must shake the tree in order to see if anything falls out.

We shook a lot of trees.

◆ ◆ ◆

"Everybody wants to know what is wrong with us," an exasperated Chris Wilson said. "This is a sensational trial and we're not making it a big deal."

Wilson, a solid cop reporter, was covering the trial of Jesse Timmendequas, a piece of trash of a man who raped and murdered 7-year-old Megan Kanka.

Timmendequas, a convinced sex offender, was Kanka's neighbor in Hamilton, and as a result, the crime triggered versions of "Megan's Law" around the country. A neighborhood must be notified if a convicted sex offender moves in.

Media from around the world flocked to Trenton for the trial. It was Mercer County's biggest trial since the death of Charles Lindbergh's baby.

The Trentonian didn't make it a big deal

While I didn't want to overplay the trial, Wilson produced some fairly good pieces from the courthouse. JESSE JUROR TOSSED OUT FOR CHEERING was one of our first big stories from the trial. One of the jurors clenched his fist and pumped his arm, when evidence was presented against Jesse. But must of the trial featured details we already had reported.

But in our world the "Pitbull" trial took center stage.

The Pitbulls were a knuckleheaded gang of mob wannabes who killed a man because they thought he was a mob rat.

Brus Post, a leader of the Pitbulls, turned into a mob turncoat himself.

His testimony against his Pitbull gang buddies set the stage for a larger trial and knocked coverage of molester trial to the back pages.

The Pitbulls were great, though. Post reneged on his plea deal with prosecutors, because they wouldn't let him wear a dress suit to the trial instead of his prison fatigues.

The front page headline was:
CRYBABY KILLER LOSES COOL

Another front page featured a witness making a stabbing motion with his arm with the headline, "HE STABBED HIM LIKE THIS."

Another time, Post called the judge Rosemary Ruggiero Williams a "slut."

The headline read: PITBULL CALLS JUDGE SLUT

There's nothing wrong with "slut" in the headline. It catches the reader's eye. It's bold, and it told the story.

Post sent us a letter blasting the judge in the trial, Rosemary Ruggiero Williams, calling her a slut. PITBULL TO JUDGE: GET BACK IN THE KITCHEN.

Every paper needs a crackpot like Post—he helped bring in big numbers at the newsstand.

On May 30, The Trentonian finally made a splash at the Timmendequas trial

At 11:30 a.m, The Associated Press moved a story about the opening arguments in the trial. The defense lawyer tried to say little Megan Kanka, an 8-year-old girl, tried to initiate the contact, not Jesse.

I looked at Paul Mickle, "We've got the lead story."

Mickle had an accelerator mentality; he was never satisfied with a story—he always wanted more. But MEGAN ASKED FOR IT wrote itself.

Schwartz, sensing the potential for a huge story, wanted to do more. He wanted an editorial. Barbara Lependorff, Jesse's lawyer, got Geek of the Year that day, beating out sure winner Sen. Bob Torricelli.

The editorial, written by Editorial Page Editor Mark Stradling, sarcastically asked for the death penalty to Lependorff.

"It's too bad Lependorff's wasn't around to defend Bruno Hauptmann back in the 1930s," the editorial said. "She would have claimed the Lindbergh baby climbed down from a rickety wooden ladder and jumped into his killer's arms, and the jurors of those days would have known exactly what to do: Sentence her to death along with her client as an example to future generations of lawyers.

"That's hyperbole, of course. We can't really kill lawyers, not even when they twist the truth and try to make it seem the victim was the instigator."

Wilson called in at 2:30 p.m. to give us an update on the trial, and we told him what the lead of his story was going to be. It jarred him at first, and he didn't think of looking at the story from that angle. He'd been hanging around other reporters all day, and they were all too close to the story to see the shocking value of this opening statement.

After pausing for a moment, it clicked in for him. "Yeah, we can do that," he said.

While all the other newspapers were focusing on the angle that the prosecutors and defense had just presented their opening arguments, we went with Defense Lawyer Says.... (OVERBAR): MEGAN ASKED FOR IT.

People were naturally outraged. Many thought we said Megan asked for it. I guess they didn't read the fine print.

The prosecutors ripped the editorial in court the next day, defending Lependorff. That proved to me that it was all one big family over at the courthouse. That prompted another editorial ripping all the lawyers involved.

"How can you say Megan asked for it?" people were demanding of us. We were the only paper to focus on this angle, simply because we monitored the AP wire. Wilson was the star of the trial, and we had it on its ear for one day. The reporters thought our paper was great, that we really had balls.

Our front page was shown on all the Philadelphia stations, and the WB network interviewed me for its lead story.

"I stand by the headline and the story," I boomed.

Schwartz was interviewed with FOX News' Bill O'Reilly and the New York Times wrote about the editorial, and Paul Mickle went on AM Philadelphia, a local news show on an ABC affiliate.

The topic: did the editorial have an affect on the jury and should this sentence of this trial be thrown out?

Mickle was great.

Wally Kennedy, the show's host, asked him what if the judge agrees with the defense and just gives him life?

"Then we'll get on his case, too," Paul shot back.

We were the center of attention, the talk of the town. This became the biggest trial in Trenton since the Lindbergh trial. The AP provided us with another great angle the following day. One of their photographers saw Megan's dad outside his house and asked him what he thought of the defense argument. "It turned my stomach," he said.

Newspapers like to avoid the media spotlight. For some reason, it is considered bad to be part of a story.

It is the best free publicity a newspaper can have.

The roar was restored.

Princess Diana's death on Aug. 31, 1997 stunned the world. Tabloid journalism was the blame for Princess Diana's death. Why didn't they just leave her alone?

Princess Diana sold. The public had a ferocious appetite to read and look at her.

If the readers didn't want to have Diana harassed, then they shouldn't read.

Then they shouldn't gawk at her pictures.

If there wasn't a demand, the tabloid photographers would have left her alone.

Behind the leadership of Bob Shields, we were methodical in our approach that night. We stopped the presses, put a new front page on, and never missed a deadline.

Movies always make it appear that stopping the presses is some dramatic ordeal, but we did it nonchalantly. It went off without a hitch, and thank God, we didn't have to lead with a political story. A newspaper is as good as its copy desk, and we did big things and made a big package.

Over 49,000 were bought that day, one of our best-selling Sunday lines ever. And it was a write-off day. Write-off days are those that don't count on the circulation figure. The number of papers actually printed was reduced because it was Labor Day Weekend.

Even with the shorter run, we had our best Sunday sale of the year.

In death, Diana was still in demand.

I didn't care what happened in New Jersey that night. We ran seven pages of coverage with 11 stories. There was even a report on who would be picked to carry the casket. There was only half a page for regular news.

The next day, Good Day Philadelphia wanted to have me on to talk about tabloid journalism. The press was being blamed for Di's death. Paparazzi photographers supposedly hounded her to her doom.

Yes, I wanted to defend tabloid journalism from the hit it was taking. But I worked until 3 a.m. the night before, and I would've had to get up at 5 a.m. to make the show. They pleaded with me to appear; apparently I was the only newspaper executive who was working at that time of night on that day.

That is really sad. This is the biggest story of the decade, at least, and all of the other newspaper executives were enjoying the three-day weekend. Editors have to get involved, especially on days like this. Diana's death was the biggest of the story in the decade; editors should be leading their teams. If it were election night, they would be there.

This would like the Giants playing in the Super Bowl—and coach Bill Parcells didn't show up for the game.

Mike Regan, who was the best features editor I've worked with, decided to go on the television show for me.

Regan did very well. He told the audience that tabloids are getting raw deals, because of the size of the paper. But religious publications have the same shape and play up sensational stories too, he pointed out. It boiled down to the fact that this was a tremendous story for us.

Our local cable news channel, WZBN, interviewed me, Paul Mickle and Sherry Sylvester about the reputations that tabloids get. The answer is simple. Tabloids did not put a drunk driver behind the wheel of Di's car and make him speed away at 90 miles per hour.

There was absolutely no backlash during our coverage. We sold better than ever. Di pushed over 60,000. And the fact was that we did a good job packaging wire stories. Even if we sent a reporter over there, there wasn't too much more they could have done.

The best column Sherry ever wrote was spawned by the Di tragedy. She said that basically Di's death was no big deal because the great princess was only a "high-fashioned clotheshorse."

"The death of Princess Diana, while sad for her children and family, is no tragedy," Sylvester wrote. "It's not even close. It is both puzzling and troubling to watch the world behaving as it is."

Later, she wrote:

"Nothing made her unique but her looks, her money and her ex-husband....The fact that the world is bent over in despair at her loss says very little about her and reveals something very upsetting about the world.

"We seem to have lost our sense of what it takes to live a life that matters. We have confused individuals who are truly committed to make the world a better place with those who get their picture on the cover of People magazine.

"The tearful millions who are overcome with grief seem unaware that being beautiful is not indicative of any accomplishment.

"They saw something they believed was real in Diana's lovely smile, despite much evidence that very little was there.

"Diana was a woman who wrote that shopping was one of her primary interests. She spent the day she died shopping. Her death has been described a 'tragic blow' for the British fashion industry.

"She is a symbol of how little we have come to expect of our heroes and heroines. We no longer require that they have personal strength and courage that are always necessary to break new ground or chart a new course.

"Instead, like the cowardly lion, we have become clueless about the meaning of courage.

"We call Diana courageous for demanding a $23 million divorce settlement.

"In a day or two the whole world will weep at the funeral of a woman who was not a great leader, a great thinker or a great humanitarian.

"She will receive an honor guard and full state funeral for being a great celebrity—someone who was famous for being famous.

"The news that millions of people seem to care so much that she died is definitely cause for fears.

"We should be crying for the shallow world in which we live."

This column ran on page 15—three days after Diana's death.

Sylvester drew the wrath of our readers—and even Trentonian staffers. Three wanted to write rebuttal columns, and years later, some staffers still harbor bitter feelings toward her because of this column.

She made TV and radio appearances about the column. She was the talk of the town—because she courageously stirred the pot.

Funny thing, Sylvester wrote political columns regularly, but people hardly noticed. She was like a tree falling in the forest.

She writes about Princess Diana; she's the center of controversy.

The public skewered her column, but they read it.

That's all that mattered.

◆ ◆ ◆

Newspapers shouldn't shy away from controversy; editors must embrace it. The Princess Diana column written by Sherry Sylvester drew fire.

We lamely tried to re-open those wounds four months later.

When celebrity and House representative Sonny Bono died when he slammed into a tree while skiing, Sylvester called Bono's death "MORE TRAGIC THAN DI."

It was a slow news day, and we knew the Bono death would lead most newscasts and newspapers. We tried a different hook to the story—by bringing up a sore spot with readers.

Sylvester wrote:

"Still for people who are paying attention, there is little doubt that the passing of Sonny Bono ranks higher on the tragedy-meter than the recent deaths of Michael Kennedy or even Princess Di.

"Bono is a man of actual accomplishments. He was not only the guy who wrote 'Needles and Pins' and 'Baby Don't Go,' which earns him a place in our cultural history, but he also represents exactly what the founding fathers had in mind when they created the congressional branch of government—a citizen legislator."

This attempt to make Bono's death more significant than Diana's fell woefully short. Most readers saw it as a transparent attempt to enrage them with Princess Diana's death again.

They didn't buy it—literally.

It sold about 58,000, nearly 2,000 papers below our average.

◆ ◆ ◆

A true editor will not be afraid of running celebrity stories on page 1—especially if a celebrity is up to no good in your market.

I considered myself the celebrity sheriff in Trenton.

If a celebrity sneaks into the Greater Trenton Area, we will get them.

In 1997, George Clooney made a mistake: He visited Trenton.

Katmandu, a local nightclub in the city, boosted that Clooney visited them a recent Saturday night. The heartthrob was in town because he was going to attend a memorial for the father of "Spin City" sitcom star Richard Kind

We tried to find out anything anecdotal: What did he eat, drink, what was he like, what did he talk about, how did the people around react?

After the dust settled, police told us that Clooney's limo driver asked them if they of any good strip clubs in the area. We also found Clooney and his party took two local girls to an area diner after a night of boozing.

This was front-page news. We ran this headline:

TV HUNK CRUISES CITY FOR STRIPPERS

We had a three-package:

—Main story about Clooney looking for some strippers and finally ending up at Katmandu. Wilson and Molly Davis crafted this lead:

"Hollywood hunk George Clooney trolled Trenton for topless bars Saturday night—but apparently decided on the scantily clad scenery at KatManDu was the hottest ticket in town."

—Sidebar on the diner, featuring the reaction from the workers. We found out he gobbled up bacon and eggs.

—We also had a story about strippers in the Trenton area and how they would have reacted if Clooney visited them. Mike Regan was forced to visit strip joints in the area and produced this lead:

"George Clooney's mild-mannered charm and boyish good looks may have taken him to the top in Hollywood, but in Greater Trenton, the swarthy stud better back it up with some portraits of famous presidents if he expects to get anywhere with local strippers."

It was a fun package and a winner at the stores. People talked about it, and in fact, the New York Post's Page Six mocked us for running an extensive three-story package: "I guess not too many celebrities come to Trenton."

Ironically, Chris Wilson, our cop reporter at the time, used the story to nail down a job at Star magazine, and a couple of years later, he was hired to work on Page Six of the Post.

A couple of days later, we had a story on the women who spent time with Clooney. We ran the headline "OUR NIGHT WITH GEORGE CLOONEY."

I offered the women about $500 apiece to become Page 6 poster girls. We would call them "Clooney's Batgirls."

They rejected the offer.

We loved dealing with sexy celebrities, and if that celebrity had local connections, we beat it like a drum.

The Globe, the supermarket tabloid, reported a story on "Ally McBeal" star Calista Flockhart. She was from Medford Lakes, N.J., a town in our coverage area; she also attended Rutgers.

She was our girl.

As the celebrity sheriff, this is exactly what I wanted to hear.

Dom Yanchunas wrote a compelling Sunday piece on the "STAR'S TRAIL OF BROKEN HEARTS."

It was a talker—and it even drew fire from my wife, Martha, a reporter for the Associated Press.

She couldn't understand why we were making a big deal out of "these losers." "They should get over it," Martha said.

Even though she was disgusted by our news judgment, it was a talker. It drew strong emotions from my wife. Under my philosophy, it is newsworthy.

Yanchunas produced a wonderful lead:

"The success of a former Burlington County beauty who now stars in a prime-time television series has prompted fond recollections from her old hometown—even while a celebrity gossip tabloid is exposing the trail of broken hearts she left on her road to the top."

The supermarket tabloids are mocked as artificial and phony. But I look at those publications as a guide to learn what readers want. These papers are the top-selling in the country. They must be doing something right.

Newspaper skeptics think these publications "make things up."

They don't.

They just aggressively pursue stories.

Unfortunately, most newspapers measure their success by the number of awards it wins.

Forget awards.

Give me readers. Covering sex and celebrities helps get me readers.

Give me booming sales. That's the best award possible.

Commentary on pop culture can be successful on the newsstands.

For example, when Ellen DeGeneres received tons of publicity over her character proclaiming her homosexuality, The Trentonian took different tact.

We were poised to do a local reaction story on it. Of course, knowing the bent of our paper and its conservative principles, we had a headline picked out before we even interviewed a single person. But, if you get the quotes to fit the headline, then the story's accurate, isn't it?

Overbar: Greater Trenton to Ellen
GET BACK IN THE CLOSET!

The dreaded climate of political correctness in our society manipulated the media on the DeGeneres story. In other newspapers, all of the stories were puff pieces. Treating this television episode like it was history. Every newspaper seemed to tout how wonderful and open-minded our society had become.

We didn't.

Because we know what our beloved Trenton readers wanted.

◆   ◆   ◆

Some reporters—no matter how good they are—don't get it.

They don't know what sells. They have no feeling what a good story is.

Chris Dolmetsch was a good cop reporter. When it came to celebrities, he didn't have a clue.

One evening, I received a call from Paul Mickle who was at home watching TV.

Mickle said earlier in the day he received a crazy tip that Julia Roberts was having this private birthday party at the Great Adventure amusement park in Jackson (which was in our circulation area). Mickle was watching "Entertainment Tonight," and it mentioned it was her birthday.

Mickle said he gave the assignment to Dolmetsch and didn't get back to him about it. I thanked Mickle for making me aware of the development.

I asked Dolmetsch about the story.

"Apparently, there is some party with Julia Roberts, yada, yada, yada," Dolmetsch told me.

Everyone in the newsroom gasped

Jaws just dropped.

Dolmetsch just gave a "yada, yada, yada" to a celebrity story.

Dom Yanchunas and I were on the story.

Editors usually live in ivory towers; they shouldn't.

A solid editor will operate like a general and grab a gun to fight on the front lines.

A solid editor must not be afraid to get his hands dirty.

I was working on this story.

We also sent our society writer Marci Shatzman to go right to Great Adventure and act as if she was covering the party.

She went there, wasn't allowed into the park and she left.

A host of cop cars followed.

Yanchunas and I went to a bar near the park and just shot the shit with people, and some patrons told us they saw her in there earlier that day.

After Shatzman cleared out the cops, Dom and I went in and found out that all the workers hang out a 7-Eleven nearby.

Dom and I staked out the 7-Eleven, and we stayed there until 2 a.m. We busted our asses, and got The Trentonian on Great Adventure's shitlist.

By talking to workers, we found out it was a star-studded private birthday party for Julia. Ed Harris, Lyle Lovett and Tim Robbins were all there. We uncovered the rides the "Pretty Woman" was on, and the reaction from the workers about meeting one of the world's most glamorous actresses.

JULIA'S GREAT ADVENTURE was a wonderful front page.

It should have been better.

If Dolmetsch jumped on the story, we might have gotten a picture of Roberts at the bar.

Like most reporters in this industry, Dolmetsch didn't understand the news value of the story. Guess it didn't change the world. It didn't have a profound impact on our lives.

It didn't matter if Dolmetsch or the rest of the industry like the story.

The readers did.

Readers, you see, ultimately determine the newsworthiness of a story.

Not Dolmetsch. Thank God for that.

Oprah Winfrey was one celebrity to sneak by us. She taped a segment of one of her shows in Princeton. It was an interview with Princeton resident and famous author Toni Morrison. We had reporters staked out outside Morrison's home.

But no luck. The irony was Winfrey's arrival in Princeton came one day after she said "the First Amendment rocks" in her reaction to a legal victory over Texas cattle ranchers.

Blackwell made sure that made the lead of his story:

"Oprah Winfrey, who declared 'the First Amendment rocks!' after she and a pack of her lawyers dodged a slander lawsuit Thursday, is celebrating her triumph by coming to town this weekend—and doing her best to muzzle the press."

◆ ◆ ◆

Dom Yanchunas covers all of his bases.

He's disciplined. He makes all his cop checks.

The Trentonian has an extensive list and it isn't rare for a reporter to use short cuts and going to the most prominent locations. It saves time and preserves energy.

Yanchunas was making the rounds and November 2, 1997 seemed like a quiet, typical Sunday.

He checked with the State Police of Wilburtha—hardly a hotbed for news.

A trooper tipped Yanchunas with a hot story. Yanchunas came up with this:

"LAWRENCE TWP—A pair of nationally known gangsta rappers were busted Saturday for carrying a loaded assault weapon in their car on Interstate 295.

"State troopers nabbed identical twin rappers Kane and Abel at about 3:55 p.m. after their red 1995 Lexus was clocked zooming north at 93 mph on Route 1.

"After pulling the car over, a trooper spotted a TEC-9 semiautomatic assault weapon, a mini machine gun, sticking out of an open bag. The gun was leaded with a 20-round magazine containing 18 bullets. No one was hurt.

"The two rappers and their older brother, who was driving the car, surrendered without protest. In fact, they seemed pleased to gain a little notoriety, State Police at Wilburtha said.

"'They kind of laughed said Trooper Carl Knudsen. 'They said this may boost their record sales.'"

And it helped us boost our own sales on a slow day.

Thanks mainly to Yanchunas' discipline.

◆ ◆ ◆

If you polled the Trentonian staff to name the two worst front pages during my tenure, two headlines stand out:

ARE THEY IN HEAVEN?

LAUTENBERG: LORD OR LOSER

Sherry Sylvester's lead story on New Jersey Sen. Frank Lautenberg's future was the worst front page during my tenure.

Funny thing, most newspaper editors would think this is a wonderful enterprise piece. An insight to the power of a senator.

Our readers rejected it.

It was boring.

Our readers hate politics; therefore, so do I.

This was one day after Mike Tyson bit off Evander Holyfield's ear in their controversial championship fight.

After the incident, we led the paper with the headline:
BITE OF THE CENTURY.
The next day, Linda Dougherty wrote a column about how crazy Tyson is.
On the back page of the "Lautenberg" debacle, we had "HE'S NUTS!" with a picture of a maniacal Mike Tyson.
Dougherty wrote:
"The Nevada police should throw (Tyson) in jail," Dougherty wrote, "for assaulting an officer in the post-fight melee as a violation of his parole.
"And the nearest mental hospital should get that white jacket around his arms, the ones tattooed with images of Chairman Mao and Arthur Ashe.
"And tie the strings tight."
Unfortunately, the back page was more compelling than the front.
But "ARE THEY IN HEAVEN?" was a winner. Hell, it was a pet story.
You can't lose with pet stories.
People love animals. Animals and tragedy equal sales.
About 40 animals died in a fire at a Bucks County, Pa., pet store. A couple of days later, a funeral was held. One of the children asked: "Are they in heaven?"
There it was a perfect lead headline.
'ARE THEY IN HEAVEN?'
Accompanying the headline was a photo with the following caption:
"Blaze survivor Samantha the toucan looks dolefully at casket containing ashes of fire victims, including numerous dogs, cats and her friend, a pet macaw."
This was dramatic stuff and a big-time seller. The package, headline and the front-page headline effectively depicted the drama.
Pet funerals can be front-page news.

We picked this story over the Trenton School District reaching a deal with its teachers to avoid a strike. Our readers prefer pet stories over dull, lifeless education stories.

For some reason, readers hold pets' lives in high regard. Sometimes, pets' deaths are more tragic than humans'.

Some of our memorable front pages involved pets:

TRAILER BARK: A tale about a Bensalem, Pa., women who kept 40 dogs in her trailer. It was the best-selling paper that week.

KILL YOUR DOG—OR ELSE!: A story about an insurance company threatening to drop its coverage for a family if they didn't kill their house dog.

MOUNTAIN LIONS INVADE AREA: A story about the numerous sightings of lions in the region.

WILD DOGS EXECUTED: A wild pack of dogs were mauling area cats, and they paid the ultimate price.

All of those stories were compelling.

When newspaper gurus mock front pages like ARE THEY IN HEAVEN?, they display their own ignorance. These stories are newsworthy with our readers.

I don't care what newspaper gurus say.

I'll take TRAILER PARK over political or education stories.

◆ ◆ ◆

I called into the office.

I was taking a rare day off—and spent it at the racetrack.

"Spent" is the key word here. I was spending—and losing—lots of money betting on some glue factory candidates.

Great tabloid editors must bet on horses. It's part of the lifestyle and the tradition. I don't know one great tabloid editor who doesn't throw some cash at some four-legged freak of nature.

Since my luck was bad, I decided to give Erik Lukens a buzz to find out what was happening in the newsroom.

The newsroom produced a winner.

Lukens told me about this groundhog that gobbled up a wildlife volunteer's diamond.

"Wow," I said.

That's one of those stories where the incident easily writes the headline:

GROUNDHOG ATE MY DIAMOND

Cindy Manion, a thirtysomething graphic artist who looked 20, put together the front page every day—under my direction.

Manion had a knack for art and producing solid front pages. She cut out the picture of the hungry groundhog and had the animal look directly at the woman who owned the diamond.

It was a hilarious front page.

Jon Blackwell took time away from covering the council clowns and wrote this lead:

"TABERNACLE—A newlywed woman lost her $3,500 engagement ring to the fast-moving jaws of an orphaned woodchuck Monday, when she reached into the furry beast's cage at a township animal shelter and feet it a carrot.

"Now, the wild woodchuck, who earned the nickname 'Diamond Lil,' had a bellyful of riches that she's apparently going to keep because ringless animal lover Lois Farly refuses to cut the rodent open and get her bauble back."

The next day, we had a tease, "GROUNDHOG 'RELEASES' DIAMOND."

◆ ◆ ◆

Newspapers take pride in covering education.

If you polled editors, most of them likely would say it is the most important beat in the newspaper.

I don't agree.

Usually, education beats are dull, lifeless and without focus.

Writers merely attend meetings and pelt readers with a barrage of boring stories.

To me, most meetings are "bored" meetings.

Three types of education stories grab my attention.

Firstly, you can't go wrong with tax increases. No reader likes them. Nobody likes to pay more of them. Tax increases usually fuel reader rage.

That's a good thing.

Another type of story is blundering administrators and teacher—who can't ensure students' safety.

The Trenton School District seemingly was reliable in the buffoonery department.

One story, 11-year-old Rajeem Denson nearly drowned during swim class at the Arthur J. Holland Middle School in Trenton. As he was clinging to life, The Trentonian discovered bombshell revelations.

With the front page INCREDIBLE TWISTS IN NEAR DROWNING, we ran the following bullet points:

- Instead of diving in, teacher sent child to bottom of pool to ID victim.

- 60 students in swimming class, but only one teacher could swim.

- District launches cover-up: students ordered to ignore cops, press; superintendent thumbs nose at investigators.

This is a case were the front page effectively depicted the story. We pulled no punches in our approach.

Mark Stradling and Erik Lukens provided a dramatic editorial:

"We want answers to two questions and we want them immediately from Trenton school officials.

"1. How did a kid who was in a supervised swimming class end up near death at the bottom of the pool?

"2. By what authority may school officials stonewall a police investigation into the accident?

"We would like to think that the answers to these questions and other will be given freely and completely. Given yesterday's performance by school officials, though, we already see what's in the works. It has all the earmarks of a typical school district whitewash, except this time we're not talking about test scores or misplaced money or curriculum changes, but a child's very life. Please! What more basic function does our school system have than to safeguard the children entrusted to its care?"

The instructor, who wasn't certified to teach swim courses, was suspended.

Trenton teachers constantly made headlines for either crime or simply being knuckleheads.

We had one front page, CITY TEACHERS CAUGHT RUNNING DRUGS, which was about two Trenton teachers were bagged on the Jersey Turnpike with $2,000 in cocaine.

The third type of story is violence at the schools.

Trenton provided us with lots of it. One time we led the front page with 3RD-GRADER BLOODIES TEACH WITH PUNCH!

Yanchunas transformed it into an issue story:

"The nation's simmering trend of schoolhouse violence came to Trenton this week as a bold, hammer-wielding third-grader slugged one of his teachers in the mouth, bloodying her face and knocking a tooth loose, authorities said."

We also once led with the story BOY SETS TEACHER'S HAIR **ON FIRE!** His classmates had claimed he did it because the art instructor is mean.

We didn't care—we got one hell of an education story out of it.

◆ ◆ ◆

It was my version of "DEWEY DEFEATS TRUMAN."

Sometimes a newspaper is vulnerable to the wires and a rapidly changing story.

Andrew Cunanan, a gay man, was on the lam—accused of several murders in Minnesota and one caretaker in Burlington County, N.J.

Then he killed Gianni Versace in Miami.

Cunanan became the top story on all newscasts.

We ran several stories about the Cunanan saga. We had several reported sightings in our circulation area. One reader believed Cunanan saw him in a Burlington County diner, and another at the Route 1 toll bridge.

Cunanan was a huge story.

One day, a gay doctor was found dead in a bedroom of his Miami home.

All indications pointed to Cunanan.

So in our first edition, we ran the headline HE KILLS AGAIN!

But as the story developed after 11 p.m. it became clear that Cunanan may be only a suspect in the doctor's death. He may not have done it.

I changed the front page for second edition, SERIAL KILLER EYED IN DOC SLAY.

I thought we were safe, but the story kept on changing. At 1:30 a.m. and the news desk was gone, and an Associated Press moved on the wire stating Cunanan wasn't linked to the doctor's death at all.

The front page had turned into a nightmare. We started with HE KILLS AGAIN and ended with KILLER ELUDES DRAGNET. I was batting .333 on accuracy on the front page. It is part of the job. The broadcast outlets can cover up their blunders. Our mistakes are out there in print, and I couldn't bring the papers back. Two-thirds of our editions had the incorrect headline because the story shifted on numerous occasions.

We went too far with HE KILLS AGAIN! If we were a mainstream paper, KILLER ELUDES DRAGNET likely would have been the lead headline anyway. It was safe, but at The Trentonian, we tried to be cutting edge.

I wanted to cut my head off with a sharp edge after that.

Venezia loved to take shots at me about the front page HE KILLS AGAIN! He took the famous picture of Truman holding the headline "DEWEY DEFEATS TRUMAN" and replaced the headline with HE KILLS AGAIN.

HE KILLS AGAIN is a skeleton that rattles in my closet.

I deserved those shots from Venezia.

In this instance, I was too aggressive in trying to sell the newspaper.

◆ ◆ ◆

As Paul Mickle would say, "Jeff Zelevansky is a newsman and a half!"

Zelevansky, who wrote the KIDS MUG CORPSE headline that put us in the right direction, gave us numerous news tips—even after he left the paper.

One night, he called to inform me about a murder at Diva's strip club. I dispatched part-time photographer Bob Castelli to the scene.

Castelli snapped up the picture of the man's corpse, uncovered, being probed by investigators.

Castelli gave me the lead photo for page 1, STRIP-CLUB BLOODBATH.

There was no question about running the picture of the corpse. Some readers complained about it, but most bought it.

It was a sensational news photo, and if it means I could sell more papers with it, I will toss good taste out of the window.

Most of the time, editors will cower with these types of pictures—thinking it will drive readers away.

It doesn't.

In fact, more people will buy the paper because of the drama that is depicted. STRIP-CLUB BLOODBATH was the second largest sale in 1997, right behind SEX IN THE MORTUARY.

The readers will never admit to buying the paper because of the front-page corpse, but they did.

The numbers do not lie.

The terrific tabloid twosome of Chris Wilson and Todd Venezia generated a masterpiece of a story:

"BRISTOL TWP., Pa—A posh strip club turned into a shooting gallery last night as a bouncer killed a man who approached the dance hall's front door, pulled a gun and opened fire, cops said.

"Jack Fletcher, 56, of Levittown hit the bouncer once in the leg as he blasted the worker at close range outside Divas International Gentleman's Club shortly before 9 p.m., said Sgt. Charles McGuigan.

"The security man, who has only been identified as 'Ron,' was able to quickly wrest the .22-caliber pistol from the muscle shirt-wearing gunman. He then fired four times right into the man's heart, killing him, McGuigan said."

◆ ◆ ◆

We watch the local noon news on TV regularly. It keeps us on top of things, and there's nothing wrong getting a story idea from the local news stations.

WCAU, Channel 10 in Philly, ended its noon newscast with a feature shots of a crop circle found at a farm in Lawrence, Mercer County.

A crop circle in Lawrence! We have a line.

Anytime you have a crop circle in your circulation area, you lead with it. It's offbeat, and crackpots will come out of the closet to claim the crop circle was done by a real UFO.

We paid for Leslie Barbaro to fly in a helicopter to take pictures of the crop circle from above. We had our lead photo.

Well, we ran a four-story package on the crop circles and crafty Chris Wilson somehow dug up some real nutcases who believe aliens landed in Mercer County.

In one of the sidebars with the headline "Aliens in Lawrence, E.T. expert sez," Wilson wrote:

"Extraterrestrial experts yesterday said the mysterious cop circle that materialized overnight in a desolate Lawrence oat field appears to be out of this world!

"After examining a photograph of the crop circle faxed to them by The Trentonian, three UFO analysts said it's nearly identical to the thousands of strange circles that have marked English fields since the 1980s.

"'It's not a hoax,' said Stephanie Ellen St. Claire, a psychic astrologer and radio personality in Tucson, Ariz. 'It's exactly the same kind of thing that's been going on in England. You're going to see a lot more of these in the U.S. now.'"

At the news meeting, we debated over the headline. I preferred "UFO MYSTERY" because we couldn't say for sure it's not aliens. So let's go with it.

Schwartz shot it down immediately, "You're fuckin' crazy. This is a prank."

So, UFO PRANK was the lead headline.

The next day, Circulation Director Jim Farrell reported the sales were solid and that we try to make it the wood again.

But nothing new developed—other than other media outlets visited the farm to catch up with The Trentonian's front page.

Well, we manipulated the front page. We made the media's interest in the farm the focus of the second day story.

Our main page 1 headline was FLYING SAUCER FRENZY with the following bullet points.

- Choppers fly over Lawrence crop circle

- Reporters flock to farmer's field

- Cops use Geiger counter to investigate

If a paper is a good seller, an editor must do whatever it takes to make the story have legs. We stretched it a bit here, but it proved effective.

◆   ◆   ◆

The Trentonian in 1997 chronicled the tragic mystery of 12-year-old Celina Mays.

Mays disappeared without a trace from a communal home in Willingboro, Burlington County. A kooky cult ran the communal home.

The Mays saga was on Mickle's hit list—right behind "Flaca" of course.

All eyes focused on the cult leader—Rev. Cerita Smith. Did the cult know where Mays was?

During the course of the story, the story took a bizarre twist—a sexual twist.

A lawyer claimed Smith's 23-year-old son Sean became a stud to help increase the sagging cult. A missing girl, sexual intrigue and a bizarre cult are a great combination for a line.

CULT BABY FACTORY graced the front page.

Mickle, with the inside headline "Sects education," did the story himself:

"WILLIINGBORO—A lawyer fighting the church Celina Mays called home is alleging that the so-called cult has become a virtual baby factory, with the group leader's son serving as a clan stud to boost flagging membership.

"It's an effort that has made at least four church members new moms—at the hands of 23-year-old Sean, the married son of clan guru Rev. Cerita Smith."

Venezia chuckles every time he hears that CULT BABY FACTORY headline—a headline that he wrote. This was one of the top five selling

Saturday papers in 1998—because the saga was a mystery with a sexual twist.

No issues were needed here.

Unfortunately, Mays is still missing.

◆ ◆ ◆

The headline was way too sensational.

Too sensational for even The Trentonian.

Sometimes headlines will seem so bizarre that nobody believes it's true. It might catch the reader's eye, but the content seems so outlandish to even buy.

Case in point, The Trentonian's issue on Sept. 18, 1997.

We led with a story about an 84-year-old doctor who is the keeper of Albert Einstein's brain.

When "MERCER MAN HAS EINSTEIN'S BRAIN IN JAR" hit the newsstands, the public noticed, but didn't buy it.

It was the worst sale of the week.

"It seemed too crazy," then-Circulation Director Jim Farrell said after delivering me the circulation report from that week. "It looked like something somebody will read in the Weekly World News."

"AL'S BRAIN TRUST: Doc sends slices around the world" read the headline on page 3.

Yanchunas provided a story with a map—detailing the locations of Albert Einstein's sliced brain. This doc had sent slices to Hamilton, Ontario, California, Princeton, Alabama, Australia and Japan.

Al's Brain gets around.

Yanchunas reported:

"HOPEWELL TWP. —For 42 years, a local doctor has been the sole custodian of one of the world's most powerful engines of scientific research—the brain of Albert Einstein.

"Dr. Thomas S. Harvey, who performed the autopsy on the Nobel Prize winning scientist after his death, keeps hunks of the famous brain in a jar of special preservatives. The brain parts are hidden in a secret Princeton location to thwart potential thievery of the ultimate intellectual property."

The Trentonian runs sensational stories all the time—but Einstein's brain proved there were limits to the wackiness. The story should have sold, but it failed miserably. It was too unrealistic.

It demonstrated that even The Trentonian has limits on the types of crazy stories it runs.

◆   ◆   ◆

Tony Wilson, who has worked at The Trentonian for at least 30 years, has seen it all.

Wilson, you see, covers the courthouse. He's covered gruesome crimes and dramatic trials.

He's a journalistic legend in Trenton.

He keeps a steady demeanor—no matter how significant the story.

One day in 1997, Todd Venezia, who was filling in for Mickle as city editor, asked Wilson what was going on.

Wilson said nothing much "just a couple of odds and ends."

"You know," Wilson said, "they did catch a 81-year-old drug dealer."

"WHAT?" Venezia screamed.

Venezia was stunned. Wilson didn't have much on it either. To him, it was just an oddity. It was a brief at best.

Stories about 81-year-old drug dealers should lead newspapers.

Venezia knew that. He dispatched Yanchunas to go to the neighborhood to get a profile to the dealer.

The line DRUG DEALER NABBED—HE'S 81 was a hit.

Yanchunas, once again, came through in the clutch.

With the inside headline, GERIATRIC JUNK PUSHER, Yanchunas reported:

"The city's oldest drug dealer my be spending the rest of his golden years behind bars after county detectives charged him yesterday with trying to peddle 51 bags of heroin.

"Eighty-one-year-old Edward "Pops" Brown who has been known to supplement his Social Security checks by selling dope, was arrested at about 10 p.m. moments after he hobbled off a northbound train at Trenton Train Station.

"When detectives from Mercer County's Special Investigations Unit pulled Brown aside, the senior citizen immediately volunteered that he had just returned from buying drugs in Philadelphia, cops said.

"Then the opiate-loving octogenarian 'reached into his pockets and pulled out 51 bags of heroin and handed them to the officers,' said Mercer County Capt. Don Ricigliano."

Most editors today scoff at a story like this. "It shouldn't be leading the paper," most of them would say. This easily was the most talked about story of the week.

A story was a brief in the Trenton Times.

♦ ♦ ♦

It was Saturday, October 11, 1997.

It was a slow week, but a sad one. Bob Shields, a fixture of The Trentonian and an innovative designer, resigned from managing editor post to join the New York Daily News.

His final front page, KING OF THIEVES, told the tale about the evil "Bank Bomber." The surveillance photo of the bandit appeared on the cover.

The "Bank Bomber" robbed 17 banks in two months by using a fake pipe bomb to force teller to fork over the bread.

I asked Yanchunas to do a story on how prolific this robber was, and how he compares to the best robbers in history.

In a story that appeared on Oct. 9, 1997, Yanchunas wrote:

"The brazen bank bandit terrorizing the region's tellers with phony pipe bombs my have set a new U.S. record for the most bank heists in a two-month span, crime experts said this week.

"The 'Bank Bomber' is credited with 17 bank heists in his 59-day, five state spree. Several agents, criminology professors and other sleuths said they have never heard of a more prolific bank robber in the region or even the nation."

As part of the package, Yanchunas wrote a "tale of the tape" comparing this bandit to John Dillinger. Here is how it appeared in the paper:

JOHN DILLINGER

Born: 1903, Indianapolis

Description: 5-foot-7, medium build, light brown hair.

Bank heists: At least 11 in Indiana, Ohio, Wisconsin, South Dakota over year.

Weapon of choice: Real guns.

Total take: $200,000.

Preferred attire: Neat blue suit, straw hat.

Also on resume: 2 jail escapes, one dead sheriff, one dead FBI agent.

End to mayhem: Shot dead by FBI agents outside a Chicago theater.

BANK "BOMBER"

Born: ???

Description: 6-foot, medium build, light brown hair.

Bank heists: 17 banks in New Jersey, Pennsylvania, Delaware, Maryland, Virginia over 2-month period.

Weapon of choice: Fake bombs.

Total take: Est. $50,000.

Preferred attire: Jeans, T-shirt, camouflage, baseball cap.

Also on resume: Just a whole lot of red-faced cops and bankers.

End to mayhem: ???

It's now two days after the story and the tale of the tape appeared in the paper. Tony Wilson was on duty. Usually, one or maybe two reporters work the weekend because not much breaking news happens. The news cycle is a tad slower.

I asked Wilson what is going on.

"Not much," he said. "Just a couple of things.

"Oh yes, they caught that pipe bomb bandit."

"WHAT?"

"And he's a prison guard."

It was déjà vu. Wilson is the master of the understatement. We led with the Bank "Bomber" at least five times, and it was an "oh, by the way" in Wilson's book.

I tried to reach Yanchunas, but for some reason, he was out looking for pumpkins.

No reporters were available, and calls were flooding in from other media outlets.

I found out from one of these television reporters that our front page KING OF THIEVES helped bag the "bomber." The bomber's colleagues at the prison recognized the photo on the front page and turned in the man who we compared to Dillinger.

We have this huge story of how this newspaper help put a criminal off the street and I have to be informed about it from a TV reporter.

Our "Bank Bomber" beat writer was hunting for the great pumpkin.

Our reporter in the building didn't realize the magnitude of the story.

And we had no reporter in sight to help.

I felt like Commissioner Gordon in Batman.

"Only one man can save us. Only one man can bring sanity to this situation."

Paul Mickle.

I summoned Mickle to help out on the package, and like a true newsman, he was willing and able.

"Tony could have done this himself," Mickle said at the time. "He's a veteran newsman who knows what he's doing."

Mickle may have been right, but I couldn't take any chances.

Mickle helped transform an 8-inch story into a blockbuster two-page package. He swooped in and saved the day.

Mickle wrote this lead:

"A Mercer County corrections officer—recognized by colleagues from his photographer in The Trentonian—was arrested yesterday and charged as the brazen bandit who used a fake pipe bomb to commit 17 robberies in five states in the past two months.

"Freddie Feliciano, 22, a corrections officer since 1995 who was robbing banks at a record-setting pace, was arrested by the FBI without incident at 6 a.m. at this Hamilton Township home."

On the front page, we had "BANK BOMBER NABBED....And We Helped."

Thanks to Shields' final front page and Yanchunas' tale of the tape, The Trentonian put a thug off the street.

Now, *that's* community service.

◆   ◆   ◆

"I know Mike Raffaele," Trenton Mayor Doug Palmer screamed at reporter Dom Yanchunas, "and he would never run a story like this!"

That story was about the mayor getting into a shouting match with a prominent restaurant owner over parking.

We did run that story—as the wood.

The headline, DOUG LOST COOL, was the best seller in the first week of October in 1997.

Yanchunas wrote:

"A city restaurateur has accused Mayor Doug Palmer of shouting profanity and intimidating him after Hizzonner waded into a parking dispute last week between the Chambersburg eatery and a nearby rival.

"Amici Milano restaurant owner Jimmy Kamies said he is furious that Palmer angrily lectured him on the business' parking dispute with nearby Marsilio's Restaurant, one of Palmer's favorite dining spots.

"Kamies charges that Palmer used profanity and virtually ordered Kamies to allow Marsilio's customers to park in his lot reserved for Amici Milano guests.

"The confrontation took place at about 10 p.m. Friday on a sidewalk near the disputed Chestnut Street lot after Kamies called on cops to ticket the cars parked on his lot.

"Palmer admits he was "angry" and excited" when discussing the matter with Kamies, but only because at the time he thought the police should not be spending their time ticketing 'Burg parkers."

This story hit home with Trenton readers. Palmer showed an arrogance because he was ticketed. And anytime a politician goes bonkers, the editor must exploit it.

Interestingly, a majority of the news staff wanted to lead with a story about a clown knocking on a man's door and tossing acid into his face.

A crazed clown was on the loose in the Greater Trenton area.

"CRAZED CLOWN should be the headline," Lukens said.

Venezia agreed. So did I.

But Schwartz is the publisher and he shot it down—emphatically.

"No one cares about a fuckin' clown," Schwartz said. "It's a dumb story."

So, DOUG LOST COOL remained the line, but staffers were stunned by Schwartz strong insistence against the clown story. It was strange, almost bizarre.

"Is Sandy afraid of clowns?" one staffer said. "You would think that after that meeting."

"Yeah," another staffer said. "Something must have happened when he was a kid. If it wasn't a clown involved, we probably would have made it the line."

A Trentonian legend was born: Sandy Schwartz is afraid of clowns.

Years later, Eric Ladley approached Paul Mickle about the Schwartz fear of clowns legend.

"If you look into it you'll find," Mickle said. "that Sandy is not indeed afraid of clowns. It wasn't an interesting story. The Doug story was better."

♦ ♦ ♦

Anytime you can get sexy pictures of Hooters girls on Page 1 and Page 3 of your paper, you will undoubtedly be successful.

When Hooters girls arrived to promote a cigar shop in the sleepy town of Newtown, Pa., it raised eyebrows—and drew rage from the business community.

It also gave us a wonderful opportunity to put the Hooters' talents on page 1.

Ralph Tasgal was assigned the story. Tasgal struggled as a writer and reporter and drew fire from Venezia daily. Tasgal lacked the aggressiveness and the street smarts to be successful at the Trentonian. He had enormous potential.

Venezia constantly rewrote Tasgal's prose.

The Hooters story was one of them.

Venezia—with Tasgal's byline—crafted this lead:

"NEWTOWN, Pa. —A cigar shop owner is creating a Hooters hullabaloo on the day this picture-postcard town's quaintest local event with a sexy scheme to boost sales by using scantily clad women to greet customers.

"Classic Cigar, a relative newcomer to town, has been dragged into this ribald ruckus after fellow bizmen got wind of the plan to hire two waitresses from the famous Hooters restaurant during Newtown's annual 'open house tour.'"

Chris Barth was dispatched to a Hooters in the Philly area to get group shots of the girls. It was an art element we needed.

What's a story about Hooters girls without a picture? A bad one.

Barth was ordered to get Hooters girls frolicking around at work. He did. He provided one playing with a hula hoop and a dramatic group shot.

For Barth, it was mission accomplished.

Now we needed a headline—one that will completely capture the sexy element of the story.

Erik Lukens—the Babe Ruth of headline writers—hit one out of the park, again.

TEMPEST IN A D-CUP was the lead headline of the paper.

A great headline. A sexy story. Sizzling pictures.

It doesn't get better than that.

◆ ◆ ◆

Crosshairs and tabloid newspapers go hand in hand.

The crosshairs are a critical tool for front-page drama.

For example, on a slow news day, we led with the U.S. planning to attack Saddam and Iraq—again.

Normally, we wouldn't lead with a dull international story. Lead with international stories and the circulation will plunge.

We needed to jazz up the cover. Make it compelling and appeal to the patriotic nature of the country.

We ran the headline U.S. TAKES AIM AT IRAQ with crosshairs right on Saddam's forehead.

Mickle loves the crosshairs; he fondly remembers the outrage the now-defunct Philadelphia Bulletin created in the late 1970s.

The Bulletin put crosshairs on the pope to reflect the pontiff's vulnerability to possible assassins during a visit to Philly.

Now, crosshairs can be placed on the beloved. Once, a crazed cat killer was on the loose in Trenton. I put crosshairs on a cat with the headline, CAT KILLER ON THE LOOSE. A pair of crosshairs on an innocent pet will capture anybody's attention.

It's effective and very dramatic.

When the hard-working cab drivers were targets of a rash of robberies, it cried for more drama.

Dom Yanchunas produced an enterprise package on the safety of cab drivers, and we slapped crosshairs on a cab on Page 1.

The headline CABBIES UNDER SIEGE became even better with the crosshairs.

Use crosshairs like it was seasoning—it can spice a dull front page up.

◆ ◆ ◆

For most newspaper editors, Election night is the Super Bowl.

Not at the Trentonian.

Politics wasn't held in the highest esteem here.

It didn't sell; therefore, we didn't care.

That was a problem for us. Sherry Sylvester, you see, was our chief political writer.

She can't sit around and collect dust.

We wanted her to emphasize personality over issues.

Issues are boring.

Today's newspapers are in awe of the dance of legislation. It's newsworthy to follow every step of a bill becoming a law.

A newspaper filled with issues is a boring newspaper.

Political personalities are vital to effectively covering elections. Florio was an easy target for the Trentonian because of his arrogant personality.

If the taxpayers are directly affected, run it.

The best political headlines are those that end with "AND YOU PAY!"

For example:

DRAG QUEENS PARTY—AND YOU PAY!

WILD JUNKET FOR POL—AND YOU PAY!

The audience likes buffoonery. When a politician is caught in a lie or is caught living lavishly with taxpayers' money.

That works.

Following every piece of legislation doesn't.

Election night is supposed to be a showcase of editorial talent. The night all of the stops are made. Everybody seems to care. Editors have to make themselves look important.

Pizza is ordered. And editors try to justify their existence.

In 1997, New Jersey has a critical election for governor. Gov. Whitman is facing a stiff challenge from Democrat James McGreevey. Every newspaper in the state is preparing for election coverage.

But not Trentonian City Editor Paul Mickle.

Mickle, you see, doesn't want The Trentonian to lead its paper with "bullshit elections."

His goal was to find another story that will knock election off.

He's the only city editor in the state with such aspirations.

"If people really cared, then they'd vote," Mickle would say.

He's right.

But election night is the Super Bowl for newspapers. Editors work into the night. Heck, they might even work longer than eight hours.

Pizza is ordered and the newsroom truly becomes a newsroom. Editors pretend to look busy, and dig into every statistic. Oh it's hectic. All of the management editorial types must be part of final product. All of the cooks are in the kitchen.

It's a showcase for the editorial talent.

Where are these guys on the other 364 days in a year?

But at The Trentonian, it's another day of finding the story that will sell newspapers.

Unfortunately, editors sit in their ivory towers for 364 days. One night a year they will approach the newspaper like it's a vital, do-or-die night.

They actually roll up their sleeves and become a part of the process.

Every day should be Election Day.

If editors had the same intensity toward the job on the other 364 days, the industry wouldn't be in its critical state.

For Mickle, it's just another day. He will have the same high intensity toward his work on every shift. Every day is played like Game 7 of the World Series.

That is refreshing.

We need more Mickles.

An editor has to look at every issue as a must-win game.

Mickle knew the elections normally don't sell.

On this day, the Trenton Strangler called him with a tip that he almost turned into the lead story. He was at WCW Monday Nitro in Philadelphia, and a couple Eagles players were there, totally bombed and yelling at the wrestlers. People in the crowd were booing the Birds. It made a messy scene.

About an hour after the Strangler's tip, we got a press release from Mount Laurel saying one of the Eagles, Steve Everitt, was pulled over for DWI.

Mickle wanted so badly for this story to be the line.

I thought it should have been too, but it was the biggest night in politics, and we led with Whitman's razor-thin victory.

It was one of the worst editorial decisions I've made. Football, boozin', and pro wrestling is an ideal combination. It's a clear-cut winner for circulation.

It beats the tightest of elections

Ironically, the big election wasn't the top-selling paper for the Trentonian that week.

A wild bank robbery and shootout in Princeton took the top honors.

A story headlined TERROR IN PRINCETON easily beats WHITMAN BY A WHISKER every time.

◆ ◆ ◆

TERROR IN PRINCETON, a story about gunmen who robbed a Sovereign Bank in the Princeton rekindled the fierce rivalry with the Trenton Times.

Both papers had motives—to sell papers.

Our targeted readers differed. The Times tried to appeal to the Princeton, suburban crowd. The coverage was more issue—and enterprise-oriented.

We targeted the blue-collar readers in the Trenton area, but also appealed to a general audience that enjoyed the Trentonian pull-no-punches approach.

We used hard-hitting crime stories to grab readers.

Two distinct philosophies separated the papers more than the half-mile between the two newspaper buildings.

In this story, three gunmen robbed a Sovereign Bank in Princeton. Princeton cops then fatally gunned down one of the robbers. The other two escaped, carjacked a 91-year-old man and dumped him during the getaway.

A hard-hitting crime story in Princeton.

The Times and The Trentonian's agendas clashed. We took pride in being the best big story paper in the market. The Times covered issues and tried to seduce Princeton readers.

The battle was joined.

Before the robbery, I didn't lose sleep about the competition with the Times. Newspaper editors today make too much of a deal out of rivalries with the competition.

Firstly, Editors get wrapped up if a story appears in the "rival" paper and they don't have it—even if the story is on page 14.

This is a waste of energy.

The editor should be primarily concerned about what's on the competition's Page 1.

That's it.

Forget what's on pages 3-14.

One time, the Times ran a story about a woman who lost her legs when a drunken driver struck her. They put the story on Page 3.

We didn't have the story.

My immediate reaction was correct. "Boy, did the Times fuck up." Blunders like that happened frequently.

I didn't care about getting beaten. We were going to lead with this story the next day. Reporter Nancy Houtz got details of the victim being an avid jogger.

OUR HEADLINE: CRUEL FATE HITS JOGGER.

The deck read: She loses legs after being struck by drunken driver.

Under the inside headline, 'HER LEGS WERE HER LIFE,' Houtz reported:

"The family of an athletic young college student cut down by a runaway car kept a grim bedside vigil last night as the 26-year-old Trenton woman struggled to recover from the crash that left her legs amputated."

This resulted in a great sale.

The readers don't look at the paper that closely to realize the Times had the same story on Page 3 the day before.

We played it better, and people thought we were the first to break the story.

Readers probably won't have the same feelings about a story on open space.

Newspapers get scooped by its rivals every day. The keys are what types of stories they are and where the stories are placed.

The Sovereign Bank robbery rocked both newspapers. Both were going to make it the lead story. We needed to maintain our blue-collar base that relished crime while the Times wanted to keep the Princeton reader.

We were defending our turf.

All of our reporters were assigned to this story. We didn't care about anything else. We had three pages of coverage on Day 1. The Times had three stories, but had an effective graphic breaking down what happened.

On Day 2, we had an 11-story, five-page package. We had stories about the manhunt of the two remaining robbers at large, an interview with a bank employee, a story about how Princeton was paralyzed with fear and one how Princeton Puerto Ricans were being rounded up as possible suspects. The Times had the identification of the robbers at large.

We didn't.

But we loved to play the fear factor. Nothing's better than a story that forces people to lock their doors—a story that makes readers stay inside. The only time these readers will go outside is to go buy our paper.

The Princeton bank robbery was one of those stories. Wild gunmen were in our midst.

On Day 3 of the coverage, we led with how police were exploring the possibility of an inside job.

HOSTAGE DATED SLAIN GUNMAN led the fourth day of Trentonian coverage. Blackwell got a tip from a source how one teller was linked to the gunman who was shot dead. We never got a chance to talk to the bank teller.

The lead read: "The robber killed in Princeton's bloody bank holdup was the ex-boyfriend of the teller he took hostage moments before police gunned him down, sources told The Trentonian yesterday."

Every night, we sent a reporter to pick up a Times. On Day 4, Dom Yanchunas grabbed a copy of the Times, and to his dismay, the bank teller we linked to the gunman said she never hung out with such a loser.

They talked to the teller. We didn't.

We fell behind in the story.

For our later editions, we bilked the Times interview. We didn't even give the Times complete credit. Yanchunas inserted the following into the story:

"But in an equally startling rebuttal, (the woman) denies that she even knew Rivera or the other thugs, saying in a published report today that she wouldn't 'associate with these lowlifes.'"

Officials at the Times must have been furious about what we did. But the ends justify the means.

The next night, the Times turned into Fort Knox. It was virtually impossible for us to get a paper at the plant. The fences were locked, and strangers weren't allowed on the Times facility.

Yanchunas and I decided to tail the first Times truck to leave the facility. It was like a scene from Hawaii Five-O with cops following the bad guys.

In this instance, a Trenton Times truck was the bad guy. We followed the truck for about 20 minutes until the deliveryman make its first drop at a truck stop in Bordentown.

We had a Times—only 20 minutes later than normal

It was a victory for the good guys from the Trentonian.

We continued this process for the next year. We would do whatever it takes to get an edge.

When a newspaper does that, the readers win.

◆ ◆ ◆

"DISGRACED!" shouted The Trentonian's front page on November 11, 1997.

The Trentonian told it like it is.

Jim Waldron, Trenton's public safety director, was forced to resign amid allegations of stealing $270,000 from elderly ladies.

We could have used a straightforward headline like "OFFICIAL BILKED $270Gs FROM GRANNIES."

But DISGRACED! was appropriate in this case. It accurately told the story. A newspaper must not be afraid about being bold.

We picked a photo of Waldron looking distressed.

Under the inside headline, WALDRON IN A CAULDRON, Venezia wrote:

"Trenton's top law enforcement official stepped down yesterday—just hours after he lost his license to practice law for allegedly bilking $270,000 from a pair of elderly widows who trusted him with their finances.

"Public Safety Director Jim Waldron, known as 'The Commish,' during his 3 1/2-year term, effected ended his legal career by signing a 'consent to disbarment' agreement yesterday.

"It's a disgraceful turn of events that Waldron had, apparently, hoped to keep quiet.

"In fact, neither he nor the city made mention of the disbarment in announcing that Waldron had stepped down from his roughly $60,000 a year job, effective immediately.

"The statement did thank Waldron for his 'dedication' and wished him luck in the future."

◆ ◆ ◆

"I have an idea," Schwartz grumbled. "How about we call this kid, 'Candy Boy'."

"What?"

"Yeah, 'Candy Boy,'" Schwartz said more convinced of his point now. "Everybody will know who we are talking about."

"Candy boy" was little 12-year-old Eddie Werner, who was murdered while trying to raise money selling candy.

The front-page headline went from HE WAS STRANGLED with a picture of little Eddie to:

CANDY BOY WAS STRANGLED

Venezia and other staffers chuckled when they heard the new, improved headline.

However, it is imperative for a headline to grab people's attention, and at the same time, the reader will immediately know what the story was about.

Mention CANDY BOY during this period, and readers knew exactly who it was.

There was not confusion; therefore, it was an effective headline.

Phones rang off the hook when the term "CANDY BOY" first graced the front pages of the Trentonian. We were called tasteless. Accused of having no compassion for the family.

I only have compassion for the readers. The sales were solid. Some might argue that the story didn't need such a "tasteless" headline. The story itself would have sold.

The headline makes it easier for the readers to make their decisions. The clearer the headline, the higher the sale. A convoluted headlined could drop a sale.

In another development, 15-year-old Sam Manzie was arrested and charged with his murder.

The next day's headline read:

GEEKY LONER, 15, KILLED CANDY BOY

The paper didn't back down from the criticism. People were gobbling up the papers at the newsstands. That's the ultimate poll.

Editors today tend to take a couple of complaints out of context. If one person calls an editor and rips the use of "Candy Boy," then it is assumed everybody is upset.

That's not the case.

Editors must realize that a caller is just one reader. One. Not thousands.

But for some reason, if somebody calls, editors start scrambling for changes. We must ditch this because some crackpot is angry.

Satisfied readers don't call to pat editors on the back.

They just buy the paper more frequently. They are the "silent majority."

"Candy Boy" in the headline did enhance sales because it told the story more effectively.

"Candy Boy" delivered sweet sales.

A year later, "Candy Boy" guided us in making the right decision.

Tony Wilson reported:

"The Ewing mom who allegedly made her troubled son live in a tiny tool shed and forced him to dig a ditch as punishment for getting expelled from school created the self-styled boot camp only because she wanted to set the troubled boy straight her lawyer said yesterday."

Our page 1 headline read:

MOM: SHED BOY NEEDED TOUGH LOVE

"Candy Boy" and "Shed Boy" sparked solid sales.

◆ ◆ ◆

It was the hardest decision in my newspaper career.

On one side, we had a very attractive local coed killed in Tasmania from encephalitis developed from a mosquito bite.

The other choice is a story of an arm with the name with the tattoo "Steve" on it found in a Trenton Dumpster.

In these instances, a newspaper can't lose. There will be a boost in the sales, no matter which story I pick.

However, I wanted the maximum amount of sales.

Todd Venezia backed the coed story. The headline would be COED KILLED BY MOSQUITO. The girl was attractive, and tragedies involving good-looking tug at the heartstrings even more.

It was an eye-popping front.

Jon Blackwell and Mike Regan strongly supported MAN'S ARM FOUND IN CITY DUMPSTER. They argued that an arm in a Dumpster will continue the tradition of the Trentonian and body parts.

Remember how famous HEAD HAD AIDS was.

Blackwell wrote a solid lead:

"Cops peered into a trash bin behind a South Trenton strip mall yesterday and made a sickening discovery—a freshly severed arm tattooed with the name 'Steve.'"

The coed story, however, was a one-shot deal. It was going to be the only day we would be able to lead with it.

The "arm" story had legs. It was a mystery, and we could lead with it in the next couple of days.

COED KILLED BY A MOSQUITO hit the newsstands.

ARM FOUND IN DUMPSTER was a tease.

Bob Jelenic called me the next day. He wasn't happy with my decision.

He did like the story choice, but we should have used the headline: COED KILLED BY ENCEPHALITIS instead.

Jelenic's headline would have served as a reader-repellent. But hey, it was the second news-related call from the owner.

Schwartz said "shit" when he heard about my thought process.

He was disappointed.

"Remember this, you can't go wrong with a story involving body parts," he said.

The next day, we led with this headline:
COPS SEARCH FOR REST OF 'STEVE.'

◆ ◆ ◆

In the newspaper business, less can be more.

For instance, when a woman's body was found in the woods on the outskirts of the city of Trenton, the police didn't give us much information.

It appeared to be a drug overdose, but nobody was confirming it.

Mysterious corpses are good for newspapers. Eric Ladley urged me to make it the wood and wrote this lead:

"A woman whose body was found by police yesterday afternoon in the wooded backyard of an abandoned building died under suspicious circumstances, police said."

I went with the lead headline, WOMAN'S CORPSE FOUND IN WOODS.

Struggling newspapers would have made a brief out of this story—assuming it was an overdose. Editors should never assume.

Assuming can only lead to trouble—and lost sales. Who am I to decide if this is an overdose. It would be arrogant on my part. This could be a murder. Why should I report otherwise?

The story was the best-selling Sunday paper for April and most of May.

Of course, the next day we ran the story how this woman died of an overdose.

◆ ◆ ◆

In a libel suit in 1995, a Trentonian reporter claimed Schwartz said the following:

"There's no point in being in the newspaper business if you can't take care of your friends and screw your enemies."

Schwartz denied making the statement.

When dealing with advertisers, Schwartz's alleged statement could have been a rallying cry.

Editors normally hate dealing with advertisers—because they believe the paper's integrity is at stake. But the ad department pays for our salaries and generates revenue for the paper.

And what's integrity if the paper goes out of business.

Some businesses won't advertise in your paper, but will expect you to cover their events (to get free advertising).

Forget 'em.

In 1997, CoreStates bank (now known as First Union) dropped its advertising from The Trentonian. But at the same time, expected us to cover its events. The bank sponsors a major race in Trenton. In 1997, we didn't send a reporter to the race. In fact, we ran only a picture and called it simply the "bike race" without mentioning the sponsor.

In a group shot on the society page, we cropped out a CoreStates executive. Why give him the free advertising?

The feud with CoreStates escalated even more. The Flyers and the Sixers played at the CoreStates Center. We refused to mention the arena's name in stories. One time, we really stuck it to CoreStates on the back page after the Flyers named Wayne Cashman the head coach.

The overline said: Call the Philly arena now…

WAYNE MANOR

As for art, We put a headshot on top of the arena and airbrushed the CoreStates logo out of the background.

CoreStates saw what was happening: they finally returned to advertising in the newspaper.

It was a victory for the good guys.

Wal-Mart and Sam's Club didn't advertise with us. Never will. So we made it a point to hammer them whenever we could.

One front page read:

MICE INFEST WAL-MART

Under the inside headline "CRAWL-MART," reporter Nancy Houtz with help from Todd Venezia wrote this lead:

"A horde of dirty mice have turned a local Wal-Mart into a varmint's paradise after the furry friends infested the store's stock and forced local health officials to shutter the in-house McDonald's

About 10 months later, The Trentonian led with:

MICE DROPPINGS ON SAM'S CLUB EASTER CANDY

Eric Ladley wrote this lead:

"An army of mice chased the Easter Bunny from the Sam's Club store on Route 1, after the dirty, gnawing rodents broke into the building and relieved themselves on 150,000 pieces of holiday candy."

If they advertised, maybe those stories would have been briefs, but both didn't, we had solid front pages. They were legitimate news stories.

Editors should be blunt with their staffs when it comes to advertisers. If you steer away from a story because an advertiser is involved, tell them.

Advertisers do get some breaks from newspapers. Nobody will admit it, but it's true. Editors have been forced to look away from stories because an advertiser is involved.

It's a part of the business of being a business.

Sometimes we hit our advertisers when it meant better sales at the stands.

The KatManDu, an advertiser, is a popular waterfront nightclub, supposedly a symbol of Trenton's rebirth. Yanchunas, who picked up a lot of stories simply by living and hanging out in the city, heard that the state was going to close KatManDu down. Venezia loved the story so much that he came in during the day to write it.

It was first thought that KatManDu would be accused of watering down its drinks. This ballyhooed nightclub getting accused of one of the worst things a nightclub can do.

Instead, we found out it was bar flies. It was only going to be closed for a couple of days. It's still a good story with the headline:
BUGS IN THE BOOZE AT KATMANDU
Venezia took an interest in the story himself:
"A nightclub that local leaders hoped would spur Trenton's waterfront rebirth is facing a stomach-turning image crisis, and the threat of the two-week ban on booze sales after the state charged them with letting fruit flies infest their liquor sales."

Schwartz came up with the headline, BUGS IN THE BOOZE AT KATMANDU—it was one of his final headlines.

He was going out with style.

In a letter to Schwartz, Gov. Whitman mentioned the headline as one of her favorites.

Advertisers do make an impact on newspaper's decisions, but the tremendous story must prevail—at all costs.

◆   ◆   ◆

The business section is the least important in the paper. Traditionally, business stories sell only when there are massive layoffs in the market.

For example, the media are going nuts about the 2002 Enron scandal. Nobody cares. Even though a lot of people's finances have been tapped out because of it, most readers don't understand it, and tune out.

In developing a business section, it is vital to develop a personality: a person who readers can connect. At The Trentonian, it was one man. Jim Fitzsimmons.

A veteran newspaperman in the Trenton market for years, Fitz had a cult following. He was beloved and a true man.

Fitz knew the game of the business department. Business editors at small to mid-sized papers must write "puff" pieces to appeal to advertisers. If a new store was opening and the owners were advertising in the paper, Fitz was there.

But Fitz focused on the human-interest element of stories. Struggling business editors will tell how great the store is and what it offers. Fitz would do a profile on the owners—briefly mentioning what the store has to offer.

When hiring a business editor, you must look for somebody who is connected in the community. A personality everybody knows.

Fortunately, Fitz also was a great journalist.

◆ ◆ ◆

During the Storm Gifford era, peace prevailed in the sports department.

Holmlund and Barrow developed into leaders. Jelenic wasn't pestering us.

Gifford stabilized the patient.

We continued to push national over local—to the chagrin of the hospitalized Jim Davis.

Davis, who suffered a collapsed lung, is "Mr. Little League" in the Greater Trenton Area. Little League used to be the centerpiece—not anymore.

One back page—featuring Rangers' Mark Messier possibly heading to Canucks—enraged Davis.

Davis calling from his hospital bed, said "what the fuck are you doing?"

"We're in the middle of fuckin' July, and you're leading with fuckin' hockey. July is Little League. Not fuckin' hockey!"

That was the only sports-related major outburst I knew about in the summer of 1997.

Hearing it from Jim Davis was a lot better than Jelenic.

Gifford—the most effective sports editor during my tenure—passed the editor reins to Holmlund, and Eric Barrow was named assistant sports editor.

The sports section was developing into a hard-hitting section. It was a far cry from burying the Mike Tyson-Evander Holyfield fight.

◆ ◆ ◆

The Trentonian's conservative readership expected us to take hard shots at President Clinton.

For most of my first year as editor, our crosshairs were also on Chelsea Clinton. The "Ivy League Princess" was considering going to Princeton, and we were prepared to assign a reporter to her full time.

We would have reported rumors our her social life, her partying, her boyfriends and grades.

We would have been the official paper of Chelsea.

The president's daughter put a pin in our balloon.

She chose Stanford.

President Clinton kept us busy however with the Monica Lewinsky scandal. Three days after the scandal broke, Stradling told me that he was writing an editorial saying that Clinton must resign. The editorial led the paper: BILL MUST RESIGN.

"President Clinton is scheduled to give the State of the Union address tomorrow night," the editorial opened. "For the good of the Union, it would be best if he kept it brief. Two words would suffice: 'I resign.'"

A paragraph later, the editorial read:

"Why should the American people be expected to tolerate this behavior any longer? Whatever pain the president may have caused in his marriage is nothing compared to the pain that this entire country may suffer as a result of his misfeasance and his arrogance. He must go—and go now, right now, before any more harm is done.

This was January—months before any other newspaper would make the same argument. We didn't need a long meeting. In order to appear even-handed, newspaper editors will have lengthy editorial board meetings and usually the argument becomes watered down and weak in voice.

The meeting about demanding Clinton's resignation lasted 15 seconds. Stradling told me what he was going to write, and I said "OK, I have a lead for Monday's paper."

Newspaper editorials need to have a strong, aggressive voice—one that will trigger an emotion.

"Use all the tools—make that weapons—at your command, including humor, sarcasm, passion, inflammatory language and absolute avoidance of fairness and objectivity to drive as many people in your community, especially the political leaders, teachers, government workers, lawyers, doctors, women, ethnic groups (but not advertisers) into a sputtering, murderous rage every day.

"If you do that, you'll produce an old-timey newspaper editorial page that may not produce Pulitzer Prizes, but will produce readers. Ain't that what it's all about."

We were the first paper in the country to demand Clinton resignation, and, in light of his future impeachment, we looked prophetic. Stradling was on the nose with everything. Our editorial got incredible play in New York.

We were talked about.

My mother, who lives in upstate New York, had even heard about it. "What the hell is my son doing?" she must have asked. It was interesting publicity. Sherry went on-air in a New York station and on ABC-TV.

With the editorial, we positioned ourselves at the forefront of public opinion. The Trentonian was not ordinary; we were different. Only once or twice a year did we ever put an editorial on the front page. The last, with Megan Kanka, got good results. It's not something you can overuse, with the right issue the impact can be tremendous. Our blue-collar conservative readership ate it up. Some thought we were jumping the gun, but you have to get people interested in your paper.

My rule is that if the issue is big enough and there is nothing else really happening that day, it's okay to lead with an editorial. The Super Bowl was that day, and we were too wrapped up in that to produce any lines. The big game is the worst night, even worse than covering an election. It was Denver versus Green Bay, and we had to make a lot of changes at the end, because I'd been anticipating that Green Bay would win. There is always a lot of scrambling, and the game ends late.

There is no question that our paper was anti-Bill Clinton.

We hated Clinton and were proud of it.

He got a great shot from the AP with his famous finger wagging, and we replayed it over and over again. The next day, when he held a press conference, every other paper was probably thinking along the lines of "Bill Strikes Back" story.

Not me.

MORE BULL FROM BILL was the real story here. We were right again. In our subhead we said, "Clinton Makes Lame Denial."

When Clinton gave his State of the Union address, all of the other media gushed over him. They went gaga, and reported how great his speech was.

We used the big hammerhead: SLICK! Underneath we had this deck: "Clinton snows 'ems in Oscar-worthy State of the Union performance."

The Clinton-Lewinsky saga was one of those scandals readers can easily understand: the president was getting a blow job from an intern and is now trying to cover his ass.

Simplicity is vital to covering scandals.

The Trentonian didn't limit its ridicule to Bill Clinton.

Hillary also was an easy target.

When Hillary when on a tour of the Northeast to promote historic preservation—she excluded Trenton.

We took exception.

Jon Blackwell, a history buff, put together a piece under the headline "GIVE HER AN 'F' FOR HISTORY."

Blackwell wrote:

'Trenton was the turning point of the Revolution, a onetime capital of the United States and an industrial center where the Roebling family designed the Brooklyn Bridge.

"But to Hillary Clinton, New Jersey's Capital City apparently has less historic merit than such towns merit than such towns as West Orange, Pittsfield, Mass., and Newburgh, N.Y.

"That's right—when the First Lady went on a tour of the Northeast this week to promote historic preservation, she paid visits to all those "historic" towns while ignoring Greater Trenton.

"Some outraged Trentonians say the president's wife deserves an 'F' in history for her neglect.

"'She goes to a dump like West Orange to talk about history—incredible!' said city historian Charles Webster. "Then she goes to Newburgh. That's a speck on the map!

"'So, what if Washington slept in Newburgh? He won battles here. He beat the British here and it's because of the Battle of Trenton that we won the Revolution. It just shows Hillary Clinton's total ignorance of history.'"

In early 2002, Webster became the business editor of The Trentonian.

But Blackwell's innovation was refreshing—he found a local angle to a national story.

More importantly, he hammered a Clinton.

Our readers liked that.

◆ ◆ ◆

Most scandals begin with a small story, then snowball into a huge unstoppable force.

This was the case with the Trentonian's coverage of the Baron Athletic Association, a social club in Hamilton Township.

On January 22, 1998, reporter Chris Dolmetsch in his routine cop checks stumbled on and wrote this story:

"HAMILTON—State troopers raided an exclusive Cypress Lane social club Wednesday confiscating more than $160,000 in illegal gambling equipment and booze, a state police spokesman said yesterday.

"State police were led to the Baron's Athletic Association while making routine inspections of licensed establishments in the area. One owner told them to check out the BAA, Sgt. Al Della Fave said.

"An Alcoholic Beverage Control Commission inspector went to the club, gained admittance—and immediately noticed signs prices of alcohol and a number of casino-style slot machines.

"Not only are slot machines illegal in New Jersey, outside of Atlantic City, the BAA had no license to sell alcohol. So the inspector immediately secured a search warrant for the premises.

"'When you find an establishment selling alcohol without a license, it immediately gives the ABC to anything,' Della Fave said. 'Rugs, paintings, anything they want.

"'Officials seized 12 slot machines, each valued at $10,000; 10 video poker machines, each valued at $3,000; more than $11,000 in cash; six roulette wheels; 10 blackjack and poker tables; two large bags of quarters; numerous bottles of liquor and 100 cases of beer.

"One club board member, whose name was not available yesterday, posted a $75,000 bond that prevented state police front shutting the place down altogether.

"BAA officials and club members approached yesterday had no comment when reached at the club.

"The club itself was charged with an administrative violation of selling alcohol without a license. State police are still investigating the case and trying to identify the main perpetrators.

"'Right now, the investigation now focuses on those people who will be held directly responsible for running BAA,' Della Fave said.

"The BAA is an exclusive social club that often sponsors charity events and donates money to worthy causes. The club donated $45,000 to the Deborah Heart and Lung Center in Browns Mills in October."

Dolmetsch emphatically believed the bust at the Barons should have been the line. I didn't even want to hear it from it him.

I was so focused on Clinton's woes with Lewinsky. No bust could knock the Clinton story off the front page of The Trentonian.

Dolmetsch's story was buried—on page 11.

It was a move I would later second-guess myself.

About a week later, Venezia found out from a high-ranking source that the Baron kept surveillance cameras, and the law-enforcement authorities seized the tapes.

And some prominent area politicians and personalities were on that tape.

Once again, I didn't make that development the lead story of the paper. Instead, led with SLICK, a package on Clinton's dramatic State of the Union speech.

Another blunder. But we had a plan. With gambling machines involved, it will be obvious that the local authorities were probing the possible link to the mob.

How else would have these knuckleheads obtained these video machines? Of course, the law-enforcement authorities wouldn't deny they were investigating any mob connections.

On January 30, 1998, The Trentonian led with MOB LINK EYED IN POLS' GAMBLING DEN. We staked out the Baron's and harassed members who were entering the building. Most of them were grumpy old men—the types who you would spot at the racetrack.

"These are your biggest fans," I joked with Linda Dougherty. "They probably read your racing selections in the paper."

The mob link story was reported by Dom Yanchunas, Paul Mickle and Todd Venezia:

"The state is probing a line between the mob underworld and a Hamilton social club that served as a private casino for some of Trenton area's top leaders, two sources close to the investigation revealed.

"The sources said the probe of The Baron Athletic Association is focusing on which area politicians and law-enforcement officials knew about mob influence on the club's illicit gaming operation—and why they did nothing to stop it."

To make matters even better, we learned that Daniel Giaquinto, Gov. Whitman's appointment for county prosecutor, was a provisional member. He had no comment.

We also found out that one of our former photographers played the slots there, and we did an anonymous story about it. It wasn't mentioned how he once worked for us. The day the Baron broke, The Trentonian had six stories and the Times had one. The only unfortunate thing was that many of the Baron members were old Trentonian readers.

Information also came out that Hamilton Mayor and Public Safety Director Jack Rafferty was a member of the Baron and had gambled there before. Mickle had taken a picture of Rafferty on previous election night lighting up a cigar, and we ran it for the first time that day.

It was a tremendous shot that made Rafferty look like an old-time political boss. We ran that picture on page 1 regularly. He eventually complained to a local TV reporter about it.

Other politicians, cops and judges were linked to the Baron. It was the town's "dirty little secret."

On Feb. 1, Sherry Sylvester wrote a column on the Baron, and it was just another reason why readers resented her. She outlined the political ramifications of the scandal. Sylvester advocated closing the place down completely, which angered many in the community. On this day we had nothing new to report, but the column helped us keep the story alive.

Nevertheless, we led with the Baron four straight days, just pounding on this apparent crime, including INSIDE THE RAID on Feb. 2.

Mickle scratched together this lead:

"HAMILTON—Some of the biggest names in Hamilton business and politics scrambled like speakeasy patrons in an old gangster movie not long before New Jersey troopers raided the casino at the Baron Athletic Association 12 nights ago.

"Insiders say dozens of men of local stature dropped cards, dice and quarters, and skedaddled outside to Buicks and Cadillacs that peeled out of the parking lot like teenagers in hotrods."

When you are covering a scandal like this you must have a story every day.

Ride this horse until it dies.

WZBN, a local cable station that we didn't consider very hard-hitting, interviewed Giaquinto and didn't ask him about the Baron. A week earlier, WZBN had a report blasting us for demanding President Clinton's resignation just one week after the beginnings of the Monica Lewinsky scandal. The television station interviewed a professor from the College of New Jersey who promptly ripped us for being biased. The TV station never got our side of the story.

Jon Blackwell wrote a story on Feb. 3 about WZBN's Giaquinto story. Blackwell called the same professor, Gary Woodward, and he admitted that WZBN dropped the ball.

I didn't mind us getting bashed, because all publicity is good. But our story really riled them up. One of their executives called us to ask how relations were between the two organizations. The story was a real morale booster in our office, because it showed how we kicked the ass of Hamilton-based news organization right in its own town.

I told the executive that we expected everyone to cover this big local story. He wanted to know if the story was driven by the fact that they smashed us on TV, and I told him no, but their insult did make us try even harder.

The scandal troubled the advertising department because Mayor Jack Rafferty was involved. An old-time Hamilton politician, he was connected with everyone in town. The advertisers rallied around him.

BARON CASINO RAKED IN MILLIONS was our March 14 headline. The state outlined its case against the Baron. The information was released late on a Friday, and it quickly turned into the lead story. We warned the ad department so they would be ready to tell their advertisers. They got really upset.

"Yeah, once all their ad friends are in jail, they won't be able to get any money," Mickle said.

A couple of days later, Rafferty, who refused to answer questions from the Trentonian or the Trenton Times about the Baron scandal, talked to reporters from WPVI-Channel 6 and WZBN.

Dom Yanchunas got an opportunity to view the tape and wrote this story:

"Mayor Jack Rafferty ended his silence yesterday about the controversy engulfing the Baron Athletic Association by making a stunning disclosure—he knew the club had slot machines but did nothing about it.

"'I saw the slot machines,' Rafferty said in a rambling television interview. 'I saw them there. I spoke to some of the fellas about them, (and thought) that they shouldn't possibly be there.'

"Then looking somewhat put upon, Rafferty admitted that he failed to respond to the machines by saying to himself rhetorically, 'Jack, you're the mayor. You should have…made the call or did what you had to do.

"'Well, I just didn't.'

In a two-month span, we led with the Baron story 14 times. The readers loved it.

I left the paper before the scandal wrapped up. The closed athletic club is now a senior center and most of the Baron members were cleared. Some people in the city are still calling it a whitewash.

Rafferty didn't run for re-election in 1999, and his handpicked successor was crushed in the election—thanks mainly to the Trentonian's aggressive coverage of the scandal. We constantly ran a picture of Rafferty puffing a cigar—looking like a boss of a political machine.

Mickle took the picture of Rafferty celebrating Hamilton council victories on Election night 1997. "We will need this photo someday," Mickle said at the time.

We did.

We ran it every day to get under his goat. "They are trying to make me look like a political boss," Rafferty whined to a local TV reporter.

We didn't care because Hamilton readers relished the story.

An editor must not lose sight of the scandal. But simplification is the utmost importance when covering scandals. Politicians possibly breaking laws are the easiest to understand.

Most of the times, scandals—like Whitewater—are convoluted and impossible for readers to follow. These are dangerous. You can lose readers quickly.

The Baron scandal boosted morale in the newsroom to an all-time high.

◆ ◆ ◆

It was the worst moment of my career. April 6, 1998.

In a meeting with Schwartz, I jokingly asked him, "make sure you don't retire until after my vacation to Hawaii at the end of May."

There were rumors of Schwartz retiring in 1998. Those rumors have floated around, but fortunately never came into fruition.

"Well, I won't be here then," Schwartz said. "I'm telling you the truth."

He lit his cigar, put it in his mouth, and took a puff. "I'm retiring at the end of May," he said.

The roof just caved in.

It was incomprehensible of the Trentonian without Schwartz.

GLORY DAYS   141

What would the Journal Register Company do?
Who would be the replacement?
Schwartz sheltered us from Jelenic's temper tantrums. He didn't take Jelenic seriously when it came to editorial advice.
Newsroom personnel always speculated how Schwartz kept the Journal Register Company at bay. Did he have pictures incriminating any of the top personnel?
That's unlikely, but a lot of JRC horror stories were surfacing in the industry. Short staffs. Brutal cuts. Editorial mandates from the central office in Trenton.
The Trentonian was insulated—thanks to Schwartz.
Schwartz, at times, ignored orders to protect his staff.
Who would protect us now?
The Trentonian was losing its editorial compass.
And maybe its shield for protection from the JRC monsters.
My Hawaii vacation was cancelled.

◆   ◆   ◆

The motives of the murders in the Greater Trenton Area can happen for the most bizarre reasons. The motives can elevate an ordinary murder to a hard-hitting story that will remain etched in people's memories.
Today's editors in the industry don't force their reporters to dig deeper for stories; therefore, the motive is never really discovered.
Or the editors will be too busy pushing issue packages to even notice that these stories are getting buried.
In a one-year span at The Trentonian, we had people slain over parking tickets, a dice game, a bottle of rum and a card game.
Chris Dolmetsch's aggressive reporting delivered the story about the man killed over parking tickets.
Of course, we led the front page with SLAIN OVER PARKING TICKETS

Dolmetsch reported:

"A Fillmore Street man, angry that a longtime buddy had borrowed his car and racked up a pile of parking tickets, gunned his pal down in the middle of the street early yesterday morning as three other friends watched."

Under the headline, SLASH OF RUM, Dom Yanchunas produced the story about murder over the bottle of rum:

"A routine speeding ticket along Interstate 195 here has led cops to a 'wonton, cold-blooded, conscienceless killer' who murdered the guy for drinking his rum last week, authorities say.

"The wanted man, Gary Melendez, 30, of Pottstown, Pa., slashed his own throat with a knife when cops tracked him down and stormed his hideout Tuesday night in Paterson, police officials said yesterday.

"Melendez is accused of viciously punching and stabbing his neighbor, 20-year-old Richard W. Wright Jr. to death Saturday after he caught Wright drinking from Melendez's half-gallon bottle of Bacardi rum in the seedy flophouse on their Pottstown Street.

When Yanchunas called the Pottstown Mercury newspaper to give them a tip and possibly get some information, the Mercury's editors didn't seem interested. Guess they thought their readers don't care about murders over a bottle of Bacardi.

Our readers do.

With the story, we ran a "headshot" of a bottle of Bacardi.

But my favorite front page on these bizarre murders was a man being killed over a card game. I originally wanted to lead with KILLED OVER CARD GAME.

Todd Venezia thought we should reach higher on this one.

"I've got it," he said. "How about DEAD MAN'S HAND?"

That was the lead headline.

We ran the headshot of the victim with a collage of aces and eights—which is known as the "Dead Man's Hand."

The best subhead in Trentonian history ran on page 3 with that story. Part-time copy editor Rob Zecker, a seemingly lifetime University of Pennsylvania student who dressed like a hobo, put his greatness as a headline writer on display.

The main headline on page 3 was DEADLY CARD with the eye-popping subhead ".22 beats two of a kind."

Nancy Houtz was the reporter on that story:

"WILLINGBORO—A friendly game of cards turned deadly early yesterday when a hotheaded player pulled out a handgun and shot his friend dead—then robbed three other players before dashing out the door, police said."

The Burlington County Times and the Trenton Times proved their mediocrity by running measly 3-inch stories depicting the incident.

We gave it the appropriate play.

◆ ◆ ◆

New reporter Eric Ladley had a gift.

A gift nobody in the building possessed.

He always managed to get the sexy picture.

You would never expect this from an aspiring political writer who just graduated from George Washington University and is working on a book about Nixon's Asian policy.

It's true. It's true.

Ladley accepted a post to become an assistant business writer for the legendary Jim Fitzsimmons.

But it became quickly apparent Ladley had a knack for hard news and more importantly getting pictures of sizzling ladies.

Those talents are critical at The Trentonian.

Ladley's magic was discovered when we sent him to Rider to get a story about the unseasonably warm weather.

And he needed to get pictures—pictures of coeds prancing the university in bikinis.

Ladley came through.

He produced a picture of some delightful dames dancing under the sun.

Normally, weather stories are buried deep inside the paper.

With these babes, the story became a very large tease with a big picture stripped down the side of Page 1.

Ladley produced a winner.

The next time we sent Ladley out to get pictures of babes in the warm weather—he proved the first assignment wasn't a fluke.

He got a picture of a lovely lady in a bikini sitting in a pool. We ran it big on Page 1.

Dom Yanchunas didn't have the Ladley flair for getting those kinds of pictures.

When he went out to interview coeds for a story, they threatened to call the cops.

They did call the office wondering who was this "weird" reporter.

Yanchunas fell short on the Ladley scale.

When we found out a Philadelphia 76ers cheerleader lived in Hamilton, it was obvious who was going to get the assignment. Our goal was to get a sexy picture of a cheerleader.

Mickle in eager anticipation greeted Ladley when he returned to the office from his assignment.

"What did you get, Eric?" Mickle asked. "Did you get a picture of this woman in a swimsuit?"

"No."

"What the fuck," Mickle said. "This is bullshit. Why doesn't this girl take her freakin' clothes off?"

"But I did get a picture of her," Ladley said. "with her leg behind her head."

The newsroom gasped.

But Mickle continued his tirade.

"Oh great, now we have a picture of her with her freakin' clothes on," Mickle said.

The picture, however, was incredible.

"It is the sexiest picture of a woman with her clothes on that I ever seen," Night City Editor Todd Venezia said.

Despite Mickle's complaints about the 76er cheerleader, Ladley's legend was growing.

Now, Ladley's uncanny ability would be put to a stiff test.

We found out Summer, an exotic dancer with whom Craig Rabinowitz, a suburban Philadelphia man who killed his wife, was infatuated, was dancing in our coverage area in Lower Bucks County.

This was a blockbuster case in our market.

We had to attack this story.

But we couldn't barge into the strip club, Divas, and tell them we're from the paper and want the interview with Summer.

We would be thrown out.

However, we needed the story.

We needed a smooth personality.

Chris Dolmetsch would get thrown out immediately, like he did when we sent him to there to interview strippers following a deadly shooting.

Scratch Dolmetsch.

We sent Yanchunas the day before to check out the place. They would recognize his face. He's smooth, but we didn't want to take any chances.

A female reporter might stick out like a sore thumb and may not get close enough to the dancers.

The king of getting the sexy pictures was summoned.

I gave Ladley $20 and asked him to go undercover and get a lap dance.

Most newspapers would think this would be unethical. To act like a customer and talk to Summer would be considered misleading.

Forget 'em.

Ladley went there and got to chance to talk to Summer.

And received a lap dance.

At first, we only wanted to get a little color to add to our main story. But Schwartz decided that this was one of those rare times when we needed a first person account. Night City Todd Venezia came up with the idea to put Ladley's picture next to Summer's on the front page. The tease read, "My lap dance with Summer," with a picture of a beaming Ladley.

It sold.

Under the headline "Writer gets lap dance to die for," here is Ladley's story in its entirety:

"I never thought I'd be writing an article like this for The Trentonian—but yesterday morning something unbelievable happened.

"It started when my editor came up to me and said:

"'Eric here's $20. Go out and get a lap dance from Summer!'

"That's right, Summer, the most famous go-go girl in the area, the sexy siren who entranced wife killer Craig Rabinowitz with her lusty lap-dancing skill and may have even driven him to murder.

"So, I went over to the club where she was performing, Divas on Route 13 in Levittown, and bough some lunch while waiting for her to appear. I wasn't there for more than 15 minutes, and she came out on stage wearing a red lace slip.

"After her act was finished, she walked form patron to patron getting tips, squeezing their dollars between her breasts.

"'Do you do lap dances?' I asked her.

"She glanced down at my Caesar salad and said in a sexy voice. 'Finish your lunch, and then I'll be by for dessert.

"She emerged about 15 minutes later and led me into a backroom where I sat in the middle of an overstuffed couch for my $20, five-minute thrill ride.

"I expected a normal lap dance, where the dancer does her act in front of you and makes a little contact. But Summer can twist herself into more shapes than a pretzel, right on top of your body. She is not your normal lap dancer.

"'What do you like in a woman," she asked me.

"'Well, flexibility is a nice asset,' I said.

"She then proceeded to demonstrate that she was more flexible than a rubber band. She un-buttoned my shirt and placed her professionally trained hands on the center of my chest, where she could feel my ever-quickening heart beat.

"'It's bound to get a little hot in here,' she said, as she took off her slip.

"She was wearing just a black thong and her chest was completely bare. All I could do was stare at her well-sculpted body.

"She started the dance off by digging her red-heeled shoe into my chest and twisting her leg around, a move that was both painful and pleasurable. Then she glided her chest across my face, and rubbed herself with her hands. She maneuvered her legs around mine, sliding her body down until she was sitting on my thighs. She moved her head behind mine and licked my ear.

"What surprised me the most was when she stretched her body over my lap and jiggled her buttocks up and down while keeps her hips still. I expected her to gyrate on my lap, but I did not expect her to give me a gymnastic exhibition 3 feet from my face.

"'Thank you very much,' she said when we were done.

"I wiped the sweat from my brow and decided to use the moment to ask her about her new found notoriety. 'How do you feel about all of the attention from the media?' I asked her.

"'Being on the news all the time is annoying,' she said.

"'What do you think of Craig Rabinowitz?

"'Well, I meet all kinds of people,' she said."

"The dimly lit club where Summer performed was much nicer than the average strip joint, with a bar surrounding the stage where the girls were performing.

"As I entered, one of the girls was finishing her act, her naked chest writhing to some dance music. The crowd was mostly men in their 30s and 40s, some wearing suits and others T-shirts and jeans.

"Summer came out wearing a red lace slip and red high-heeled shoes. Her acted included gyrating on the floor to Seal's 'Kiss From a Rose' and grabbing the brass rail between her legs and turning upside-down. By the end of her act, the red slip was off and she was bare-chested and wearing just a black thong.

"'That was a very athletic act,' I said. 'Especially, how you grabbed the pole.'

"'You can't be afraid of the pole,' she said. 'I was when I first began, but now I feel I can do just about anything up on stage.'

"It really was quite an act.

"And after I finally finished my meeting with the area's most famous stripper, I could honestly say that she is good at what she does.

"But I don't think I'd kill my wife for her."

Howard Griffin, an advertising big wig at the Journal Register Company, was disgusted by The Trentonian's front page that featured Ladley smiling like he was the bird who just swallowed the canary.

He ripped the paper.

Schwartz responded:

"Howard,

"I just got the circulation report for the week ending on April 25, 1998. It was a bad week.

"But still you should know since you're such a great fucking newsman that the lap-dancer was the second best day of the week.

"Have a nice day.

"Sincerely,

H.L. Schwartz III."

In a couple of months, the paper will be taking hits from the corporation—without the screw-'em attitude of Schwartz.

Trouble loomed.

◆ ◆ ◆

The phone rang. It was Mary Mooney.

Mooney, a former night city editor and shining star at The Trentonian, was working for the Allentown Morning Call.

Mooney has sound news judgment. And she had a hot tip. Allentown's mayor blasted the city Trenton in the Morning Call.

A day earlier Money magazine ranked the Trenton area (that includes Princeton) No. 1 in living conditions among medium-sized metro areas in the Northeast.

Allentown Mayor William Heydt, whose city ranked No. 15 on the list, told the Morning Call: "Trenton is first? I wouldn't put too much credence in this study if it ranks Trenton first. I wouldn't go there with an Uzi."

Heydt had crossed the line. No outsider is allowed to pick on Trenton. We insiders can pick on it all the time, but anybody else will feel our wrath.

I dispatched Leslie Barbaro to Allentown—an hour and a half drive—to find some dumps in the city.

She had no problems find blight.

In fact, she took a picture of a "WELCOME TO ALLENTOWN" sign with a scrap recycling facility in the background.

Barbaro, a true photojournalist, also talked to Allentown residents, who promptly ripped Heydt.

"I don't think much of the police," 72-year-old Allentown resident George Eck said. "We tell them all about the problems (drugs dealing near his home), but they don't do nothing.

"I don't think too much of the mayor either. He doesn't do much here."

Trenton Mayor Doug Palmer was quoted in Eric Ladley's story as saying: "I challenge him to come here without an Uzi. I am convinced that when he sees the waterfront, great restaurants and rebuilt housing, he will change his mind."

We always relished picking on the smooth Palmer, but when an outsider attacks Trenton we rallied the troops behind the distinguished mayor.

♦ ♦ ♦

Gov. Christie Whitman's daughter, Kate, helped sell papers—sometimes more than her mother.

No, it wasn't because of her important contributions to society or charity.

She had trouble with the law.

Just before I became editor in January 1997, she was the focus of a front-page lead story. On her way to her mother's State of the State speech, she drove on the Jersey Turnpike. But when she exited the Turnpike at Exit 7A, she didn't have enough money to pay for the $3.15 toll.

That was front page news at the Trentonian. The story said:

"The toll-taker ordered her to fill out a routine form promising that she would mail the money later and the whole episode caused a flap within the Turnpike Authority when toll-takers complained that their bosses seemed to handle the paperwork with kid gloves."

Whitman was enraged with the story, and complained to Schwartz.

In June 1998, Kate, while visiting friends at Lehigh University, got into trouble again.

Under the inside headline BEERY EYED, Dom Yanchunas reported:

"Gov. Whitman's 21-year-old daughter, Kate, stirred a pile of new trouble for her mother this weekend after cops handcuffed her and placed her under arrest for tossing an open beer can on the ground.

"The officers, who had minutes before warned Kate Whitman to throw the can of Bud Light in the trash because she was drinking in public, charged the governor's offspring with littering.

"Whitman then stood in the rain and wept as she repeatedly apologized to the arresting officer. She also complained that it's not easy being the daughter of a governor, the cop said."

Most newspapers made this a brief. The Allentown Morning Call reporter wondered why we made a big deal out of it. The Morning Call covers the Lehigh Valley.

We, of course, made it the wood with the headline, COPS BUST GOV'S DAUGHTER.

Whenever a relative of a politician gets into trouble, it's front-page news. We found that out with the Bush daughters in 2001.

What made this story more compelling was the sob story Kate tried to push.

Poor Kate, she has it tough because she is a governor's daughter. Readers love this stuff.

They weren't holding any pity parties for Kate.

◆ ◆ ◆

Irene Bagley was unhappy.

Unhappy with my news judgment—on a holiday no less.

"How can you lead with this," she moaned, "on Easter Sunday."

"This" was NUCLEAR MENACE IN OUR MIDST, a story by political reporter Dave Neese about how officials could not account for a nuclear missile that had been missing for 30 years.

Neese wrote:

"It's surely one of the biggest—and potentially most dangerous—objects anyone ever misplaced.

"It's a mass of material weighing two to three tons—and possibly contaminated with deadly plutonium.

"The lost object is the debris of a 47-foot tall nuclear missile with an 18-foot wing span."

The news was more important than any holiday. Newspapers tend to shut down on holidays, but I believed a newsroom must maintain its intensity these days. Every day counts. Today's holiday newspapers are filled with fluff. The reader doesn't need to be told that "today is Thanksgiving."

They want to know what's new. Feature stories about "Black Friday" won't cut it.

Bagley, despite our Easter Sunday differences, was a damned good newswoman.

One Thanksgiving night, Bagley, our obituary clerk, sent out a reluctant reporter on a major story about a woman who died falling off her horse during a holiday fox hunt.

A dramatic story and Bagley mobilized the troops.

I took pride in our holiday front pages like these:

5-FOOT GATOR ON CITY STREETS

WOMAN KILLED DURING FOX HUNT

BEAUTY SHOP BANDITS

CRASH SEASON: A story about the rash of holiday accidents

An Editor must press the accelerator at all times—even on holidays.

Remember one of the biggest stories of the 1990s happened on a holiday weekend.

Princess Diana died on Labor Day weekend.

◆ ◆ ◆

The period from May 1998 to mid-June was a time period of tragedy for the paper.

- A pressman died of a heart attack.
- A member of the circulation department committed suicide while working his route.
- Emil Slaboda, the legendary editor who carried the paper through the period when the Times was owned by the Washington Post, died of a heart attack.
- Tim Hogan, a former Trentonian controller who was promoted to become publisher in Taunton, Mass., committed suicide.

- Karen Pugh, who ran the dispatch department, died in a fiery automobile accident after a wild chase with Burlington County police.

It was a period of tears for the paper—a bizarre set of circumstances. We felt cursed.

◆ ◆ ◆

Tim Hogan's death sent the entire newspaper reeling. Hogan, who was an easygoing, yet very efficient controller, committed suicide. He battled depression—a problem no one in the building realized he had. He hid it well.

Too well.

Hogan was a good controller and a great man. Depression will never take that away from his legacy.

It took the Taunton, Mass., authorities nearly six days to find the body. So, there was hope that Hogan would still be alive.

Schwartz wrote the story about the discovery of the body. It would be Schwartz's final story in his illustrious career.

A story he never dreamed he would write.

◆ ◆ ◆

While Tim Hogan's suicide a front-page story in Taunton, Mass., Karen Pugh's death led The Trentonian.

It seemed like a typical Friday night at The Trentonian.

Paul Mickle was in the office late to prepare the weekend budget. Editors usually have to prepare stories in advance for the weekends—which are less hectic than news days during the week.

Dom Yanchunas was the night cop reporter. The night cop shift was in rotation among the reporters. Yanchunas, Houtz and Dolmetsch would each work this 4 p.m. to midnight shift once a month.

Yanchunas was there the night of Emil Slaboda's death. It happened about 7 p.m. on a Friday night. Usually with obituaries, you might have one done in advance.

We didn't have one ready for Emil Slaboda.

But Yanchunas scrambled together a piece, Mark Stradling produced a column and Mickle gathered pictures depicting a great career.

We ended with a two-page package.

Slaboda probably deserved the entire paper.

He was a giant in Trenton.

Hours before Pugh's death, it was a relatively slow news day. We were planning to lead with a story how a man—who once served time in the Mercer County Prison—had plotted to kill Attorney General Janet Reno.

It was a weak lead—with a very thin local hook.

It seemed like a typical Friday night. Pugh, 44, was there until about 6 p.m. The dispatch department is in charge of dummying the paper. It determines how large a paper is and where the ads are located.

Generally, the dispatch department makes sure the paper has a proper ratio between ads and news copy.

Karen Pugh supervised the dispatch department. She also was an emergency medical technician.

I was having dinner with my wife at a nearby restaurant when my Breaking News Network pager buzzed.

The BNN is an organization of geeks who listen to New York, New Jersey and Pennsylvania police scanners and report it over a pager.

So my pager buzzing wasn't unusual. It rang every 10 minutes, but most of the time it wasn't an incident in the circulation area.

This time it wasn't.

It indicated a woman had died in a fiery crash after a wild police chase in Browns Mills, Burlington County.

Burlington County is in our circulation area.

I rushed to the office.

The bar was low; this could be a lead story. A thin story about the man plotting to kill Janet Reno wasn't going to sell many papers.

A deadly crash after a wild cop chase will.

Yanchunas confirmed the information. We had a line.

WOMAN DIES IN FIERY CRASH.

We didn't have the identity of the woman involved. Yanchunas scoured the area for information.

Getting the ID is the most important part of the process in covering the victim in an accident or murder.

It provides a human-interest part of the story. An element that hits home with the readers. People tend to think that accidents cannot happen to them. But when they read the hobbies, characteristics and picture of a victim then it makes it apparent it can to anybody.

Accidents are tragic.

Usually newspapers would just run a brief—as most did in this case. Most newspaper editors think they are above menial accident stories. They have more enterprise packages to report.

We led with this accident for the first edition—before we knew the identification.

Jose Mendez, who was a computer systems manager, called into the office. He asked for the reporter covering the accident.

When he asked Yanchunas what was the color and make of the car involved in this Browns Mills accident.

When Yanchunas told him it was a red Toyota Celica, Mendez said "oh, shit" and hung up the phone.

Mendez called back and told Yanchunas Karen Pugh was missing and she drives a red Toyota Celica.

After about a half-hour of scrambling, Yanchunas got it confirmed: it was Karen Pugh.

When Mickle heard the news, he said "Oh, my God, oh my God."

Then in the same breath, "I think we have her picture and it's on her desk."

He strode over and plucked her picture off her desk and handed it to me for the front page.

Karen Pugh's tragedy was the lead story.

Yanchunas wrote this lead:

"A longtime Trentonian worker and mother of three died last night when she lost control of her car at a traffic circle here and barreled headlong into a tree, authorities said."

The stunning news rocked the newspaper. There were staffers who thought we overplayed the story.

Members in the other departments didn't believe the facts—she couldn't have led cops on a wild chase.

She must have had a diabetic seizure. Why don't we report on that?

One worker in the mailroom contended that the chase was racially motivated. Pugh was black, and the cop profiled her.

It was one of those stories people in the building came up with excuses for Pugh's actions. It was an attempt to save her legacy. They were throwing everything against the wall—hoping something would stick.

Nothing did.

Our approach toward stories is the same for every story—and would not change just because she worked for the paper.

The family was angered over the story and day-to-day coverage.

In the newspaper industry, we deal with facts.

We had the facts of the story correct.

She didn't have a diabetic seizure. The chase wasn't racially motivated.

Pugh went through a red light, went 90-mph, wouldn't pull over when cops ordered her to, and then she crashed into a tree. She died.

Those were the facts.

Nobody in the office would accept that. Her family was considering a lawsuit.

Pugh was a wonderful person. She was jovial and cared about people. It was a pleasure to work with her.

Ironically, none of the other major newspapers made a big deal out of this story. It was just another accident brief. The story wasn't newsworthy enough for those papers to run on the front page. Funny thing, all of those papers' circulation went down over the previous year while ours increased.

This was a dramatic story, and we run these type of stories.

No matter who the victim is.

◆ ◆ ◆

On May 22, 1998, H.L. "Sandy" Schwartz III walked out of the door the final time.

It was a dark day.

Schwartz was the embodiment of The Trentonian. We gave him four front mock pages. When a beloved person leaves for another job or retires from the newspaper industry, a mock page with a humorous story is given. It's all for yucks.

Normally, a worker will receive one.

Schwartz received four:

- One was a front page with a cutout of Schwartz's head with the headline "HEAD HAD AIDS: Virus found in outgoing publisher's noggin! The overbar read "NEW TWIST IN GOLF COURSE SHOCKER!
- One story about the breaking development of Schwartz being a "closet liberal" who is crusading for gays.
- One featured how the "great fuckin' newsman" Schwartz cracked the mysterious death of socialite Emily "Cissy" Stuart. Beloved in Princeton social circles, Stuart was slain in 1989. Her killer was never caught. Schwartz vowed the story would never let the story go. We ran anniversary stories for nine straight years.

- And finally, a story how Schwartz was nabbed in the Baron scandal with a sidebar how computers are now replacing copy editors.

By noon, Schwartz was gone.
We were left with wondering what's next.
Schwartz protected us from the corporation.
Now, we were at the mercy of Journal Register Company.
They were running the show.
Jelenic said at Hogan's funeral he had already hired a new publisher—and we was going to start in the next couple of months.
It wasn't me.
Thank God. Schwartz would have been a hard act to follow.
But I was appointed acting publisher.
And I would have to put on one hell of a performance.

2

THE 'EVIL' EMPIRE TAKES OVER

It was 9 a.m. May 23, 1998.

My home phone rang; it was Bob Jelenic's office. The president and CEO of the Journal Register Company wanted to have a discussion with me concerning the paper and what I'll be doing.

As Mickle would say, "oh boy, egad!"

The Journal Register Company is located on 50 State Street in Trenton, it is located on the 12th floor, one floor above the Associated Press' Trenton bureau.

This is where the nightmarish, sports-related calls would come from.

A box score mistake here, a missing story there and problem with the transactions.

All of those complaints came from there.

Most of those complaints never reached the editorial department. That's because Schwartz shielded us from them.

Jelenic's henchman, Chuck Pukanecz (vice president of news) was nonexistent when Schwartz was there.

One time, Pukanecz called me about putting police blotter in the paper. Police blotter works in small-time community rags, but not in Trenton. If done effectively, the blotter would take two or three open pages daily. A lot of space and resources would used. Not good for a newspaper that relies on big stories.

I asked Schwartz about Pukanecz, he said, "don't ever listen to Pukanecz, he doesn't know what the fuck he is talking about."

Schwartz should know.

Pukanecz worked as a reporter and an editor at The Trentonian. He eventually became editor of the Norristown Times-Herald during the strike by the newspaper guild. There would be pictures of the brave Pukanecz crossing the picket line to produce a paper. In my opinion, you cross the picket line and your stock will rise at the Journal Register Company.

Pukanecz, who once worked as a correspondent at the Philadelphia Inquirer, never worked full-time at a major newspaper.

But he crossed the picket line and eventually became a big executive at the Journal Register Company.

I never listened to him.

Now, I might have to.

◆ ◆ ◆

Jelenic wanted the paper to be more straightforward. Don't be excessive.

Translation: No more SEX IN THE MORTUARY or SEX KITTENS IN THE CLASSROOM.

He wanted us to be straightforward.

He told me the next publisher would be more community minded. Schwartz, he said, is a newsman, who thought he would be violating his values if he got to close to people.

Jelenic also said the next publisher knew absolutely nothing about the editorial side. The publisher, he said, would be pretty much hands off the editorial side.

That's good, I think.

This new publisher was going to be a marketing whiz and be involved in the community. Trenton Times Publisher Richard Bilotti,

Jelenic said, is at every community gathering. We had to get somebody to offset Bilotti.

Jelenic then outlined his thoughts about the sports department. He was convinced somebody in the department is out to get him. Somebody is sabotaging the operation. Somebody is making intentional mistakes in the section—just to irritate him.

Jelenic believed local sports was the franchise.

Jelenic was wrong.

Local sports as a front page lead didn't sell. In fact, the two-worst selling papers in 1997 were front-page leads involving the surging Steinert boys basketball team.

They bombed at the newsstands.

Schwartz thought these numbers might silence Jelenic once and for all about local sports.

It obviously didn't.

Jelenic was going to be involved in the day-to-day operations of the paper. I was going to be his point person.

Jelenic said the paper had to remain conservative editorially. No problem.

Jelenic said "Geek of the Week" had to go. Big problem.

Other than the Trenton Strangler, this editorial feature was one of the top features in the Sunday paper. Politicians would scope the paper weekly—just to make sure they weren't the top geek. Jelenic, in order to make the paper more beloved in the community, is scrapping the "Geek of the Week."

Jelenic said every editorial had to be faxed to the Journal Register Company for review. The Trentonian had strong voice. It pulled no punches. For some, the Trentonian's plain-speaking editorials were like a punch in the gut. Jelenic feared lawsuits.

Jelenic had fired a bombshell.

Our editorial pages were the best in the state. The editorial page editor Mark Stradling and his assistant Erik Lukens would be outraged. They might bail. While they were tremendous editorial writers, they were dependable advisors. They attended the news meetings. About 60 percent of the time, Lukens wrote the lead headline.

Losing these guys would be devastating.

The meeting lasted about 20 minutes.

It felt like an hour.

◆ ◆ ◆

I returned to the office, and wasn't sure where to work: my office and Schwartz's former place.

Schwartz gave me the key to his office and his company car. Marilyn Ellis, Schwartz's colorful administrative assistant, urged me to take the office. If Ellis said I should do it, I must.

About an hour later, an enraged Jelenic ordered me out of the office and must give my keys of the company car to Production Manager Rocky Gallo. He said I'm not the publisher, and in essence not worthy to sit in the chair.

Gallo was ordered to clean the car and returned it to the parking lot of the Journal Register Company.

Jelenic, the company's CEO, had nothing better to do than to worry where the acting publisher was sitting.

◆ ◆ ◆

As expected, Stradling and Lukens were angry. It was one thing for Schwartz to read the editorials before the paper went to press, but they didn't to subject them to the scrutiny of the suits at the Journal Register Company.

They saw the writing on the wall. Without Schwartz around, the Journal Register Company would sink its tentacles into The Trentonian.

For years, Stradling and Lukens believed the Journal Register Company was a bunch of rotten county rags. The Trentonian was the second largest paper in the chain—behind the New Haven Register.

It was clearly the best paper in the chain. The best read. The most dependable. In their view, that was because Schwartz prevented Jelenic and Pukanecz from getting their hands on it.

No Schwartz was gone.

No protection from their misguided ideas.

Three days later, Stradling, a fixture of the paper, gave his resignation. He wasn't sure where he was going to do next.

Lukens also gave his notice. My top adviser and headline writer was headed to become the editorial page editor in Bend, Ore.

I wanted to bend over and throw up.

In a month, both were gone.

♦ ♦ ♦

Lukens, who single-handedly generated more sales for the paper than any other employee, did manage to rattle Jelenic's cage in his final days.

One of Lukens editorials was rewritten by corporate. Mistakes were inserted into his story.

Lukens fired off a letter to Jelenic—letting him know if he was going to change one of his editorials, he must run them by Lukens.

Jelenic was furious. During his conversation with me, he called Lukens "a kook."

So in Lukens farewell page we ran the headline, "HE'S A KOOK!" with his picture.

◆　◆　◆

The Trentonian became a slightly duller paper during this period. We just were going to be straightforward. The best stories were running on Page 1.

That's all that mattered.

Jelenic was good to deal with. Other than his sports obsession, he understood what sold on the news side: crime.

Chuck Pukanecz didn't.

Pukanecz considered crime stories a drug. It gives you an immediate high, but doesn't have long-term effect.

Crime stories are addictive.

Our readers wanted crime stories.

Pukanecz wanted to have reporters follow Gov. Whitman like a celebrity. State workers like to read about her, Pukanecz said. She might run for president in 2000.

Whitman, a celebrity? Whitman interesting?

Pukanecz proved he was a minor-leaguer in his conversations with me. He goes back to the days of Florio.

Florio was a winner at the newsstands because he raised taxes and arrogantly boosted how he make a tough decision.

Florio was a perfect foil for the paper.

Whitman wasn't.

Whitman getting re-elected by a razor-thin margin wasn't even the best-selling paper for the week. In fact, the issue was a distant second—behind a crime story.

When she beat that jerk Florio, it sold 82,000—the largest sales in at least 20 years.

It was because Florio lost—not Whitman winning.

I ignored Pukanecz.

◆ ◆ ◆

Jelenic loved celebrity coverage.

"If Susan Anton comes to Trenton Country Club," he said. "You cover it."

Susan Anton? The golden girl?

That was no problem we regularly cover celebrities and their hijinks.

And when MTV settled its beach house in Seaside Heights, we sent a reporter daily. We got pictures of Baywatch babe Donna D'Errico, Alyssa Milano and Rebecca Romijn-Stamos.

All pictures we played prominently on page 1.

Jelenic wasn't going to get any disagreements here.

◆ ◆ ◆

Jelenic hated the look of Page 6, however.

He thought we had been running ugly girls. He wanted to see a significant upgrade. Even though they were local girls, Jelenic wanted "cleaner-looking" girls.

He wanted models.

We had a free-lancer provide us with hot women. But they were limited about five a month.

We needed more.

We hit the MTV beach house for babes who were going gaga over the stars.

We only got a handful.

After consulting with three Page 6 gurus Mike Regan, Todd Venezia and Andy Hussie, we came up with a plan.

It is in two-step battle plan.

Bring back the Page 6 contest. Every month, the readers would vote who is the sexiest Page 6 girl. The winner will get $1,000 and one of the readers who voted for her would snare $500.

This was cut because of budgetary reasons.

It was a popular stable and it boosted sales because we would run a poster of the winner each month. And people would buy the paper in bulk to stuff ballots for their favorite girls.

The readers relished this.

Taking advantage of his fury over ugly girls on Page 6, I convinced Jelenic to bring the contest back.

A big victory for the readers.

The next step was to find classic, popular Page 6 girls. Run weekly stories about how Page 6 helped make their dreams come true.

We started referring the girls as "Page 6 models."

Model is a more sophisticated term.

Women dream of becoming models—so we started running house ads with a collage of babes.

It said "we make your dreams come true." Become a Page 6 model.

Guys who always wanted to become a big league player would participate in fantasy camps. They would dress in uniforms, and play with former big-leaguers.

We looked at the new Page 6 as an opportunity for women who dreamed of being a model to live out their fantasy.

Some women would think they would be a lock for winning $1,000.

The classic stories allowed us an opportunity to put another hot babe on Page 1, and at the same time, help boost Page 6 in getting better looking women.

Who would write and take pictures of these classic women?

The choice was obvious: Eric Ladley.

Ladley was a proven commodity with getting babes in the paper. Ladley had a perfect record in snapping the picture of gorgeous women.

Ladley's first assignment was to work on one of our most beloved Page 6 models. She was easily in the top three in popularity. She was a legend with the readers. Maybe we can talk her into mounting a comeback while at the same time return Page 6 to its glory days.

Ladley was sent to interview Julie Nist.

◆ ◆ ◆

Julie Nist once defended Page 6 on the Maury Povich show.

She was tremendous.

She did a more effective job of telling the women's groups to stick it than then-Trentonian Editor Gale Baldwin.

She was in essence the spokeswoman for Page 6.

Who would be better to lead the charge in an effort to return Page 6 to its glory?

She was now running a landscape business and was getting divorced.

She went back to her maiden last name, Scully.

While working on the story, Ladley tried to convince her to make a comeback. She said she would consider it after her vacation cruise.

But Ladley got enough for her story.

When Ladley was getting her to pose for the picture to run with the story, she said, "guess you want a little cleavage."

Of course.

That was the Ladley magic at work.

She probably wouldn't have said it to another reporter.

Less than six months later, that Ladley picture would become internationally known.

In Ladley's story, Nist said: "I'm going on a two-week secret vacation. When I get back, I'll be tan rested and ready, just like Richard Nixon. I'm a little afraid I won't win, but I plan to lose another 2 pounds. Look for me in July."

During her "two-week secret vacation," Scully fell in love with a Greek seaman.

When she tried to end the relationship a few months later while living with him in Greece, he killed her. Cut off her head and threw it into the ocean. He placed her body into a suitcase.

It was a grisly murder that drew international headlines.

◆   ◆   ◆

In June 1998, Andy Hussie was appointed Page 6 coordinator. Hussie, the smooth-talking newspaper veteran, would ease the photographers' pain by helping arrange photo shoots and develop a system of payments.

He would be in charge of quality control.

Hussie then stumbled into the same problems the photographers did. Girls were nagging him for payments and making appointments and not show up.

Hussie was frustrated, but continued because this was Page 6—a proud tradition of the Trentonian.

◆   ◆   ◆

"Why don't you have Page 6 Men."

That question comes up frequently at social events.

I give a simple answer. They don't sell papers.

In the early 1990s, the paper did try to showcase Page 6 men—in fact it was a poster.

It failed.

Male readers will not buy a paper that features a good-looking guy in a swimsuit on the cover. Their masculinity is threatened.

Women, on the other hand, love talking about—and trashing—the Page 6 models.

Those same women will watch the Miss America pageant and trash it for the entire three-hour broadcast.

That is a significant group of women.

Another set of women believe Page 6 is a showcase of beautiful women. It provided an opportunity for up-and-coming models.

To be successful, we needed those women to actually pose for the page. More importantly, those women had to be local.

◆ ◆ ◆

Eric Ladley was more than just a master of getting babes on the front page.

He became one hell of a reporter.

He demonstrated this on Memorial Day weekend in 1998.

Ladley was mild-mannered. He give you blockbuster news in a totally normal voice. He kept his cool.

For example, on May 25, 1998, I came into the office to set up the paper.

Ladley came over.

He rattled off a couple of developments, and said four people were murdered at a Bucks County party.

Four people murdered at a Bucks County party!

That's the lead story.

They slayings turned out to be drug related.

Ladley was able to scratch together a four-story package that covered two pages.

Because the murders were drug related, the slaying was a brief in most of the local papers. Once again, the racist nature of the industry reared its ugly head. If the slayings occurred in Princeton, it would be the end of the world.

It happens in a slum in Bristol, Pa. Then nobody cares.

Four lives were snuffed. Four families and neighborhoods are without a loved one.

That's still a compelling story that leads the newspaper.

But they are black, Hispanic and poor. Not white and wealthy.

Newspapers are sliding, and instances like this are why.

You select the stories that draw human emotion. A reporter must bring the victims back to life, and paint a picture of their lives. Good or bad. It tells a story—a compelling human-interest story.

Four people being murdered at a party is news. Unfortunately, most papers didn't even give it the time of day.

Guess those compelling features on libraries are more important.

◆ ◆ ◆

During the period we didn't have a publisher, we produced solid, straightforward front pages. Even though we might have been slightly duller, we were keeping the circulation up.

That's all it matters.

Here are some examples of front pages during this period:

TIED-UP WOMAN FOUND DEAD IN FIRE

NEWBORN DEAD IN GAS STATION TOILET

FORMER CITY FOOTBALL STAR DIES

TROOPER PROBED IN FATAL DWI CRASH

KILLER HIRED TO RUN CITY DRUG COURT

3RD-GRADER BLOODIES TEACHER WITH PUNCH

COPS: SERIAL RAPIST IS PRISON GUARD

SLEEPING-GAS RAPIST ON THE LOOSE

All of those front pages told the story. The Trentonian under Schwartz had headlines filled with "bizarre" or "strange new twists" or "chilling."

These headlines were straightforward and clear. They also were dramatic. In the newspaper business—especially tabloids—there is an urgency to come up with clever headlines. Those cheapen the story.

Be concise. All of those stories are sensational. More importantly, they were clear enough for the reader to know what the story is about during those critical 10 seconds of deciding if he was going buy the paper.

◆ ◆ ◆

The announcement came on June 23, 1998.

David Bonfield, a former advertising executive with the Journal Register Company, is the new publisher of The Trentonian.

Advertising executives become publishers. It is typical of the industry. A publisher who has an editorial background like Schwartz is rare.

Most ad people are good business people. They want to sell papers and are skilled with the budget.

Most editors today whine about budgets, the bottom line and the lack of resources. Editors in those instances must become leaders and must effectively prioritize the coverage. If most editors had unlimited resources, then there would be newspapers filled with even more garbage about wastewater and open-space.

That's crap.

Bonfield had more of a calm demeanor—especially compared to an icon like Schwartz. Born in Philadelphia and raised in Tennessee, Bonfield attended Brigham Young University. Bonfield, who was 48 years old when he was named publisher, also worked at San Francisco Examiner and Los Angeles Daily News.

Jelenic needed an ad and marketing expert to help boost a struggling ad department. The ad department was in the dumps and needed direction.

Bonfield seemed very uneasy, very nervous the first time he came to The Trentonian. He wasn't self-assured and didn't have the presence Sandy had. He seemed skittish and unsure of what he wanted to do.

In a meeting later, Bonfield told Mickle and me to examine two newspaper markets like Minneapolis and Los Angeles.

Minneapolis and Los Angeles?

We lived in a region filled with two newspaper markets. Philadelphia and New York. The Trentonian reader can relate more to Philly and New York than Minneapolis.

We were in trouble.

♦ ♦ ♦

Schwartz stories are like those about Mickle. There are a lot of legendary stories. They might not be true, but they are consistent with the personality and therefore are believable.

There was an alleged confrontation between Bonfield and Schwartz in the early 1990s that is a Trentonian legend.

Bonfield, an executive with the JRC at the time, was visiting The Trentonian. Schwartz stopped Bonfield in the parking lot and told him to get the "fuck out of here."

Schwartz threw Bonfield off the premises and told him to never come back.

A Trentonian legend.

Knowing Schwartz's personality, it might have been true.

Schwartz protected the paper from corporate. He didn't need a suit from the corporate offices to tell him how to run the paper.

♦ ♦ ♦

July 13, 1998 changed The Trentonian's history forever.

That date could be marked as the official date of decline of the paper.

It was David Bonfield's first day.

Dealing with a new boss was uneasy for anybody.

When that boss totally disrespects your body of work, you are in trouble.

Bonfield detested the Trentonian—thought it was sleazy.

He was going to clean up the "sleaze" left by Schwartz.

On the first day, the Associated Press came out with a report of a 84-year-old Hillsborough man accused of rape.

It was an incredible story.

Bonfield didn't believe the story was true. Somebody must have made up this story. He was questioning the credibility of the Associated Press.

He didn't think it was newsworthy. He wanted to lead with the front page "PORK BEEF," a story about a boring state political issue.

I explained to him this is a talker. It's not every day an 84-year-old man is accused of rape. He wanted us to double-check the story. We did before he even asked. It was only because the Associated Press only ran a brief. We wanted a full-fledged story.

The problem was that this guy tried to come across as an authority of editorial.

Because he was publisher, he knew more about editorial direction than everybody combined.

He didn't.

Jelenic told me that Bonfield "had no clue about editorial side."

But Bonfield was trying to tell us what to do from Day 1.

We were in really big trouble.

◆ ◆ ◆

"The Quaker Bridge Mall calls us irrelevant," Bonfield said.

"What?"

"The Quaker Bridge Mall will not advertise in our paper," he said, "because they think the paper is irrelevant."

Apparently, that's a bad thing.

Well, the Quaker Bridge Mall would be quick to call us irrelevant. We ran a story about a tot falling off a chair and dying when her head hit the floor at a photo kiosk.

The stool story was irrelevant in the mall's view. Read the lead by Chris Dolmetsch:

"A day at the mall turned into a heartrending nightmare for a Hamilton family last week after their 6-year-old daughter tumbled from a stool while posing for a baby picture and smashed her head on the floor."

Try telling that little girl's parents their story is "irrelevant."

Guess it is irrelevant when Quaker Bridge officials told us there was no pigeon poison on the roof, and after Todd Venezia checked the roof there was pigeon poison.

Bonfield seemingly didn't care about kids dying at the mall and lies about pigeon poison. He believed the Quaker Bridge Mall's claims.

In his eyes, we were irrelevant.

Bonfield started to attend community meetings—with politicians and public leaders. Money was spent for golf outings at nearly $800 a pop.

Politicians weren't too fond of the Trentonian. The Trentonian didn't go gaga over them. Actually, ripped them for hypocrisy.

Bonfield started to rub elbows with the elite.

The elite was sending him one clear message: We were sleazy with a sleazy audience.

Bonfield seemingly wanted the area's elite to hold him in high regard. He didn't want to hear criticism from the "in-crowd."

With that the editorial direction of the paper changed.

The Trentonian reader, the blue-collar reader, was going to be cast aside like some worthless piece of trash. Ironically, the paper was popular with younger readers, and according to these whiz marketers, those readers are ideal to advertisers.

The Trentonian seemingly didn't want to serve them anymore.

Times were changing.

◆ ◆ ◆

The first target in Bonfield's crosshairs was the Page 6 poster tease of the Monday poster.

The tease picture used to be large on the front page—stripped down the side.

It was a eye-catcher and a big-time seller.

With the poster, we were probably the only paper in the country that had its largest sale on the Monday.

Newspaper editors need to be innovative in boosting circulation. Sunday is the slowest news day of the week. In the newspaper world, everyday counts the same. The centerpiece poster and large picture on Page 1 was popular.

The readers wanted it. We serve our readers.

But Bonfield's elite crew thought it was trash. Bonfield knew he couldn't trash the poster altogether.

"There are too many boobs on the front page," Bonfield would say constantly.

Those boobs were selling papers.

But Bonfield is the boss, and if he wants to reduce the size of top-selling tease, then fine.

We only ran a headshot of the poster girl on page 1.

Sales plummeted immediately.

We lost nearly 2,000 papers off the Monday paper just by reducing the tease.

The move itself knocked the circulation down to 56,600.

Monday wasn't the newspaper's best-selling day anymore.

◆ ◆ ◆

The emphasis of the paper quickly took a political turn.

Bonfield wanted the paper to be more on top of the state political scene. Like Pukanecz, Bonfield eyed the state worker.

State workers are more interested in political stories than crime, right?

Bonfield wanted the paper to have a "TAX RAGE" page, demonstrating the tax waste in New Jersey.

The concept was right, but it would have been repetitious after a couple of weeks, and it takes up space from more important items—crime and breaking news.

Issue-related stories started to become typical leads.

We led with the announcement of the new school superintendent in Trenton.

We ran the headline: SAVE OUR SCHOOLS

The sales stunk.

So did the front page "IT STINKS" about story about Parsons, a company the state was paying to take over the motor vehicle inspection system.

The story was solid, but it failed to galvanize the readership.

A successful newspaper cannot be liked by everybody.

A great newspaper will have enemies—like politicians who have been hit hard by the paper. A great newspaper will stir the pot and pick stories that will generate strong emotions.

Now, Bonfield, in my opinion, was cuddling up with the political elite. Hitting golf balls with state senators, Dining with mayors. Bashing the paper's heritage.

The Trentonian's slogan used to be: "Love us. Hate us. Read us."

Under Bonfield, it seemingly became: "Like us. Like us. Please!"

He heard that politicians disliked the Page 6 girl. He wanted to come out with two editions of the paper, The regular Trentonian and "Trentonian Lite," which didn't have the Page 6 girl.

He even recommended a Page 6 guy to run every Monday. The paper would feature a classy male—dressed in a tuxedo.

The paper was going soft.

And so were the sales.

◆ ◆ ◆

The newspaper was a labor of love for me.

Under Bonfield, it was labor.

News meetings with easy decisions became long, dragged out affairs.

One meeting, we had a beheaded body found in a Dumpster. Actually, the head was found in one Dumpster and the body was in another.

This is a vintage Trentonian story.

Bonfield didn't want to lead with it. Actually, he was leaning toward a story about a gas tax getting rejected. Gov. Whitman had proposed a gas tax, and we made it the front-page lead with the headline FURY OVER GAS TAX. The paper didn't sell too well.

The rejection of a gas tax wasn't going to sell extra papers. Bonfield nevertheless tried to chop down the beheaded story.

"It would be exploiting somebody's tragedy," Bonfield would say against any of those crime stories.

But our readers love crime stories; they are automatic sellers.

In my opinion, Bonfield didn't want these types of readers—the working-class reader.

For Bonfield, being respected by community leaders is better. Much better

But Bonfield's attitude toward the working-class reader in 1998 is typical in the industry. Today's newspapers want to be appreciated in the rich of the community.

Why?

If a newspaper appeals to a richer people, then it is more suitable to advertise in it. Also, editors and publishers like cuddling up with the powerful politicians. It makes them feel important.

Bonfield wanted advertising dollars and to be rubbing elbows with politicians.

He was willing to ditch the average Trentonian reader to do it.

Bonfield made a terrible miscalculation. By ditching the average, working-class reader, The Trentonian was neglecting its base of circulation.

The numbers were falling.

Sliding circulation numbers are a horrible trend for advertisers. No advertiser wants to put money into a sinking ship. Actually, if a newspaper demonstrates growth, it become or legitimate for an advertiser.

Advertisers want to see more bang for the dollar, and low numbers will not help.

The Trentonian was about to fall to 55,000.

◆ ◆ ◆

The Trentonian takes pride in its hard-hitting local news coverage.

Bonfield, in 1998, would pick a story that would provide him the least problems.

When a New Jersey State Trooper was accused of stealing $2,100 from an accident victim, Bonfield couldn't understand why the story was newsworthy.

"Why are we making a big deal out of this?" Bonfield said.

State troopers are supposed to be trustworthy—and it is diabolical for one to steal money from a crash victim.

Bonfield didn't want us to lead with it. The publisher wanted us to lead with an advance on the Starr Report—just like every other newspaper.

The Trentonian wasn't just any other newspaper. It went against the grain on stories. What made it great is that it picked offbeat stories as the lead. The Trentonian's stories drew emotion—compelling the reader to buy it.

This story about the State Trooper was local. This story was hard-hitting.

The publisher—in his ignorance—tossed away about 2,000 extra sales.

Todd Venezia was frustrated.

"(Bonfield) treats us like kids," he said, "like we don't know what we're doing. He really has no clue."

♦ ♦ ♦

Bonfield, who has hired for his marketing skills, relied heavily on readership studies.

Readership studies are nonsense.

Usually, in readership studies readers—in order to appear intellectual—will lie to the pollsters. In all of these studies, the readers will want more "good news, local sports, more issues stories and way too much crime."

These same studies indicate that seven out of 10 people do NOT slow down when they drive by an accident.

However, the circulation numbers don't reflect the desire for "good news."

"Feel good" stories bomb at the newsstands. Local sports only appeals to a very limited audience, and papers leading with issue stories usually collect dust at the newsstand.

Bonfield said the reader studies indicate that only 3 percent of the people pick up the paper because of the front page.

He believed it.

The paper was doomed.

The front page is the marquee for the newspaper. It reflects what the paper considers the best story. Those polled didn't want to appear dumb and say "yes, I'm lured in by those sensational headlines."

But they are.

Those reader studies would indicate our readers don't want to read stories about an intern allegedly having sex in a mortuary with a funeral director.

But they do.

The sales hold the truth.

In my opinion, Bonfield couldn't handle the truth.

His approach was failing—at the newsstands.

Marketing gurus like Bonfield will pitch the "Total Readership Number." It is a number derived from a study totaling the number of people who actually read the paper—not sales. Bonfield touted this number over the circulation figure.

But once again, the circulation number is objective; it is real. A "Readership Number" is subjective—usually produced by a group that is getting paid by the newspaper.

The sales' number was in the dumps because the typical Trentonian reader was discarded.

In Bonfield's world, if one politician liking the paper means 10 average Trentonian readers would stop buying, he would take the politician.

♦   ♦   ♦

The Trentonian sunk to 55,000 with a lead story, DOW-N WE GO.

It was the first time since 1971 The Trentonian had a sale of 55,000 on a non-holiday or write-off day.

Wall Street stories generally flop on the newsstands. The average guy doesn't give a damn about it.

Bonfield did.

"This has an impact on everybody's lives," Bonfield said on the Dow story. "Everybody who has 401K is affected."

Most Trentonian readers don't have 401K and don't care about business news—unless Fitz is writing something about a new Italian restaurant in Chambersburg.

In 1997, we led with "FALL STREET" when the trading was halted after the Dow plunged more than 500 points.

It was the worst sale of the year—it beat out the Steinert High School basketball team.

♦ ♦ ♦

Bonfield actually believed The Trentonian could win a Pulitzer Prize for its coverage of emissions.

"This story could win us the Pulitzer," Bonfield would say often.

Forget the Pulitzer Prize.

Ironically, The Trentonian won to First Amendment awards for public service during my tenure. One story by Dom Yanchunas detailed how prisoners were possibly getting free satellite TV, and the other was a tax piece by Dave Neese.

Under the headline "CORREC-TV," Yanchunas' straightforward report on satellite TV in the pokey lit the fuse to reader fury.

"If you're a criminal and you like satellite television, be sure you get arrested in Mercer County. The county prison may be wired for Primestar."

The inmates didn't get satellite TV—thanks to The Trentonian.

Awards are nice, but they don't necessarily prove a newspaper is successful.

The most important measure of a newspaper's success is sales. I'd rather see the paper increase by one paper a year than to put out a Pulitzer Prize-winning product that sees a sag in sales.

For some reason in the industry, a newspaper today is measured by the number of awards it wins.

Maybe that's why the newspaper business is dying.

♦ ♦ ♦

Bonfield seemingly wanted to be liked by everybody he considered "important" in the community.

Bob Jelenic was No. 1.

Jelenic's complaints about box scores and local mistakes were ignored by Schwartz.

Bonfield took those complaints seriously.

Every morning, Jelenic would rip the sports section to Bonfield; and every morning, Bonfield—who didn't have a clue how ridiculous these critiques were—would call me seeking answers.

The duo of Holmlund and Barrow were sailing in tranquil waters before Bonfield arrived.

Bonfield brought a storm that would force them to abandon ship.

The sports section was at its peak before Bonfield arrived. After all of the turmoil from Jelenic, we manage to put together a hard-hitting, crisply designed sports section.

Jelenic hardly complained during the summer I was in charge.

When Bonfield arrived, the calls came flocking in.

In my opinion, Bonfield seemed convinced that somebody was sabotaging the sports section. Bonfield claimed he was getting it a lot worse from Jelenic than we were. Problem was, nobody felt sorry for Bonfield.

Bonfield didn't like Holmlund and wanted him out.

I managed to save Holmlund until he made a tactical blunder.

In a dramatic turnaround, Jelenic suddenly didn't like the excessive coverage of the Trenton Thunder, the Double-A baseball team affiliated with the Boston Red Sox.

He wanted road trips halted.

The problem was, the Thunder were in middle of the road trip when the edict came down.

I told Bonfield to let beat writer Larry O'Rourke finish the trip.

Bonfield wouldn't allow it.

O'Rourke, who was once sports editor at the paper (who wasn't), was forced to leave the pressbox during the game against the Binghamton Mets.

It was embarrassing for O'Rourke—and the paper.

All of the sports writers at the scene now knew of one paper they wouldn't be sending their resume to.

Holmlund wrote a memo to me and copied it to Bonfield stating he is opposed to the cutbacks in coverage in the Thunder coverage.

Holmlund, in essence, put a bulls'-eye on his forehead.

The next night, there was a mistake in the Thunder box score.

Two days later, there wasn't an extensive advance on the upcoming Thunder homestand.

Bonfield and Jelenic believed that Holmlund and O'Rourke were making mistakes on purpose.

Both received memos that were copied to the corporate office.

Jelenic, a president and CEO of the chain, was making sure the proper punishment was handed down because of a box score mistake.

Both were told they might be terminated if it happened again.

Days later, Holmlund resigned and walked out.

We lost our sports editor.

I told Bonfield to hire Eric Barrow, the assistant sports editor.

Bonfield wanted a man who had kids. He believed a family man would appreciate Jelenic's concerns about local sports.

Barrow was single and didn't have kids.

Bonfield had lunch at Einstein's Bagels with Barrow.

"Eric, you're black, right?" Bonfield said. "What do you think of our Tiger Woods' coverage."

Barrow hated golf.

Bonfield apparently assumed all blacks had to be interested in Tiger Woods.

Barrow knew he had to leave the paper.

He was shopping his resume.

◆ ◆ ◆

Hamilton Jack Rafferty, a target of Baron scandal with The Trentonian, became a golfing buddy with Bonfield.

After that, the scandal became buried—or so it seemed.

In my opinion, Bonfield had his motives. Rafferty carried the key to advertising dollars in Hamilton. With his new friend, Bonfield wanted The Trentonian to back off the story about the Baron.

Bonfield would constantly say Rafferty was "misunderstood."

In fact, Bonfield wanted the editorial side to fork over the negatives with the famed picture Rafferty puffing to cigar. Bonfield was going to give them to Rafferty.

Photographer Leslie Barbaro and City Editor Paul Mickle told Bonfield the negatives are "missing."

Mickle insists even today he doesn't "know where the photographs are."

It's one thing to produce positive stories about advertisers for advertising dollars. Hell, you can write negative stories against non-advertisers—if they are true. But Bonfield crossed a line when he wanted to bury a scandal that drew flocks of readers.

Bonfield, in my opinion, didn't care—about what the popular blue-collar readers from Hamilton thought.

He was targeting a smarter, more community-oriented crowd.

That meant the Baron scandal was put on the back-burner.

Forget about what the readers want.

◆ ◆ ◆

One Friday in August, Todd Venezia was filling in for Paul Mickle. The news was flowing in:

- A good-looking niece of a late mobster was missing.
- A Chambersburg man was accused of getting his 6-year-old nephew drunk. The nephew was in serious condition after falling down of some stairs.
- A member of the Crew—a group of boys who were accused a making a large Swastika in middle of a Burlington County cornfield—was missing. The Swastika made national headlines it

was discovered by a plane in 1996. He was expected to attend a hearing in a couple of days.

It was a blockbuster, yet frantic day for Venezia.

In the news meeting, Bonfield arrived late and glanced at the log.

"Ah, nothing's going on," he said tossing the paper on the conference table.

Those in attendance were speechless. Venezia couldn't contain himself.

"What do you mean nothing's going on?" Todd fired back at him. "This a great news day."

Bonfield was taken aback by Venezia and his brashness from the beginning.

For Bonfield, there were no state political stories; therefore, no news.

To the others, he was clueless.

Venezia thought he was nuts.

Bonfield reluctantly allowed us to lead with the story on the missing suspect.

In my opinion, Bonfield had three interests: state politics, being popular in the social scene and doing anything Jelenic wanted.

When Mike Tyson came to Trenton to apply for a New Jersey boxing license, it was blockbuster news.

We had a 10-story package, and I had Dave Sommers, a new cop reporter, trail Tyson the entire day.

He followed Tyson, who bought a candy bar at the Princeton Hyatt Regency.

For our readers, this was a huge story—especially when Tyson lost his cool at the hearing.

MIKE GOES BERSERK AT HEARING was the lead headline with a 10-story package and work by four reporters. The day before we had a package (MIKE'S READY TO RUMBLE) with an editorial written by Venezia saying New Jersey must let Iron Mike fight. "Because of...time served and because the bounty in store from a Garden State Tyson fight, New Jersey should give Iron Mike a chance to fight again."

Both Tyson issues sold like hotcakes.

During these days, good-selling days meant trouble for the paper.

Jelenic, who according to legend once demanded the paper to lead with a rainout of a Little League baseball game, thought the paper went overboard on Tyson. Jelenic was silent when we had nearly 50 stories in three days during the Boston Red Sox's visit to play an exhibition game against the Thunder in Trenton.

Bonfield, of course, agreed with Jelenic—too much Tyson.

It didn't matter what the sale was.

Guess Tyson is too much of a Neanderthal for the "new sophisticated readers" of The Trentonian.

Princeton residents weren't interested in the Tyson saga, and at the time, it was all that mattered.

Another blow for the average Trentonian reader.

♦ ♦ ♦

The Trentonian readership under Schwartz was the hardcore conservative guys, like cops, who truly loved us. The working-class people, who loved it when we ripped Florio, they were our bread and butter. The Reagan Democrats. Our appeal came from our blue-collar nature.

Bonfield's strategy would ultimately fail, because he alienated The Trentonian's base. When he later went against the cops in an election on police department reforms, the cops were hurt and felt abandoned.

The cops were starting to hate a paper that once focused on covering crime.

The Trentonian used to galvanize conservatives just by its nature. That was our strength, and it was something we were losing. Probably 80 percent of our readers didn't support Clinton.

One time in a meeting, Bonfield questioned why we opposed President Clinton so much. Clinton was popular in the polls, and because of this, the paper should be more supportive of him.

Bonfield was disconnected from the *real* Trentonian reader and those people were starting to ditch the paper.

◆ ◆ ◆

The Trentonian editorial staff despised Bonfield.

They didn't like him, or more importantly, didn't respect him.

A leader doesn't have to be liked or win popularity contests. Respect, however, is vital. Everybody on the editorial side thought Bonfield was in way over his head to be publisher.

"Why doesn't Jelenic do something with this buffoon?" one staffer remarked. "(Bonfield) doesn't know what he's doing at all."

"Jelenic has to see that circulation is in the toilet," another staffer asked in the same meeting. "He's got to do something. We will lose everything."

One clear day, that every staffer will remember as "the Day of the Biker War."

A biker was critically wounded after being attacked by a rival gang in Chambersburg.

We have a biker war in the heart of our readership. This is a huge story. We had a six-story package mapped out.

On the same day, a beloved leader in the community died. Sam Plumeri Sr., the man who helped bring baseball back to Trenton, died at 82.

Bonfield ordered us to lead with Plumeri.

Bonfield had met with Plumeri the week before, and thought our readers would be more interested in his passing. Plumeri was important in social circles—beloved by the elite of the community.

The readers he wanted to appeal to—not the old Trentonian readers.

DEATH OF A LEGEND beat out the biker war.

Plumeri's death is news; it probably would have been an obvious lead most days. However, a wild biker war is breaking out in the heart of our readership. Nobody was safe walking at Chambersburg at night.

> The Trentonian wasn't interested in those readers anymore.
>
> Those readers were tossed on to the side of the road.
>
> The politicians were the in-crowd, not the guy who works the gas station in Hamilton.
>
> The decision outraged the staff. Reporters couldn't believe the Trentonian would pass on the opportunity to lead with a biker war.

Earlier in the month the paper had a story about a man who killed his best friend and tried to make it look like a mob hit. He cut his pal's corpse into little pieces and spread it throughout the Greater Trenton Area.

This was a story that had body parts—an automatic lead in Schwartz's book

Houtz, with Venezia's help, wrote this lead:

"A 21-year-old township man enraged over a homosexual advance from his 58-year-old roommate, bludgeoned the older man with a hammer, then sawed his limbs off with a hacksaw to dispose of the body, police said."

This story wasn't compelling enough for Bonfield.

The story was teased; we led with a story about Parsons.

Another issue over the weekend we had a pregnant woman stabbed to death in front of her child.

The child, thinking her mother was sleeping, baked cookies in the same room as her mother's corpse.

A vintage Trentonian story. Well, for the old Trentonian.

It was a Sunday—I made the decision to lead with it.

PREGNANT WOMAN STABBED TO DEATH was the lead story.

It was a solid seller.

Bonfield was outraged.

"We are exploiting tragedy," he said. "This story wasn't put into its proper context."

That's right we did exploit tragedy—because our readers want us to publish heartwrenching stories like this. They vote with their wallets. The story was a hit.

Bonfield threw out this election—believing it makes the paper appear more sleazy.

Guess the paper was sleazy with his golfing buddies.

They were more important than what a Chambersburg resident wants to read.

Bonfield had a major problem. While he could articulate what he didn't want, he failed to outline what he wanted.

You cannot run a paper on what it shouldn't be.

It has be follow a plan—it should be your ideal product.

In my opinion, Bonfield wanted all of the community leaders to like the paper, but he didn't know how to do it.

Most of the staff started to look for new jobs. Many were getting ready to leave.

◆ ◆ ◆

Vacancies were the last thing I needed in 1998.

I was now dealing with a publisher who is a poster child of why newspapers were declining. A publisher who isn't interested in what the average reader wants—dissing them for the political elite.

Dealing with a publisher who had no guts to protect his staff from Jelenic's ranting.

Journal Register Company had to save money.

In early September 1998, we had no managing editor. Bob Shields took his design magic to New York to work for the Daily News a year earlier. We never filled the vacancy.

We had no editorial page editor. I was forced to ask Mike Regan to work on the editorial pages two days a week.

We didn't have a sports editor and our assistant sports editor, Eric Barrow, was about to take a job with the Los Angeles Daily News.

No Shields. No Stradling. No Lukens. No Holmlund.

Top talent, never replaced. All of the vacancies must be approved by Jelenic before being filled.

Because Journal Register Company had to save the money.

A frustrated Barrow was gone. He accepted a position with the Los Angeles Daily News. Bonfield finally offered him the sports editor position—after Barrow accepted the Los Angeles job.

It was over. The sports department was stripped down. Holmlund and Barrow were the future of the sports department—they led the smoothest period for the department in at least five years.

I saw the writing on the wall.

Every time I would rebuild the sports department, Jelenic and Bonfield would tear it down. Over and over again.

Over messed up box scores, transactions and poor skiing agate. People were threatened with their jobs because a box score didn't add up properly. Chris Baud, the No. 3 person on the sports desk, was nearly fired because he didn't run complete college football scores.

Schwartz gave us protection from such absurdity. Bonfield didn't.

The news side was losing steam. Reporters detested Bonfield—knowing he would bounce potential lead stories. People were complaining to them that the paper was turning soft.

It was already soft.

Nothing is more demoralizing for a reporter to have story bounced because of a jittery publisher, who claimed he knew it all.

The paper was in a major slump.

Page 6 was in a decline. Bonfield had the Page 6 contest scrapped, and rejected most of our local models. He wanted all-American looking girls—even if they weren't local. The local girls, which was the reason why people enjoyed the feature in the first place, were getting cut back.

Babes from Los Angeles started to grace Page 6. The local girls made the page a novelty.

People would buy a biker rag to see good human flesh.

Bonfield was trying to placate some community groups, but not having local girls hurt him.

Supporters of Page 6 didn't like the page anymore because the girls weren't local, and groups that opposed Page 6 still hated it.

Nobody was happy.

Schwartz's legacy obviously was being uprooted. Piece by piece. Everything we did to stop slide triggered by the price increase was being shot down.

"People who have done more for the community than you think the paper is sleazy," Bonfield told me.

But I knew what the readers wanted.

Forget circulation, the power brokers in the community were more important. If circulation slides, so be it.

I had to leave.

I submitted the following resignation:

To: David B. Bonfield
From: Michael A. Raffaele
Re: Notice of Resignation
Sept. 16, 1998

> This memo is to inform you that I am resigning from my post as the executive editor of <u>The Trentonian</u> effective Oct. 1. It is my firm belief that the editor and publisher must be in agreement on managerial style, editorial philosophy, and how to utilize available resources to achieve the newspaper's objectives.

> Under the current circumstances, I feel it will be mutually beneficial for the paper and myself in the long run if I seek other opportunities elsewhere.

It was over.

◆ ◆ ◆

After giving my notice, I started to drift away from the day-to-day operations—especially on the weekends. It was the best way for the editorial staff to be prepared for my departure.

On Sept. 15 the day of my resignation, the paper led with MUM'S THE WORD on how Clinton is keeping quiet on the Monica Lewinsky scandal. Bonfield wanted us to lead with that over a man shooting at a cop during a wild chase in the city.

The headline was bland—a far cry from BILL ZIPS HIS LIPS just eight months earlier.

Pukanecz made the news decisions on the weekend of Sept. 20, and he wore his minor-league uniform.

He produced pathetic headlines with putrid news judgment.

On Sept. 20, the paper led with N.J. STILL LIKES BILL.

Firstly, an overwhelming majority of Trentonian readers detested Clinton, and a simple rule in headline writing was violated.

Never use "still" or "continued" in headlines because it implies that nothing new has occurred.

Meanwhile buried underneath the weather on page 8 of that edition, Eric Ladley wrote a story how a gas station worker was robbed and shot at by robbers. One bullet grazed the worker's head—he was lucky to be alive.

It would have made a perfect line.

But Pukanecz put it in a place where it made little impact. I easily missed the story the first time I looked at the paper.

The next day he led with a Mark McGwire story. Big Mac and Sammy Sosa were embroiled in their pursuit of the home run record. In a game in Milwaukee, McGwire belted No. 65.

He would have slugged No. 66, but the umpires ruled it a double they believed the fan reached over the wall to catch the ball.

Replays were clear that Big Mac shot should have been a home run.

Pukanecz went with the headline, GROUND FOOL DOUBLE, which made no sense.

Meanwhile, a 19-year-old woman was clinging to life after being struck in a vicious hit-and-run by a drunken driver.

That story took a backseat to Big Mac; it was one whopper of a mistake.

I couldn't wait until Oct. 1.

◆ ◆ ◆

Eric Ladley delivered a fine story for me in my final week. Monica Lewinsky was romantically linked to an Australian man she met while she was visiting Princeton.

Monica in Princeton? Romantically linked to an Aussie scientist who at one time lived in Princeton. That's a huge.

Ladley tracked down photos of the scientists. It cost the company $100; Bonfield wouldn't fork out a penny more.

MEET MONICA'S P'TON FLAME was the lead headline. The overline is my personal favorite: "He's Crocodile Brain-ee!"

Ladley wrote this lead:

"The identity of the mysterious Australian "boyfriend" who made Monica Lewinsky go gaga during a junket to Princeton University has been revealed.

"According to the Sydney Morning Herald, Monica's new obsession is a young, brilliant scientist Dr. Chris Burns, who is a research fellow in organic chemistry at Sydney University."

We produced a solid seller on my final week.

◆ ◆ ◆

October 1 was a simple news day—under Bonfield.

We were going to lead with a lead with a Whitman story—saying she probably won't run for president in 2000.

Chuck Pukanecz was going to be running the day-to-day operations of the paper after my departure.

The staff didn't respect "Uncle Chucky."

To them, he was a minor-leaguer who kisses Jelenic's shoes with no news judgment.

As I was leaving, it was revealed that Yankees' Darryl Strawberry had colon cancer—in middle of the playoffs.

This is a huge sports story. In order for a newspaper editor to be successful, he must be able to effectively cover three elements: news, sports and sex (celebrities).

This was a no-brainer. Strawberry should lead the paper.

In my last act as editor, I had the lead story changed to "STRAW HAS CANCER."

Later, Pukanecz returned to the office. He wondered why I changed the line. Whitman was more interesting in his view.

He was seen staring at the front page. Staring at the page.

Wondering if I had made the right decision.

The downward spiral of the Trentonian was about to be accelerated.

3

THE DARK AGES

I wandered over to my paper box. Once an editor, now I was a reader. A reader who worked as an assistant city editor for the Philly Daily News, now about to decide if I was going to buy The Trentonian.

Thousands of these decisions are made every day.

The Trentonian headline read, "BALLOONACY" with sketched pictures of balloons.

One day after I left, the Trentonian led with a story about kids being trampled during a Wal-Mart free balloon giveaway. A dramatic story.

Kids were rushed to the hospital.

Instead of running the headline: KIDS TRAMPLED AT WAL-MART, the Trentonian ran a cute headline on the incident.

Bonfield said I used to exploit tragedy.

Now, the Trentonian was mocking it.

I didn't buy that issue.

The Trentonian became totally unreadable.

I stopped even looking at the Trentonian's covers after the paper had the headline "PARENTS MAKE BEST TEACHERS"

That's lame.

I knew the circulation was in a free fall.

The Chamber of Commerce loved Bonfield and if headlines like "PARENTS MAKE BEST TEACHERS" got the thumbs-up from the Chamber, it was great.

The Trentonian was toast in my eyes. I wasn't the only reader who had such thoughts.

◆ ◆ ◆

The exodus had begun.
Todd Venezia took a job with APB online.
Mike Regan departed for the job at Fox News Web site.
Dom Yanchunas bailed to work with my wife at the Associated Press.
Jon Blackwell headed to the Asbury Park Press.
Larry O'Rourke left for the Allentown Morning Call.
Nancy Houtz left for the Metro daily in Philly.
Jim Fitzsimmons retired.
All—in my opinion—disrespected Bonfield and Pukanecz—and left because of the lackluster direction of the paper.
Jim Farrell was terminated on New Year's Eve in 1998. He went to the Courier Post in Cherry Hill.
Guess the circulation numbers were sagging, and Bonfield couldn't blame himself. Therefore, Farrell had to go.
It took the paper nine months before it hired a new editor. At least eight people were offered the job—at least eight people rejected it.
Norm Bell, a veteran newsman, accepted the position in May 1999. He couldn't believe how an editor like me would resign over the changes.
Bell, a large man who looked like Santa Claus, believed the paper was better under Bonfield.
Bell made a decision that would draw attention—because the industry started to realize the Trentonian was going soft.
He made the worst news judgment in the history of the paper. It knocked my infamous "LAUTENBERG LORD OR LOSER" off the books.

Ambrose Harris, a notorious piece of trash who raped a woman, killed her with a bullet to the head and dumped her corpse under a bridge in Trenton, bludgeoned to death a fellow death-row inmate—"Mudman" Simon.

"Ambrose killed the Mudman!" Mickle shrieked. "Ambrose killed the Mudman!"

For one day, the newsroom was electric.

Nancy Houtz worked on three stories—by herself.

Also this day, Gov. Whitman announced she wasn't running for the U.S. Senate.

This was a no-brainer.

Harris was a saga that drew readers. The search for the woman's body and the trial (this guy had the nerve to stick his middle finger at the judge) captivated and enraged readers.

Harris sold papers.

Christie—especially after she became governor—didn't.

This editor decided to lead with "CHRISTIE NOT RUNNING."

Basically, he claimed more people would be talking about Whitman at the "water cooler."

A horrible move.

An hour away from the scene of the story, The Philadelphia Daily News kicked the Trentonian's butt. This never happened under Schwartz's watch. The Daily News ran the headline "GOOD RIDDANCE" with a picture of the Mudman.

People were talking about the Daily News' front page.

And ridiculed the Trentonian's lack of news judgment.

A New Jersey magazine stunned by this news decision wondered if the paper was losing its edge. I was interviewed saying we would have led with the Ambrose attack. There would have been no doubt about it. The Trentonian was no longer a watchdog, gritty paper.

It was boring.

It was a matter of time before the sports mistakes would take its toll on Bell.

Under the constant complaints over box scores and transactions from Jelenic, Bell resigned in September.

He lasted four months under Bonfield.

Fourteen months on the job and two editors came and went in the Bonfield regime. That's nine months with Pukanecz holding the post.

◆ ◆ ◆

Jim Davis is passionate about local sports and its coverage.

Passionate enough to take the sports editor position.

Crazy enough to take the sports editor position.

Davis thought Jelenic didn't like the national focus I had. Davis shared the same philosophy; therefore, in his view, Jelenic wasn't *that* bad.

Davis didn't know how much Schwartz protected the department from the bullshit doled out by Jelenic.

Bonfield couldn't protect the staff from Jelenic.

Davis, who was hospitalized with a collapsed lung a year ago, had to deal with the stress of taking complaints from Bonfield and Jelenic every morning.

It didn't matter how late Davis worked the night before.

His phone would ring early in the morning. It was Bonfield complaining about a sports mistake.

Bonfield began getting involved in Jelenic's circles in local sports. He occasionally attended Laine Jelenic's soccer games.

Jelenic would complain constantly that Laine's statistics (mainly assists) didn't add up correctly. George O'Gorman had to explain officials have a different approach in handing assists in soccer than hockey.

The complaints had no signs of slowing down.

Davis was.

After nine grueling months on the job, Davis resigned and assumed the his reporting position.

Davis had a new appreciation for Schwartz—and the job he did protecting the department.

That was the case for most of the sports department. Most of the workers didn't like Schwartz when he was publisher.

As soon as Bonfield arrived, they noticed the tremendous job Schwartz did in keeping Jelenic away.

Sometimes the sports department was under siege with Schwartz.

But that was once every couple of months—even Schwartz couldn't stop all of Jelenic's criticisms.

Bonfield didn't slow the criticism; in fact, he was worse to deal with than Jelenic.

Bonfield's incompetence was making Schwartz even more legendary in the office.

That was Bonfield's worst nightmare.

♦ ♦ ♦

If Bonfield was Richard Nixon, Schwartz would have been John F. Kennedy.

The Schwartz legacy hovered over Bonfield. Everywhere he went, there was Schwartz. Most of the front pages on the walls of the paper, were under Schwartz's watch.

Bonfield removed a front page with the headline GIRL, 14, RAPED ON STAIRS with a poster girl right next to it. The juxtaposition of the poster girl enraged women's groups because it implied the raped girl was scantily clothed.

It was a hot-seller.

Schwartz used that front page as a rallying cry against the "politically correct" nature of the newspaper industry.

Bonfield took down that front page.

He desperately tried everything to make the staff forget about Schwartz.

Even visual reminders.

Bonfield removed all pictures of Schwartz out of the building. One staffer said that Bonfield claimed pictures of Schwartz showed disrespect for current publisher.

Don't worry. The next publisher won't be putting up any pictures of Bonfield.

Eric Ladley quoted Schwartz in a story about the grisly slaying of Page 6 model Julie Scully. Schwartz was the best person linked to the paper to be interviewed. He was the one who put her in the paper.

Bonfield was angry.

He told Ladley never to interview Schwartz for this—or any—story again.

Schwartz, the former publisher, was banned from the paper.

♦ ♦ ♦

The Trentonian featured headlines that either didn't make much sense or lulled the reader to sleep.

DAY CARE FOR SCHOOLS

BALLOT BEDLAM: This was selected over an area man being arrested for murders in New Mexico.

31 DEMS TURN ON BILL

SUICIDE WAS KILL SUSPECT

ELECTION OVERLOAD

'PIGS AT THE TROUGH'

'ROCK HARD' Against Slapping Clinton

CHRISTIE MYSTERY: Is she running for president?

HOLIDAY WISHES COME TRUE: This was picked over a bus accident killed eight in Sayreville, N.J.

SHOOTING OFF AT THE MOUTH

IS THE PRICE RIGHT?

PREZ'S JERSEY POINTMAN

Dull, lifeless stories.

Finding a replacement for Norm Bell took a year.

After an exhaustive search, they turned to the man who has been the foundation for the newsroom during these dark ages.

Paul Mickle.

In September 2000, Mickle was named editor of the Trentonian. It was a lifelong dream come true.

To deal with Bonfield's grief for more than two years, Mickle more than earned an opportunity to lead the Trentonian.

Mickle would last less than a year and his downfall—sports.

◆ ◆ ◆

Mark Schiele, who worked with Pukanecz in Norristown, was named sports editor shortly after Davis stepped down.

Mickle and Schiele were pounded with criticism about the section. It never met Jelenic's ridiculous standards.

Bonfield offered little help—other than to reinforce Jelenic's concerns.

As Mickle and Schiele were feeling the heat, I was boosting the circulation of the Lebanon Daily News.

After working at the Philly Daily News and ABCNEWS.com, I got the itch to become the editor again.

The Lebanon Daily News, a 20,000 PM daily about 30 minutes away from Harrisburg, seemed interested.

I was hired as the editor of the Lebanon Daily News in September 2001—the same month as Mickle's promotion at the Trentonian.

The Lebanon Daily News immediately turned from an irrelevant community piece of trash to a hard-hitting newspaper that everybody talked about.

I hired Eric Ladley as night city editor. The paper became only one of seven daily newspapers in Pennsylvania to show circulation increases in its daily and Sunday number. We used a simple formula: Hard-hitting local news.

There were no bake sales and extensive meeting coverage—a fixture in county rags. This county rag really rocked. The paper featured stories about naked men romping the city, a serial convenience store robber (the Turkey Hill Bandit), animal accidents, fires and other mayhem.

Ironically, I encountered the same problems in Lebanon as I did under Bonfield in Trenton.

Publisher David L. Smith wanted to be liked too.

◆ ◆ ◆

"People are starting to dislike the paper."

Publisher David Smith was coming off a vacation during which a murder-suicide occurred in West Lebanon. We had seven straight days of coverage while he was gone.

He was back.

He wasn't happy.

"This looks like something I would see in the New York Post."

I wanted to say, "thank you."

He, however, meant it as an insult.

Critics started to come forward, he said. The paper was losing its base. He was using subjective data—his sense.

But the facts were simple. More people read the Lebanon Daily News that week in at least five years. We *were* connecting. The readers voted: They like the paper.

The Lebanon Daily News was one of seven daily newspapers in Pennsylvania that showed increases in its daily and Sunday circulation numbers in the previous six months.

Smith wanted a meeting—with City Editor Paul Baker and News Editor Karol Gress.

The city editor and news editor didn't like the direction of the paper either.

Two weeks later, we had that meeting.

"Why are people hating this paper?" Smith asked, opening the meeting.

Hating the paper? This paper's single-copy sales went up nearly 10 percent, about 20 percent in the week in question.

The paper was better than it was before.

But the friends of Smith, Gress and Baker were critical. They used them as examples.

Once again, the only true objective measure of a newspaper's success was getting ignored.

A newspaper isn't successful when a couple of friends like it. And it isn't a failure if a handful of people dislike it.

The circulation figures showed the Lebanon Daily News was a success during my tenure. The sales soared despite a recession. The recession has been a convenient excuse for most editors.

The Lebanon Daily News fell victim to a thin-skinned staff.

A winning newspaper produces strong emotions. People like it. They hate it. They read it. That was the Trentonian motto under Schwartz.

A successful newspaper sells.

It was that meeting I knew I couldn't work at the Lebanon Daily News much longer. We hit a ceiling. Not being able to cast off the dead wood of a staff handcuffed me. Despite a mediocre staff, the paper had reached a much higher level. It became a must-read publication. People were buying more than ever before.

I had to leave. But where to go?

◆ ◆ ◆

A close friend told me that Chuck Pukanecz wanted me to call him. Call Chuck?

Returning to the Journal Register Company couldn't be that bad. I knew what to expect. Working at MediaNews Group became unpredictable. The staff in Lebanon was too soft and the publisher wouldn't let me replace them.

The workers at the Journal Register Company are more battle tested.

It also was nice to feel wanted.

After numerous conversations with Pukanecz one thing became clear.

I might be headed back to The Trentonian.

Returning to the Trentonian and working for Bonfield.

The impossible seemed possible.

The pieces were falling in place for me to make an unlikely return to the Trentonian because the paper was falling apart—again.

◆ ◆ ◆

Mickle was demoted from the editor spot in May 2001 because Bonfield claimed Mickle was still acting like the city editor while he held the top spot. Mickle, according to Bonfield, didn't hold the reporters accountable, and there weren't enough local stories in the paper.

Mickle was replaced on an interim basis by a man named Baldwin.

Tom Baldwin, that is.

Baldwin, a former correspondent in the Middle East for the Associated Press, became the fourth editor to work under Bonfield.

But the same problems persisted.

He was unable to fix the sports section. Pukanecz and Bonfield were hounded by Jelenic to fix these "mistakes."

Like previous editors, it was Baldwin's turn to get pounded.

◆ ◆ ◆

Paul Mickle had a meltdown.

Mickle dealt with Bonfield's jittery nagging for three years. Mickle had seen all of the great lines that would sell more papers shot down. All of the best workers—in an attempt to bail out of a sinking ship—leave for lesser paying jobs in isolated places like Scranton, Pa.

His staff was being replaced with inferior workers who didn't have the same zeal of attacking stories. The staff—like the paper—became soft.

Through it all, Mickle remained positive.

"I will stay here until I'm shot," he would constantly say. He would also say "Bonfield was starting to see the light" on news stories.

When he was editor, he couldn't have a sick day without Bonfield pestering him. His cell phone rang constantly.

One time, Bonfield told Mickle's wife to hand Paul the phone in the shower.

Three years of that treatment started to get the best of Mickle.

A meeting with Baldwin—a person Mickle hired as his city editor—sparked the outburst.

Baldwin met with Mickle to tell him that he must start working on weekends.

Mickle went berserk. It triggered an explosion that Mickle had bottled up.

"THIS IS BULLSHIT!" Mickle said.

According to witnesses, Mickle claimed this was an attempt for JRC to fire him to cut salary.

Bonfield heard Mickle's raging from his office and Bonfield told Mickle told him that he'd better calm down—or he will call the cops.

Mickle didn't calm down.

Bonfield called the cops.

Mickle was taken away—by cops.

Mickle had worked at The Trentonian for 20 years. He was an icon. He was beloved.

Now, he was being taken out of the office—disgraced.

Bonfield had an undercover officer posted in the office for the next three days—just in case a rampaging Mickle returned.

A week later, Mickle returned—on the job.

Mickle apologized for his outburst. Bonfield knew the importance of having Mickle in the newsroom because of his knowledge of local stories. You cannot fire an icon—no matter what he does. Mickle had been a good soldier for this paper for 20 years.

Mickle's record spoke for itself.

He was back where he belonged—behind the city editor's desk.

◆ ◆ ◆

Baldwin was doomed.

He believed cricket results would sell papers. He thought bake sales and flea market stories should run on page 2.

Circulation didn't improve.

Most importantly, Baldwin—like the people before him—never was able to correct the "chronic" sports problem.

For nine years, Jelenic has been hunting for the person who has been sabotaging the paper.

He still hasn't found that person.

Baldwin had major health problems and was forced to be hospitalized indefinitely.

No editor and no answers.

My phone rang. It was Pukanecz.

I'm scheduled to meet with Bonfield about becoming the next editor.

My word.

◆ ◆ ◆

Bonfield and I met at the Journal Register Company offices in Trenton.

It was a bizarre, surreal meeting. I once vowed I would never return to the Trentonian offices.

It was clear my return was imminent. Never make promises you can't keep.

The meeting was awkward.

Bonfield stressed the paper is more disciplined in a lot of areas.

He said the paper was better off than it was three years before.

In fact, Bonfield said he found the combination that sold papers: it was hard-hitting crime and sex scandals.

Politics, he said, don't sell that much.

Hmm. Sounds familiar.

Three years ago, Bonfield mocked that approach. Now, he's embracing it. Circulation must be really bad for this turnaround in Bonfield's attitude. But it was this that convinced me I should return to bring The Trentonian to glory.

I felt there was a slight chance for the paper to be saved. The Trentonian had to be tougher than the Lebanon Daily News staff.

Bonfield said the only problem with me was that I couldn't take criticism too well.

How can somebody argue against that? If I say that I can take criticism, then I'm not taking that particular criticism too well. It just reinforces the argument.

I told Bonfield I'm more mature than I was three years ago, and I feel the most comfortable in The Trentonian offices.

The meeting lasted about 40 minutes.

I was scheduled to meet with Jelenic in five days.

◆ ◆ ◆

The Jelenic meeting was nearly a replay of what it was in 1998.

The news department lacked fire.

The sports department makes too many careless mistakes.

But he was more concerned about horse racing. He complained that Linda Dougherty's horse racing selections weren't getting into the paper consistently. Her picks need to run every day.

Jelenic stressed the need for consistency in the sports section.

It was odd that Jelenic was more concerned about horse racing. Nobody—other than Schwartz—cared about the sport before. Dougherty used to get frustrated over being neglected and not properly edited in the paper.

Now the spotlight seemed to be on her.

Later, I discovered that Jelenic is starting to buy horses; hence, he developed of keen awareness of Dougherty's work.

Jelenic—a prototypical Type-A personality—can galvanize you when dealing with him on a one-on-one basis.

He would make a tremendous football coach.

Three days later, I was hired to return to the Trentonian. My first day was Sept. 5.

At the end of our pivotal 15-minute meeting, Jelenic had me ready to tackle the Trentonian. Dive into this stiff challenge headfirst.

Unfortunately, the water in this pool was very shallow.

4

RESTORE THE ROAR?

Before starting any job, the editor must study the paper and circulation.

It's almost like working on a football scouting report. You must be able to locate the strengths and weaknesses. Find out where the paper can make significant improvement for circulation growth.

Jelenic was right. The news side lacked passion. The wire stories seemed more compelling. Reporters weren't digging enough into stories to reveal the human-interest element into the story. Multiple-story packages that made the Trentonian a big-story paper didn't exist.

The reporters seemingly were taking the cop reports and throwing them into the paper. Interviews with victims or their families seemed a rarity. The human-element of these crime stories was missing.

Eye-popping stories were getting buried.

The reporting was lazy. The layouts lacked pizzazz.

Page 1 didn't have any flair. It was thrown together each night without much imagination.

Page 1 needed to show some life. This is the first step in improving circulation. Make Page 1 compelling, and your circulation will reflect that. Eventually, the content must match the flair on Page 1.

The Page 1 headlines stunk. They usually made no sense. On Sept. 5, the day I arrived, the Trentonian led with a headline SHOOT THE MESSENGERS.

This was a follow story about a prison break. It made no sense, and the reader would not know what the story was about if they quickly looked at the headline.

Both Page 1 and the content inside were garbage.

I had an emergency three-step plan:

- Bring more flair in the design on Page 1.

- Make sure the Page 1 head was clear and immediately understandable.

- Bring back the big-story approach for the paper. If a major story occurs, all of the reporters will contribute to the package. We needed to get a reputation of being the best at covering big stories. On Sept. 4, the Trentonian fell woefully short. We also needed to dig deeper in normal crime stories to find a tragic hook.

But more disconcerting was the circulation numbers. The Trentonian dropped to 48,500 on its daily number and 39,000 on Sunday.

A disgraceful number.

Bonfield is lucky to be still employed. Circulation is the won-loss record for an editor and publisher.

During my previous stint as editor, we flirted with the 60,000 daily mark and 46,000 on Sunday.

The Trentonian had lost more than one-sixth of its circulation number in three years. There was no price increase—just readers not buying the paper anymore.

Bonfield's tactics in the first year of the paper scarred the readers. The paper became dull, and a significant number of the readers bailed.

One aspect is critical when you analyze the circulation numbers. The number will never level off. It will keep on sliding until the editor drastically improves the product.

At 48,500, The Trentonian's circulation had hit its lowest point in 33 years. The Times circulation daily average held at 78,000. The great newspaper war in Trenton was becoming a mismatch.

The Trentonian was ravaged over the past three years.

◆ ◆ ◆

My arrival stunned a downtrodden, beaten staff.

"You're crazy," one staffer immediately said. "I really thought you were smart when you left when you did."

"You're crazy" was the phrase that usually greeted me when I met with the staffers who worked with me before.

The morale in the newsroom felt like a damp blanket.

The newsroom was quiet. The energy zapped.

Fewer bodies in the editorial department, and the remainder of the staff was beaten down.

Or they lacked passion.

No wonder why the Trentonian was in a endless slump.

The newsroom became dull.

It didn't exist.

Other than Mickle, who was beaten down considerably, the paper lacked the fire needed to be successful.

Three years earlier, the Trentonian had a "fuck the world" attitude. The team bonded together and put out one hell of a product.

Mickle, who worked endless hours before, now had a punch-clock mentality. He came in at 10 a.m. and was gone at 6 p.m.

Nobody was willing to go the extra mile for a paper run by Bonfield and Journal Register Company.

Pukanecz would hover in the building, but his presence didn't help. In fact, it worsened.

Nobody in the office—other than new business editor Pam Dawkins—respected Pukanecz. They didn't respect his abilities.

Three years. Four editors. And most of the time the paper was looking for an editor.

During this period, the reporters and editors didn't have the proper guidance. The news pages were thrown together and the reporters developed bad habits because they lacked a leader. They didn't dig enough for stories to find the human element—and likely Bonfield, a man who generated little respect, shot down a lot of their stories.

Ironically, the sports department was in a lot better shape than news.

◆ ◆ ◆

On Sept. 4, Mark Schiele was fired as sports editor.

According to Bonfield, Jelenic was so sick of the sports section that he said either Schiele, Bonfield or Pukanecz will be fired.

Someone's head would be on the plate.

Bonfield and Pukanecz quickly fired Schiele.

Now that's the Bonfield version of the story.

Cynics in the editorial department believed the Schiele firing was a cost-cutting move. Since I handled both editor and sports editor jobs before, it saves money for one guy to hold two jobs.

To the critics, this was the Journal Register Company way.

Nobody told be about Schiele's firing until I arrived. On my first day, I also became the sports editor.

Pukanecz and Bonfield told me to be primarily concerned with the sports section; news could do the job themselves.

They were wrong.

The news section was the reason the circulation was dropping like a rock. News sells the paper—not local sports.

This sports department was hard-nosed and self-sufficient. The staffers had a passion for the job. While George O'Gorman was working on three 20-inch stories, news reporter Jeff Edelstein was cranking out one 5-inch brief.

O'Gorman's department was under fire—not Edelstein's.

News Editor Mike Christel is much more proficient doing sports pages; he struggles with the news section. Because of the pressure on sports, he moved to news. He moved to news because nobody cared about the section. The heat's off Christel.

The news' slide triggered the Trentonian's collapse, but nobody seemed to care.

Except me.

Except the sports department.

The sports department was jaded. It was like Bosnia. Another bomb or threat won't make any difference. They were beaten down so much they were numb to any more threats.

Nobody notices the news mistakes, they said.

Bonfield prepared me the following memo (including typos) on what to watch for in sports (my comments are in Italics):

September 4, 2001

Mike Raffaele
Sports Priorities

1. Consistency—although improved we still lacked consistency and have errors and omissions on a frequent basis. Racing picks and bankroll, sports agate transactions, Roxy's picks (latest line), Down on the Farm, Sport agate running on website in direct violation of company policy, etc. In short, the sports editor needs to ensure a complete, accurate and competitive package each day. Tom Baldwin has been in the hospital for the last month, and that has hurt us. He still doesn't know when he will return. Mark Schiele lacked the management consistency to get it done.
   Consistency improved, but not enough to save Schiele's job. Bonfield had to say the paper improved somewhat in the past three years. Baldwin being in the hospital probably made little difference. He had little impact on this consistency; if he did, we would still be editor.

2. Tease the new environments—We have been inconsistent in teasing upcoming new features out front and in paper. Sometimes we're great. Other times we keep it a secret. This is true

for news side as well.

Oh, a problem with the news department, it cannot be. Bonfield is right on this issue. The paper had key items buried in the paper—teases can only help boost sales. The paper wasn't effectively teasing what's inside.

3. Sports Internal controls—We do a pretty good job at sign-off pages, but at times key personnel sign off pages they clearly have not read. A huge issue to address.

4. Deadlines—We need to better manage deadlines, which will help alleviate some of the sign-off issues mentioned above.

5. Weekends—Although improved, there is a tendency of some in sports to try and exit early on weekends and take short cuts. This happens less frequently during the week, but is still and issue. We miss breaking stories because of this. Insure this is fixed on news side as well. It would be good to work this weekend and make an assessment and report your findings on Monday, Sept. 10th.

6. Seasonal planning—Each season needs a budget and game plan. From Pros, High School, College, we need to know who's covering each team and who is the backup if they're out for any reason. The same is true for the desk and those with pagination ability.

7. Competitive Tools—Each day, the night sports crew tie-out the paper versus the Times and our daily log. Also, they leave a copy for me and should leave one for you now that you're here. Also they leave a voice mail indicating a wrap up of Trentonian versus the Times coverage. (We get an early version of the Times from Brauninger News—If they have something significant we don't try to recover as best we can for three or two star editions.)

How much does Bonfield expect the sports section to do? They might as well clean the toilets while they are at it. Isn't the news section in a competitive situation. Why can't they do the comparison?

8. Website—Sports needs to be consistent on uploading the Internet Product. We'll discuss in detail with Lori German. No sports agate, box scores, lists of rosters, or other content that would drain sales or potentially multiple sales from our circulation department should be uploaded. There is a memo from corporate I'll get for you.
This is typical example of Jelenic's obsession with box scores. He's convinced if the sports department loads local boxes on the site, the circulation will sink. I guess that's a reason why the circulation has dropped nearly 12,000 in three years. Box scores are being loaded on the Web site. How about the news?

9. Byline count—We have been averaging over 100 bylines each week in sports. Well above counts of previous years. We want to keep that discipline and manage by expectations by reporter.
Byline counts are usually a tactic done by a county rag to ensure they fill space in the paper. Fuck the quality of the stories. It's quantity.

10. JRC Web—Pro and college content is provided via JRC web exchange. We should have a daily routine of monitoring submissions by our Philly and Connecticut and New York, and New England papers. If a story is up there we must use it unless Chuck Pukanez indicates content is optional.

11. Space Budget—Usually we run 16-20 pages depending on multiple factors. If there's little or no local schedule, at times we may cut back to 12-14 pages. This needs to be discussed with me in advance based on the need.

12. Packaging—We need to continue to work on presentation. We need to ensure predictability of day's features run and focus on the flow of the section. Photos and other graphic and typographical tools need to be developed to make the section look more professional, consistent and user-friendly.
He's right. The paper lacked any sort of packaging skills, and this was killing the paper's circulation much more than agate on the Web.

13. Weekly Mtgs. —You should meet weekly with selected senior writers and desk personnel to ensure priorities are taken seriously.
With all of these priorities, the average person in the sports department would have to work about 82 hours a week; I don't think they have the time for this.

Let's review this document weekly for the remainder of the year to make sure we're on track.

Thank you,

David Bonfield

This was the first memo issued to me from Bonfield. Incredible. To me, it obviously was an attempt to cover himself. If Jelenic complains about anything, Bonfield could just say "well, Bob, Mike has a memo outlining all of these problems."

But news remained unscathed.

The *real* problem wasn't addressed.

◆ ◆ ◆

Rocky Gallo, the Trentonian's production manager, seemed eager to see me.

He sat me down, and told me "the paper hasn't made a deadline in months."

"What?"

"The paper hasn't made a deadline in months."

Bonfield—with all of his talk on accountability—had a paper that hadn't made a deadline in months. When a paper fails to make deadline, the circulation sinks because the paper is on the stands for a shorter period of time.

The earlier the paper hits the stands, the better the sale.

The direction of the newspaper was completely wrong.

The publisher was touting the importance of local sports for the paper. "That is the franchise," he would repeatedly say.

The front page was bland with a weak, murky headline and the paper couldn't make a deadline. Bonfield made only a passing reference on deadlines—it was the shortest point on the memo.

There should have been a memo on deadlines.

Missed deadlines were killing circulation—not box scores on the Internet.

The paper lacked the discipline to succeed. The corporation was beating up the wrong people.

This memo and the Gallo conversation made me regret my decision to return.

I was only two hours on the job.

◆   ◆   ◆

After two hours, I discovered our strength was the sports writing of the paper.

The newsroom lacked energy.

It seemed only the sports writers like George O'Gorman, Scott Esposito, Rich Timlen and Jim Davis gave a damn about anything.

But they were considered the weakest link of the paper.

It was extremely frustrating for the sports department to even have any pride. They see a mediocre news product and the sports department is considered the problem because of a box score mistake.

One bond that united the staffs: Everybody hated Bonfield.

They blame Bonfield for the decay of the paper. The demoralized staffs. The lack of energy in the newsroom.

All Bonfield's fault.

"They sports department thinks I'm Hitler," Bonfield once said.

So does the newsroom.

◆ ◆ ◆

Our lead story on the first day was the capture of escaped killer Terrence Brewer.

We ran a large mugshot of Brewer with the headline:
GOTCHA!

It was my first Trentonian front page since STRAW HAD CANCER. I was reunited with Sam Guerrero.

Guerrero, who I nicknamed "Sam the Man," worked in Gallo's department as a graphics designer who had the knack for eye-popping design, but he was restricted by the editorial staff's incompetence in putting together front pages. The news department didn't have the vision for Page 1. They hardly ever provided Guerrero with art, limiting his ability to showcase his artistic talent.

The editorial turkeys were preventing "Sam the Man" from soaring.

"Sam the Man" was the most important employee to help me initially boost the circulation of the paper. He was the most important employee in the building, and nobody realized it.

I will provide a rough concept on page 1; Guerrero would execute it.

Cindy Manion, who worked with me in 1998, was only allowed to work on ads. So, it was just Sam and I.

Page 1 had to be my highest priority because it was the lure to snaring the readers. A more sophisticated, eye-popping cover will override all of the shortcomings of the paper.

We had too many shortcomings.

For the early portion of my return, Sam was literally the man.

◆ ◆ ◆

We were at a major disadvantage when Brewer was nabbed. He surrendered in front of the Trenton Times; in fact, he called the paper informing them he was going to turn himself in.

Convicted killers feel more comfortable with the softball Times.

Scott Frost, who rose from part-time sports clerk to night cop reporter, managed to get enough to make the story the line. Frost didn't mention the Times by name in the story; he just gave their address.

I told him to write it that way. If somebody reads in a Trentonian story that Brewer turned himself to the Times, the reader might be apt to buy a copy of the times for more details.

Exploiting its advantage, the Times had more details and ran a picture of the handcuffed Brewer. We only had his mugshot.

The Times buried us. And it wasn't Frost's fault.

You wouldn't have known it the next morning.

◆ ◆ ◆

Barbara Whitehouse, Bonfield's administrative assistant, summoned me to his office when I came to work at 10 a.m.

Being summoned the first thing in the morning isn't good.

Jelenic had called. He wasn't happy.

But it wasn't about the Brewer story.

It was sports, of course.

Bonfield said Jelenic called the section "gray and boring."

Jelenic said the Times had more transactions than the Trentonian. That's bad. We're idiots because the Times had more transaction agate.

But the Times had a brief on Canadiens center Sakku Koivu.

Koivu, the heart and soul of the Montreal Canadiens, was diagnosed with abdominal cancer. This is a significant story. The AP moved a brief at 1:46 a.m. that morning. The Times ran two paragraphs of it in a briefs package.

The Trentonian sports staff was too busy doing paperwork in the Times comparison and uploading the Internet to catch something on the wire at 1:46 a.m.

For Jelenic, that brief might as well been a 500-point headline.

Forget about the Times totally dominating us on the lead story. A brief on C7 was causing us agony.

For not having this brief in the paper, I was forced to write a memo, threatening an employee's job.

The CEO of a newspaper chain is riding herd on a newspaper because a two-paragraph brief didn't get into the paper.

We were idiots for this—we were not off to a good start.

◆ ◆ ◆

The next couple of days I stressed simplicity in the news approach and tried to bring pizzazz to the front page.

The lead headlines were:

WITNESS'S WEEK FROM HELL: A story about a man whose testimony helped convict Terrence Brewer and we interviewed him about his fears of a possible revenge from the escapee. It was a generally a slow news day.

Mike Fay, who replaced Jim Farrell, in 1999, said the sales for the GOTCHA front page was 50,000. That's a great number now. In 1998, I would have been forced to look for a new job if I posted that number.

Sequels usually never sell as much as the original. Even though we will get a fairly good sales number, the onus will be the change the topic of the lead the next day.

FATAL WRECK: A fatal accident involving an ambulance took the lead honors on Day 3. The simplistic approach is what the paper needed. We ran a large photo of a twisted ambulance with the straightforward headline. It told the story.

The news meeting that day was a nightmare. Crazy headlines were tossed about like AMBY HORROR. With the current state of circulation, we needed people to understand what the story was about. AMBY HORROR would just cheapen the story. Somebody died in this wreck.

Simplicity sold, and it was paper's best Saturday edition in months.

POL ARRESTED IN GO-GO BAR MELEE: Dave Sommers nailed this story about a councilman who was involved in a struggle at a Bucks County, Pa., strip joint.

Sommers was the only reporter I hired in 1998 that was there in 2001. At the time, he was the best cop reporter in Bucks County and still is.

Actually, Sommers left the Trentonian in 1999 to start Web site on Bucks County news. Since **www.bucksnewsnetwork.com** failed to generate enough money for him to survive, Sommers was rehired by Mickle in early 2001.

He was easily Mickle's best hire.

Sommers was the only reporter who had link to the glory days—he understood what I meant by restoring the roar of the paper.

The paper now was merely a paper tiger.

With an unyielding passion for the job, Sommers seemingly never slept. A true newsman always on the prowl seeking stories.

Sommers still ran his Web site; in fact, he scooped our paper regularly.

It didn't' matter.

Sommers covered Bucks County. The paper read more like a publication based in Bucks County because Sommers was able to nail down the best stories—all from Bucks.

A strong emphasis on Bucks County hurt the paper in its core area—Mercer and Burlington counties.

It was all because Sommers was so much better than the rest of the reporters. Because of this, I was forced to move Sommers to the night cops beat.

Sommers, who was probably the fourth or fifth best news reporter in 1998, was clearly the top dog in the 2001 Trentonian.

◆ ◆ ◆

Today's Editor likes to whine.

Why is readership sliding? And please get out those crying towels. A lot of sob stories.

Generally, an editor will claim the organization is not providing the financial backing to be successful. Limited recourses equals declining sales, they say.

What a world-class cop out.

If today's editor had unlimited resources, then we will get a lot more of the junk newspapers are doling out. More types of zoning stories. More blockbuster sewer stories.

"We are not getting enough money to get the top reporters," an Editor once whined to me.

When I worked at the Lebanon Daily News, resources were limited.

But hiring practices based on personality and ambition will offset it. If somebody looks at your newspaper as a stepping stone, they will take the measly salary you are offering and make the most of it.

If a reporter claims the money isn't enough, don't hire him. The reporter doesn't have a personality to fit in your organization. This business is an industry based on passion for the news.

The journalist shouldn't give a damn about money, but rather, relish the exhilaration of gathering the news. This should outweigh the money.

Two of my best reporters at the Lebanon Daily News were the lowest paid—making $410 a week. That's less than the wage of some Burger King workers.

They looked at the paper as a step to getting to the next level. I didn't expect them to be around after a year.

Both were gone in seven months. But they contributed to the betterment of the paper.

Surround yourself with ambition and that will offset the limited funds.

Look at budget cuts as a challenge to your leadership. Make your team better despite the odds.

I know I can put out an effective, must-read newspaper with three aggressive reporters. In essence, we did at the Lebanon Daily News. The other reporters didn't buy into my philosophy. Their stories were buried in the paper. The publication was making incredible strides without them.

The higher-paid reporters at the Daily News were the least effective, in my view. This is a 20,000-circulation paper and for most of the workers it's an apex of mediocre careers.

The Trentonian in 2001 had loads of dead wood—a demoralized staff that detested the publisher and corporate so much that it lost its passion to gathering news.

The main adjustment for an editor with fewer workers is to reduce the reliance on beats. Focus on breaking news. Make them all general assignment reporters if you have to. Decide which beat is most important (usually it's the largest city in your circulation area) and scrap the other beats.

The Trentonian will become a day-to-day operation.

The Trentonian didn't make the best hires during October 1998 to September 2001. There was crying because Journal Register Company didn't provide enough resources. The salary for a starting reporter dropped from $550 a week to $519.

As the cost of living increased, the salaries decreased.

Before, the Trentonian used to be the second paper for most upstart reporters who want to work at big-time papers; now with its sliding circulation and lower salaries, it was now a first job for most reporters.

It will require more coaching from the editors.

◆ ◆ ◆

One new worker in the Trentonian who had loads of personality was Stephen Row, the night city editor.

Row is a minister with one hell of a temper.

His tantrums were legendary. One time, he smashed a mug during an argument with night cop reporter Scott Frost.

Such passion for the job was refreshing. One moment he could be soft-spoken, then in the next instant, he turns into a raging lunatic.

It kept the news reporters on their toes.

That's what you need from a night city editor.

◆ ◆ ◆

Molly Davis is the only editor who had the right to whine.

Once the "SEX KITTEN IN THE CLASSROOM," Davis rose through the ranks to become features editor

Actually, she was the only features person left and got the position by default.

Davis' department once consisted of five people.

In 1997, it was run by Mike Regan, the best features editor who worked for me. Regan had a feel for stories people would talk about, and he managed to utilize his staff to producing front-page worthy stories.

Regan had four reporters working for him.

Davis has one. Herself.

The Journal Register Company, once considered the features department as critical to building readers, now cut down the department to one person: the features editor.

Features is usually a secondary department in the paper. Newspapers can successfully operate with a limited features department.

Davis would have to do the same. She had no choice.

♦ ♦ ♦

The Trentonian was a baptism by fire for Joe Dyton.

Dyton, a 21-year-old senior at Rider University, got a full-time copy editing job at the Trentonian. Usually, college students don't get full-time copy editing jobs.

But this is the Trentonian sports department.

Like pro wrestling, sports staffers might get unexpectedly socked by a steel chair—providing an opportunity for another worker.

In the past six months, the Trentonian's sports editor and two assistant sports editors were either fired or stormed out never to return.

All because of a jittery publisher who had to blame somebody for all of these perceived problems.

Part-time sports clerks were elevated to full-time copy editors.

Joe Dyton was one of them.

Dyton, a solid copy editor, was forced to learn his trade under the heat of the Journal Register Company. The constant scrutiny would have forced out normal 21-year-olds.

Not Dyton.

The Journal Register Company doesn't have any age discrimination. If you mess up, you are an idiot—and it doesn't matter how old you are.

Dyton was new to the business and was learning on the job.

One thing, Dyton will remember: always run the college football scores on the agate page.

Jelenic went bonkers because he didn't see the Syracuse football score in the Trentonian. His daughter, Laine, attends Syracuse and he visited her to see a Syracuse-Auburn game—a contest between two unranked teams.

To his dismay, it didn't appear in the paper. Not even a brief. He probably wouldn't care if we didn't have the Michigan result in the paper.

Dyton was under fire.

Dyton who has seen three of his supervisors banished was never told he had to run complete college football results in the paper.

He still almost lost his job.

He received a memo—with a threat of losing his job if it happens again.

The sports department was so unsettled because of the constant changes or terminations. The new workers really didn't know what it was supposed to do at times. Dyton's so-called mistake was a result of a void in leadership. No one sat him down and told him the basics.

That's probably because those people were fired for mistakes on the horse racing page.

Jon Davis, another part-time clerk who was elevated to full-time copy editor, was suspended for a week for a blunder on the horse racing page. Davis is talented, but didn't have the ability to be a solid copy editor.

But he was thrust into the situation because of the lack of stability created by the publisher and CEO.

The turbulence was only beginning.

◆   ◆   ◆

When he looked at the agate page on Sept. 10, Bob Jelenic was furious.

The Trenton Times had 8 inches of transactions on its page; the Trentonian only had 3.

That means The Trentonian offices were about to be rocked.

The CEO apparently measured transactions agate—as the circulation of his paper dropped.

But the problem was, Jelenic believed mistakes like that were killing the newspaper—not weak front pages.

Copy editor Jay Dunn received a memo stating mistakes like this transactions "blunder" happened again—he would face disciplinary action.

Cutting transactions is normal for most newspapers—but Jelenic would rage.

Sports staffers were jaded. What would you expect from a staff that has been bombarded with this for three years?

One staff member believed that Jelenic was hounding the paper to run the transactions in its entirety because his son, Lee, was playing in the low-level United Hockey League. Jelenic, the staffer believed, couldn't directly complain about not having the UHL transactions in the paper.

Jelenic claims all of the transactions should run.

That includes the UHL.

◆ ◆ ◆

David Bonfield must be held accountable for the Trentonian's demise for the past three years.

In my opinion, his cowardice and yearning to be liked has drove the paper to new lows.

He had to be liked by the community and more importantly, Bob Jelenic.

He, in my opinion, couldn't give a rat's ass about the development of the paper.

Bonfield bought Jelenic's raging as legitimate. Hell, Jelenic is the boss, but sometimes you have to tell the boss he's wrong. You need to stand up for your staff.

Even if it is the CEO of a large newspaper chain.

Bonfield created the circulation mess in the first place. He came in with an approach that he wanted the paper to be not like Schwartz's.

He uprooted it. The Schwartz staff bailed. The front pages became soft.

Circulation fell.

He left Jelenic have free reign over the sports department.

The quality of the personnel decreased—leading to more mistakes in the paper.

More calls from Jelenic.

Since the circulation is sliding, Jelenic had a convenient excuse to blame it on the sports department.

Bonfield playing corporate politics drove the paper into the ground. Every editorial decision had to go through Chuck Pukanecz.

Seemingly, if the paper made a tactical mistake and Jelenic raged, Bonfield could say Pukanecz approved of the move.

Bonfield would be covering his bases.

Pukanecz, in my opinion, didn't want any part of The Trentonian's woes. He didn't want to be linked to the paper at all.

Corporate jockeying at its finest.

Staff members, in my opinion, became sacrificial lambs for Bonfield. If a mistake occurs in the paper, Bonfield could discipline or fire the worker or write them up to show Jelenic he was doing something to solve the problem.

But constant turmoil means you lose your top workers and you settle for those with lesser skills. Workers with lesser skills produce an inferior product.

Hence, it is a publisher who is putting out a mediocre product to keep his job.

The readers are the ultimate losers. As was I for returning to the job.

◆ ◆ ◆

"HE'S BACK!" read the Trentonian's front page on Sept. 11.

Michael Jordan was returning to the NBA for "the love of the game."

That was big news for the Trentonian readers. Our readers love Jordan.

We had tease of a Rider University student believed to be sick because of bad beer. A big brew scare in Rider. That's great news. Anytime you have a story about poisoned alcohol, you are successful.

We had a package on a string of home invasions in the region. The home invasion package was the lead story—until Jordan made his bombshell announcement. Home invasions sell papers. Anytime you have home security as an issue, you are in good shape for sales.

The back page led with a story about the New York Giants getting drubbed by the Denver Broncos on Monday night football. A late football game usually means readers will be buying your paper to read about what happened after they went to sleep.

It had all of the ingredients to be a solid sale.

It wasn't.

All of those stories had little meaning at the end of the day.

5

THE STORY OF A LIFETIME

It was 9:25 a.m. My hotel phone rang.

I didn't leave the Trentonian office until 3 a.m. Ate dinner at 4 a.m. and didn't go to sleep until 5 a.m.

Whenever the phone rings at about 9:30 a.m. and you work for the Bonfield Trentonian, it means trouble.

Usually, Jelenic will call at 9 a.m., ream out Bonfield and by the time the publisher gathers himself, he calls the editor at 9:30 a.m.

This was bad news. Real news.

It was Barb Whitehouse, Bonfield's administrative assistant.

"A plane has hit the World Trade Center," She said. "Dave wanted you to know about it. He wants you in the office as soon as you can."

Our world has changed.

By the time I got to the office about 25 minutes later, a second plane slammed into the second tower.

By the time I collected my thoughts, the Pentagon was struck by a plane. Another plane crashed near Pittsburgh.

The two towers collapsed.

At 10:30 a.m., we had the biggest story of our lifetime.

◆ ◆ ◆

"We've got dead," Mickle repeatedly screamed through the newsroom.

We were going to have a lot of local deaths in this tragedy.

People are scrambling for theories. Workers in other departments huddled around the television looking for answers in this surreal setting.

This was still a news story. Our approach will be the same as KIDS MUG CORPSE. Just get the facts and we'll effectively present the story.

A solid editor doesn't have the time to reflect and realize the magnitude of the story.

You had to get the damned story.

The local hook to this story is that "we got dead."

Those towers were filled with people from our circulation area. Princeton, Trenton and Bucks County residents commute to work

The stories are there; and we must get them.

In terms of approach, this story was just like KIDS MUG CORPSE.

But this story has a lot more angles and everybody in the building will be working on it.

◆ ◆ ◆

Whenever faced with a blockbuster story, the editor must keep a focus—make sure all of the reporters know their roles.

The last thing you need to happen is two reporters working on the same angle.

Every reporter wants to be a part of this story—contribute in some way to history. What we did today will be looked at for the rest of time.

Anybody who breathes and works in this business wants to be a part of it.

Everybody wants to help; therefore, confusion reigns.

But The Trentonian's legacy was at stake. We will be remembered for what we did on this day.

We wanted to have an extra edition, which is a special issue printed on the spot.

Bonfield and corporate waffled for two hours on this. What are the costs? What does this mean for circulation? Do we take a couple of pages out of the Michael Jordan issue and replace them with the attack?

Or do we do a special edition just dealing with the attack? Maybe 12-20 pages. The action needed to be decisive. We are assigning general stories for the next day's paper, but our focus would change significantly if we produced an extra.

Nobody would make up their minds.

We sent reporters to the Trenton, Hamilton and Princeton train stations. There, we maybe can find people who escaped the terror attacks or know possible victims.

We did find one Hamilton woman who worked at the Trade Center, got out and immediately took a train home.

She talked to The Trentonian first.

We sent a reporter to blood banks—people were already flocking there to provide help.

We put together a general reaction story. Rich Timlen, a sports reporter, said more people in Trenton wanted to talk more about Jordan than the actual attack.

That's Trenton.

We gathered political reaction.

We mustered together a story about security.

A reporter was sent to schools to see parents picking up their kids in fear.

We assigned a story to Pam Dawkins, our business reporter, to work on talking to political experts on what this means and what kind of group could have plotted such an act of terrorism.

Free-lancer Bob McNeil scrambled together story on how this attack rates in U.S. history. We compared it to Pearl Harbor and how this attack is much more devastating.

The reporters were launched into action, but we still didn't know the status of the extra edition.

Finally, at about 12:30 p.m., we were going to do a 16-page extra edition. We had to get the edition completely done by 1:30 p.m. We had to be on the streets by 3 p.m.

When a paper moves to produce an extra edition, it requires pressmen and circulation departments to bring their workers into the office and work overtime.

It's costly.

In days like this decisions had to be prompt and decisive. Bonfield wiggled and squirmed—unable to make a decision without consulting the corporate offices.

It slowed production.

This was the first extra edition in the history of the Trentonian.

The front page had the headline UNDER ATTACK with a picture of the trade center from a distance in flames.

The back page had the headline NATIONAL NIGHTMARE with people frantically getting away from a collapsed tower.

Dramatic stuff. Our legacy was preserved.

The layouts were solid, and we had five locally written stories with a plethora produced of stories produced by the Associated Press.

We were effectively documenting history.

We printed about 10,000 copies of the extra and 9,000 were sold. An unbelievable sale. Only 10 percent of the printed copies weren't sold. Normally, about 18 percent return rate is considered good.

With the special section done, we had early deadline for the regular edition.

We were planning to run 23 pages of coverage. We would have done more, but we simply didn't have the time or the resources to be effective.

We had to be done with the paper at 10:30 p.m. —an hour earlier than normal. This is with a newshole that was about four times its normal size.

A lot of work was ahead.

◆ ◆ ◆

Dave Sommers has a nose for news.

He can find a local hook at anywhere.

We knew we were going to have local fatalities in this story. It was obvious, but how many would be reported in the early going.

Sommers was one of the first reporters do find out that one of the pilots on one of the planes that hit the towers was Vic Saracini, a Bucks County resident.

A local angle uncovered in the biggest story of our time.

Sommers managed to dig up a photo of the victim. He was the first face from the tragedy.

Unfortunately, there will be many more.

Lisa Meyer, a thirtysomething reporter with little journalistic experience, was stationed at the Princeton Train Station. She was to try to talk to as many people coming off the train. She stayed there for nearly 10 hours. At 11 a.m., we let her leave her post.

But she noticed there was a lot of cars still parked in the station. Usually the lot is vacant at this time of the day.

Most of the lot was full.

That's when the magnitude of the tragedy hit home.

Mickle was right. "We got dead."

◆   ◆   ◆

Mickle was adamant about the headline for the Sept. 12 edition. This headline will be remembered for the rest of time. This front page will be what grandparents will use to show the magnitude of the terrorist attacks.

These front pages will be etched in our memory.

For The Trentonian, these issues provided us with a forum to regain the readers we squandered away in the past three years.

Those readers who were leisurely discarded by Bonfield might reconsider and return to the paper.

The front page had to be dramatic.

Mickle kept on saying "ACT OF WAR."

Pukanecz wanted TERROR AT HOME.

I initially leaned toward BASTARDS. Mickle keenly disliked that headline for the right reason: We used it before.

On the day after the Oklahoma City attacks in 1995, we ran the headline GET THE BASTARDS.

You cannot dispute Mickle's memory.

We went with TERROR AT HOME, because it reflected that this was a terroristic attack on our soil. We always felt as a nation we insolated from terroristic attacks. It was a rude awakening. We put the headline on top of a close-up picture of the planes smashing into the second tower.

It was a devastating front page. It would sell papers.

Mickle was mocked by some for saying ACT OF WAR. Staffers thought is was too strong to put war in a headline.

Mickle was so passionate about this headline is that he called me from home at about 11:30 p.m. after the press started running to tell me we made the wrong decision. President Bush used the phrase "act of war."

The New York Post and New York Daily News used "ACT OF WAR."

Jelenic thought we should have used BASTARDS.

This frantic day showed that the news staff when pushed can muster up the passion to be successful. The cogs with the right guidance can put together one hell of a product.

The 1998 staff wouldn't have done much better.

It was refreshing.

I left the office at 1:30 a.m. feeling upbeat about the direction of the paper. We can put out a winning newspaper with this staff.

In about 10 hours a pin would pierce my balloon.

◆ ◆ ◆

The red light on my office phone was flashing.

Somebody left a message.

It was Chuck Pukanecz.

Whenever Pukanecz calls, there's trouble.

Since it's Sept.12 maybe we would be given a break from the sports bullshit.

We weren't.

Pukanecz left a message stating we missed a Rutgers baseball brief; the Times had it. A pitcher for the Scarlet Knights apparently was honored by Baseball America. The Times ran two paragraphs; they might as well had put the story on page 1—ahead of the terroristic attacks.

I'm the only editor in the country who received a complaint from the corporate offices about the sports section on Sept. 12.

Mixed-up priorities.

The world is forever changed. It occurred about 45 minutes away from the office, and scores of our residents were killed.

But The Trentonian did not have a Rutgers baseball brief in the paper.

Somebody would need to be written up—again.

Every memo sounded the same—if you do this again, you may be terminated.

Firing somebody over a Rutgers baseball brief is like giving the death penalty for a parking violation.

I guess we would have sold a ton of more papers if we had that brief in the paper.

◆ ◆ ◆

Mike Fay's world was wonderful.

Nothing's better than an act of war. It sells a hell of a lot of papers.

Despite not having a brief on the Rutgers baseball team, the sale soared to 66,000.

It was the largest issue during Bonfield's regime about 17,000 above the daily average. About 4,000 ahead of SEX IN THE MORTUARY.

If a story is 4,000 more than SEX IN THE MORTUARY, you have a winner.

Wars sell.

The paper sold more than 80,000 papers when the Gulf War broke out.

The act of terror provided an opportunity to recover the readers we lost in the last three years. People who left the paper bought it on Sept. 12. Hopefully, we will have retention in sales.

Every newspaper generated big sales on Sept. 12. Keeping a portion of those readers is now the key.

Before Sept. 11, sales jumped over the 50,000 mark in my first week. The jazzier approach on the front page was working.

Guerrero was getting the job done.

Now, during this period, the reporters needed to step up.

We needed to follow the trail of local victims. That means calling funeral directors, politicians, police departments and fire companies for possible reports of missing people.

The struggle of retaining readers rested on the coverage of local angles—not national. People are able keep track of national story with network television and the 24-hour cable channels. We needed to exploit the local angles; our local hook was the considerable amount of victims from our area.

We had nearly 20 pages of coverage on the second day. We had five stories on victims.

Our front page had the headline: SHOW NO MERCY with the famous picture of the firemen raising the World Trade Center flag at Ground Zero.

Copies of that particular front page were in demand.

◆ ◆ ◆

Dave Sommers has a "Forest Gump" quality to him.

Great reporters have it.

They stumble into a story—even when they are lost working on another one.

Sommers was working a story on Jim Berger, a Yardley, Pa., resident who was an business executive at the Trade Center. Berger was credited of saving the lives of most of his staff in leading them out of the building. Berger died heroically.

A touching story.

While trying to find the Berger residence, Sommers stumbled onto a movie set—and there was heartthrob actor Mel Gibson.

Gibson was shooting promotional shots for the movie *Signs*. He was outside the Langhorne Presbyterian Church—keeping a low profile.

But Gibson was bagged. Sommers snapped his picture and we ran it on Page 17.

We still push celebrity stories—even during our nation's darkest hour.

◆　◆　◆

Day 3 of the coverage featured a front page with Osama bin Laden and the headline MARKED MAN!

President Bush was played prominently on Days 4 and 5 with YOU WILL HEAR FROM US, with a picture of Bush at Ground Zero and UNITED AGAINST EVIL, a story about how Bush is building an international coalition.

Keeping a fresh hook on Page 1 of such an ongoing story is difficult. The story did have legs, but to lead with something other than the attack would be cheap.

While we had nearly 60 people perish during the attack—none of the stories warranted page 1 play. Normally, if any of these people died tragically in separate events—we would have 60 different front pages. But this event was too big to focus on one person.

That was until we found out about Todd Beamer's heroics.

A Cranbury resident, Beamer, 34, a sales executive, a father of two and a former star athlete in Hightstown High, led the charge on Flight 93. He said "Let's Roll" as he led a pack of passengers to derail the terrorists' attack.

The plane crashed in Western Pennsylvania—far short of the Washington D.C. destination. All of the passengers on board died.

"Let's Roll" became the rallying cry of the nation.

The man who said it was from our circulation area.

He was the face we needed to humanize the story.

On Day 6 of the coverage, we led with OUR HERO SAVED CAPITAL.

It was a winner.

In the main story, Vice President Dick Cheney hailed the passengers.

"Without question, the attack would have been much worse if it hadn't been for the courageous acts of those individuals on United 93," Cheney said.

Bush honored Beamer's wife, Lisa, during a dramatic speech to Congress and the nation 10 days after the attack.

Beamer would become a fixture in The Trentonian.

◆　　◆　　◆

After 10 days of covering the attack, the staff started to get depressed.

Day in and day out of interviewing families who lost loved ones started to tax the staff emotionally.

During that time, the Trentonian ran at least five stories a day on local victims. We ran an extensive casualty list.

It is imperative for reporters not to get too close to their topics. The staff was getting too close.

Jeff Edelstein, a colorful personality of the newsroom who needed a little more seasoning in this reporting skills, was devastated. The job was draining him emotionally.

Other reporters started to follow.

Mickle, the same man who took the picture of Karen Pugh seconds after we discovered she died in a fiery wreck, kept the pedal to the metal.

Mickle kept pressing the staff on the fact that this is history. It seemed at times Dave Sommers was the only reporter who passionately dove into the story.

The others were too emotionally connected.

It is said that city cop reporters often burn out after two years because of dealing with tragedy every day.

This was the biggest tragedy of them all.

Our readership was wounded.

During these times, the editor must keep the staff on the ultimate goal—getting the story. There cannot be emotional attachment. Be aware of the reporter's feelings, but they should know the stories are the most important.

Also, it provides the victim's family with a memory—a well-written story in the story will give the families something they will cherish forever.

The staff was worn out, and getting weary of the story.

It was December when to stop leading with it on the front page.

◆ ◆ ◆

Like most Americans, David Bonfield was mad as hell.

Angry over the attacks, he directed his venom toward Middle Easterners.

Convinced that area Middle Easterners weren't doing enough to help the cause, Bonfield wanted to have editorial board meetings for the Mideast Americans to defend themselves.

"What are they doing to help the American cause?" he wondered.

We were bogged down with these meetings, and Bonfield wanted answers.

Every day, we were asked if we had anything on the Mosques.

To appease Bonfield, we ran a story on Sept. 30 featuring local Afghans saying that the Americans will never capture bin Laden with the headline: YOU WILL NEVER CATCH HIM.

But Bonfield wanted more, and never eased on this angle.

◆ ◆ ◆

On Sept. 19, the paper might was well had the word "FUCK" in capital letters on Page 1.

We were facing the death penalty for another parking violation.

The front page led with the funeral for pilot Vic Saracini. The headline read WORLD MOURNS LOCAL PILOT.

A dramatic front page that didn't sell too well. It seemed when we led the front page with patriotic themes, the sale was much stronger. Mourning a local pilot didn't boost the national pride.

All that didn't matter.

The mugshot of sports writer Jack Kerwin next to his high school football column was too big in the paper. It appeared to be larger than the other column mugs.

There was a mistake in the local schedule. West Windsor-Plainsboro South does not play today—they played yesterday.

Jelenic was furious.

So was Pukanecz.

Of course, so was Bonfield.

During the biggest story of our lifetime, the corporate offices of Journal Register Company is upside down because of a mugshot being too big and a mistake in the local schedule.

Later in the day, Pukanecz sat me down.

"If you are fired in a month from now," he said, "I won't be able do anything for you."

Hmmm. Let me see. We had cut down transactions, a mistake in the local schedule, a headshot that ran too big.

Of course, let me not forget about the Rutgers baseball brief. I should have been more concerned with that than the terroristic attacks.

Fire me, please.

"I want you to be focused solely on sports," he said. "Let the news side handle the terror stories themselves."

Pukanecz didn't realize the news side woes and Bonfield's mismanagement of news stories in the past drove the circulation down.

Of course, the circulation slide was triggered by trimmed-down transactions.

Right then, I knew my days were numbered in Trenton.

I wasn't going to be selling my house in Lebanon, Pa.

My wife wasn't going to be quitting her job with the Associated Press in Harrisburg, Pa.

There are reasons why bad newspapers struggle.

The Trentonian's bigwigs actually believed the agate page of the paper was more important than page 1.

At least they made that impression.

◆ ◆ ◆

Scott Esposito is a survivor.

In 1997, he didn't put Lee Jelenic on the all-county team.

Since then, he, in my opinion, was in Bob Jelenic's doghouse.

Somehow, Esposito still has a job with The Trentonian. Esposito was the most improved worker on the staff and will be a great sports editor someday.

Even though he probably will never hold a management position in the chain because of his actions in 1997, he now covers the Trenton Titans, a team in the East Coast Hockey League (ECHL).

In late September, Esposito was unable to cover a critical Titans preseason game against the archrival Reading Royals.

In our warped world, every time the Titans hit the ice—it's a life or death situation.

We needed to find somebody to step up. Esposito's backup, Rick Timlen, had to cover college football, and all of the other reporters were at high school sporting events.

Joe O'Gorman got the call.

O'Gorman, a part-time reporter and George's brother, is a class act, and was willing to cover this game—even though he never wrote a hockey story before.

O'Gorman knew about the politics of the situation. Hockey was a hot potato, and he was doing this for the team.

The Titans came out with a crucial 4-1 win in the preseason ECHL opener.

After the game, O'Gorman was trapped in an elevator in Sovereign-Bank Arena. He was stuck for about 20 minutes.

He still managed to file a game story with a box score with minutes to spare before deadline.

But there was poison in the box score.

O'Gorman, who never did a hockey summary in his life, didn't give an assist to Titans' Ben Stafford in the box.

Stafford, you see, played hockey with Lee Jelenic in Yale.

The big guy caught the mistake.

It was the end of the world.

Or so it seemed.

At this paper, it seemed more important than the coverage of the terroristic attacks.

O'Gorman, Chris Collins (the page editor) and Storm Gifford (the person who proofed the page) received memos written by Pukanecz under my name. All were threatened with possibly losing their jobs.

O'Gorman who did me the favor for covering the event was blamed for "hurting the credibility of the paper."

Bonfield didn't want to hear about O'Gorman's favor. He must be written up for the mistake.

And the publisher wonders why nobody apparently respects him.

Pukanecz then produced a memo telling the staff how to proof pages.

It was a condescending memo written by an executive who never did a sports page at newspapers larger than 40,000.

Now, he was telling the sports department how to proof pages.

He was considered minor league with county rag views. He has reached the apex of his career.

Bonfield thought Pukanecz was an editorial genius.

That in itself would indicate Pukanecz had problems.

In fact, Bonfield thought the memo was an exceptional teaching tool, and he wanted the memo to be posted throughout the building.

One member of the sports department was frustrated looking at the memo.

He tore it down.

When Bonfield noticed the memo was torn down, he wanted me to track down the culprit.

Bonfield wanted him fired.

Another death penalty for a parking ticket.

I never found the suspect.

◆ ◆ ◆

The terrorist attacks led The Trentonian from Sept. 12 to Oct. 5—that's 24 consecutive days.

Easily a Trentonian record.

We had front pages ranging from WE'LL GET THE BUTCHERS, HOW WE WILL WIN, WHERE'S THE BUTCHER? and AMERICA PREPARES FOR BIO-TERROR

The streak snapped when the Hamilton police chief was suspended in light of accusations of sexual harassment.

But in the first edition of that issue, we led with THE SPIRIT OF AMERICA—a story about how Beamer's "Let's roll" has been Bush's phrase to rally a demoralized nation.

The circulation was rolling—we were averaging about 52,000 papers—about 2,500 above average.

It's all because of the attack.

An editor must figure out when to stop leading with a hot story. A story could become overkill; readers will become tired of seeing the same topic on page 1 every day.

Our goal was reader retention. We were in danger in losing them if we continued to ride the attacks.

It also is difficult for an editor to keep the story fresh—finding a new angle. We led with this story for 24 straight days.

We needed a change.

The decision, however, was made for us.

◆ ◆ ◆

Airstrikes over Afghanistan started on Oct. 7. We were officially in a war.

While we should have used Mickle's "ACT OF WAR" on Sept. 11, the attacks gave us the opportunity to use the headline that is an easy winner at the newsstands.

We love easy winners.

A 600-point headline WAR graced the cover the Trentonian with a collage of Bush, bin Laden, the burning Trade Center Towers and planes.

A brilliant piece of art work by Sam Guerrero. A masterpiece.

It was a front page we prepared for in advance. A newspaper had to be prepared just in case it happens late at night.

From an ideal standpoint the later an event happens in the day, the better.

If a breaking story occurs after 6 p.m., it is better for a newspaper because it's after the 6 p.m. local news. We actually might be the first source of information for the public.

If it happens after 11 p.m., it is perfect.

The odds are that most readers will be sleeping and won't know about the story until they see the paper the next morning.

The later the breaking story, the better the sales.

Unfortunately for us, the bombing started at about 1 p.m. Everybody will know about it.

Therefore, it required a special front page that people will buy for keepsakes.

We ran eight pages of coverage, and our sale was about 56,000—thanks mainly to Guerrero's cover.

The next day, we had to lead with the war.

Ideally, I wanted a picture of the damage from the bombings. A rubble shot with the headline, TAKE THAT!

But from a dramatic standpoint, this is a pathetic war. We had pictures of the enemy in middle of dust bowls. Afghanistan was reduced to rubble during its war against the Soviet Union in the 1980s.

The pictures were more laughable than hard-hitting.

"*That's* the enemy," copy editor and key advisor Andy Hussie said. "This is a joke."

We had to lead with the second day of the war. We couldn't use the headline BOMBINGS CONTINUE.

The words "continue" and "still" are killers to headlines. Both indicate that there are no new developments in the story.

But we had to lead with the second day of bombings.

Thank God for Guerrero.

Guerrero crafted a brilliant front page featuring the collage of planes, bombs, the Afghans with the headline PAYBACK!

We didn't have any news, but we had one hell of a dramatic looking front page.

That can overtake the lack of content.

Sam was the man.

◆ ◆ ◆

"The anthrax came from Trenton!" Paul Mickle screamed with his voice reaching a higher pitch as he delivered each word. "Anthrax came from Trenton!"

"What?"

"This is *our* anthrax!" Mickle said. "The anthrax that infected (NBC anchor) Tom Brokow's assistant was mailed from freakin' Trenton.

"It's *our* freakin' anthrax."

My God, it is *our* anthrax.

Trenton, N.J., just became the center of the world. The middle of the biggest story of our lifetime.

In the newspaper business, we take possession of every thing that's local.

For example, Todd Beamer lived in *our* circulation area—he was *our* hero. The man who paid the ultimate price to save the capitol.

He was *our* guy.

Now, Trenton, which already had a tarnished reputation to the outside world, now has another scar.

It's *our* anthrax.

Trenton makes anthrax, the world takes.

Unbelievable.

Trenton may be a haven of terrorists, but for now, it was home for every prominent newsperson in the world.

◆ ◆ ◆

Dave Neese, a onetime statehouse reporter who was The Trentonian's editorial page editor, had to get away from all of this—he took a vacation to Morocco.

A Midwesterner, Neese had a short-wave radio with him on his journey. He was listening to foreign newscasts.

He couldn't speak any of the languages, but with every newscast, he understood one word, "Trenton."

"Trenton" kept on creeping up in all the newscasts. It was their main story.

"What the fuck is going on over there?" Neese thought.

Trenton was on the world stage.

◆ ◆ ◆

On Oct. 13, the night of the revelation of the outbreak, I was supposed to attend a Chamber function. It was supposed to be my first attempt to reaching out to the community.

All of the bigwigs were supposed to be there Hamilton Mayor Glen Gilmore and Trenton Mayor Doug Palmer. The letter was mailed from the Hamilton Post Office with the postmark of Trenton.

The story was more important. Forget about the community service.

Upstart reporter Linda Lisanti and Mickle did a tremendous job in crafting an eight-story, five-page package.

The headline read: ANTHRAX MAILED FROM TRENTON—in about 400 point.

It was powerful.

Gilmore and Palmer didn't attend the function, but neither made a big deal of the anthrax on the first day. This was an important chapter in the biggest story of our lives. Trenton and Hamilton were at the center of the universe.

But they didn't want to panic.

Until they saw The Trentonian front page.

They immediately called a Sunday morning news conference to quell fears, but the Hamilton Post Office was used by possible terrorists.

Anthrax can be deadly.

It created alarm in the community.

◆ ◆ ◆

It was Oct. 15.

My cell phone rang.

Usually, this meant a blockbuster story has developed like anthrax or trouble is brewing in the corporate offices.

It was Bonfield.

Jelenic was unhappy.

I committed a sin that seemingly was second behind a box score blunder.

I moved a standing element in the paper.

Jelenic and crew believe that standing elements must run on the same page every day. Normally, that is true. For example, the police blotter must run on Page 8. One day, I didn't—I put more terrorism coverage on that page to keep the package together.

Bad idea.

Jelenic claimed moving the blotter off of page 8 was like getting ready to play golf and forgetting the golf ball.

These standing elements, they believe, can boost circulation. Help break the slide.

Dramatic news stories end the slide—not standing elements.

In the Sunday paper, Page 4 has Dave Barry's column and a feature called "Week's Worth."

"Week's Worth," written by Jeff Edelstein, was compilation of the top, offbeat stories of the week with covers of the last seven Trentonians. It has been in the paper since 1999.

It is a complete rip-off of a New York Daily News feature. But the Daily News editors are smart enough not to run it on Page 4. They bury it.

The Trentonian on Oct. 14 featured the bombshell discovery that the anthrax letter is from Trenton. We had a four-page package. In order to keep continuity in the package, I moved this "Week's Worth" to Page 17.

Bad move in the JRC world.

"You don't own the paper," Bonfield said. "You can't make decisions like that on your own."

From that point on, I would need corporate approval before I would move a standing element—even if anthrax breaks out in the area.

◆ ◆ ◆

This anthrax was known as "Trenton anthrax" in headlines.

TRENTON ANTHRAX HITS CAPITOL: The story dealt with an Anthrax letter addressed to Sen. Tom Daschle from Trenton.

TRENTON ANTRHAX STRIKES AGAIN: The story about the New York Post editor receiving an anthrax-laced letter.

We gave it a personality.

Fear gripped the region. Emergency workers racing to all corners of the area on reports of white powder.

One time, workers raced to a Dunkin' Donuts because somebody noticed white powder in the shop.

We had an anthrax scare in our parking lot; a worker noticed white powder on top of her lemonade. The emergency crews—and TV crews—flocked to our parking lot.

We had a story about a anthrax prank involving crushed mints got a couple of area students arrested.

The area was in turmoil.

So was our office.

◆ ◆ ◆

While we were being bombarded with anthrax scares, Bob Jelenic was angry.

The Trentonian didn't have the results of the PGA Southern Championship on the agate page. The Southern Championship in Magnolia, Texas, was a second-tier PGA event—there was a bigger event that featured the top stars at the Western Open.

But in this world, the Trentonian is losing readers because of blunders like this.

Copy editor Jon Davis, the son of Jim, was terminated.

Davis made a lot of mistakes, but because of all of the firings before, Davis was placed into a position in which he was destined to fail.

The miscue on the agate page was the last straw.

In a stable work environment, Davis would have been a reporter—not a copy editor. But in knee-jerk move, The Trentonian hired him as a copy editor because of shortage of bodies on the copy desk.

A shortage created by terminations.

"This is management by terror," one staffer said. "They are doing this to save money. How can anybody work under these fuckin' conditions?"

◆ ◆ ◆

Rich Timlen is a loose cannon.

While extremely talented, Timlen, who was my first hire as sports editor way back in 1997, can do dumb things that are not related to journalism.

One night, he discovered a letter in the office that looked similar to those with anthrax. It was addressed to the editor.

We were concerned we could have been a target for the alleged terrorists. We considered ourselves a pull-no-punches paper like the New York Post. If they can get a letter, so can we.

Timlen crossed off the word "Editor" and put in "Jay Dunn."

Walking into the sports department, Timlen said "Jay, I have a letter for you."

Dunn was terrified. The letter did look similar to those anthrax letters.

The next day, Dunn was ready to press charges against Timlen saying "it was somebody pointing a gun at you."

He was right.

Bonfield and I met with Dunn, and Timlen's job was in jeopardy.

It was a foolish move—especially in light of the anthrax scares.

Dunn decided to drop the threat of bringing up charges.

Timlen was spared.

If something like that happened again, he would be terminated.

◆ ◆ ◆

It took two weeks before the readers were sick of anthrax. Our circulation was flattening out at about 49,000 to 50,000.

We had to keep it above 50,000.

Mike Fay stepped down and Edward Kelly, who worked in Bridgewater, N.J., took the post.

Managers under Bonfield were constantly changing. Jim Callahan, the controller under Bonfield for nearly three years, resigned—shortly after Bonfield told him "controllers are a dime a dozen."

Vic Billak replaced Callahan.

The infamous "dime a dozen" speech is typical of Bonfield. It was a defense mechanism. Instead of standing up for his workers in the heat of battle, he gives them the "dime a dozen" speech.

I received the "dime a dozen" speech when I complained I needed help in the sports department.

I wanted to hire Eric Ladley, who worked for me as night city editor at the Lebanon Daily News and was a former City Hall reporter for The Trentonian.

And boy, could he get pictures of babes.

I was both the editor and sports editor, and I needed somebody to help me with the administration of the sports department.

Ladley was an ideal choice.

Even though I had numerous vacancies, we needed corporate approval to fill them.

I complained to Bonfield about this. And I got the "dime a dozen" speech.

"I know you are upset," Bonfield said. "I know you may leave over this. But hey, editors are a 'dime a dozen.'"

The lack of standing up for his managers really hurt Bonfield.

He knew I was working 14 hours a day in the office—doing two jobs.

He didn't fight for the positions. While Jelenic ravaged the department with ridiculous complaints over the agate page, Bonfield didn't stand up to his boss for his staff.

He agreed with him.

He was a matador with corporate. Never standing up for the staff.

He never gave his staff a reason to work for him.

During his time as publisher, he's been through three controllers, two advertising representatives, five editors (you have to count me twice) and three circulation directors.

All tossed aside because Bonfield never defended them when the going got tough.

In my opinion, Bonfield left the managers taking bullets.

It was clear nobody in all departments liked or respected him. He was despised.

Schwartz had enemies in the building, but he stood up for his staff when needed. He was respected.

Bonfield, in my opinion, wasn't respected.

6

BLOODBATH

The Trentonian kept at 50,000—about 1,500 more than when I started in September.

The Sept. 11 attacks and the anthrax situation derailed the newsroom. It felt like we were operating in an emergency mode for the last two months.

Despite the pitfalls thanks to Jelenic and Bonfield, the paper was getting better.

"People are talking about the paper again," Sommers said.

We were connecting with the core readership we discarded three years earlier.

Sommers was a part of my plan to show actor Danny Glover's liberal colors.

We received word about Glover schedule to give a speech against the death penalty in Princeton.

It was a wonderful opportunity to get an easy front page lead.

I told Sommers to ask Glover about bin Laden. Should the butcher die?

It was painfully obvious for Glover to say no. Someone giving a speech against the death penalty will not arbitrarily say "bin Laden must die."

When Glover says he should die, we have a line.

Easy pickings.

Glover said bin Laden shouldn't die, and called the United States a "nation of terror."

You don't say those things when the country is at war.

We ran the headline SPARE BIN LADEN'S LIFE.

We were flooded with hundreds of e-mails expressing outrage over the story. Across the nation, people were boycotting Glover's work. Oliver North picked up the story and so did the Drudge Report.

The paper was drawing nationwide attention.

The roar was getting restored.

Through December, the crime-oriented lines were compelling enough to keep our circulation above 50,000. It was a significant victory for us.

We ran front pages like:

HIGH-SPEED TRAIN KILLS 3 TEENS

STEPSON SLAYS BARBOR

STEPSON SLAYS BUCKS HORSEMAN

GUARDS FIGHT TO DATE EX-CONS

2 WOMEN DIE IN COP CHASE

MADMAN STABS INFANT

MURDER AT HAMILTON FACILITY

This growth seemingly didn't matter for Jelenic and Bonfield if the sports section was a mess.

◆ ◆ ◆

After a three-month wait, Eric Ladley returned to The Trentonian as associate sports editor on Dec. 7.

He was being tabbed the savior of the sports section.

For the first couple of weeks, he lived up to his billings.

"The section has looked really good," Bonfield would say.

By the end of the week of Dec. 18, the roof was going to cave in—with Pukanecz saying "Ladley and (I) could go back to Lebanon for all I care."

A turbulent week.

◆ ◆ ◆

Rich Timlen was called The Cockroach.

The man had covered high school hockey for five years, and miraculously still had a job.

He survived.

He was on the firing line several times, and pulled off a Houdini act and escaped.

The Cockroach outlasted several nuclear outbursts from Bonfield, Pukanecz and Jelenic.

The Cockroach finally got squashed.

The Lawrenceville hockey tournament is considered by some CEOs who run newspaper chains as a prestigious showcase of the top high school hockey talent.

Timlen covered the tournament a year before and Lawrenceville lost a handful of games. The Big Red was playing in the ninth-place game of the tournament, and Timlen, who had worked two straight 10-plus hour days asked then sports editor Mark Schiele if he can leave early.

Schiele said OK.

Lawrenceville, the only area team in the tournament, won the game.

The next day, Jelenic raged.

Timlen received a memo stating—he faced possible termination. Timlen should have known better than to ask to leave such a "big" event early. He faced termination—even though his boss told him it was all right to leave.

Timlen somehow got out of the predicament and kept his job.

Long live the Cockroach.

This year, I told Timlen he had to cover all of the Lawrenceville games. He understood.

He covered all of the Lawrenceville games.

Nothing else.

The other games in the tournament involved teams not in our area—our readers don't give a rat's ass about Nichols from the Buffalo, N.Y., area.

Timlen reported who won the tournament, but all of the scores didn't appear in the paper.

On December 17, 2001, Bonfield was in a budget meeting with Jelenic—deciding the financial plan for 2002.

It was at this meeting they decided Rich Timlen would be terminated.

All because he didn't run all of the scores from the Lawrenceville hockey tournament.

Jelenic on the spot said everybody was expendable, and "the sun will rise again tomorrow."

The sun set on Rich Timlen.

Timlen, during our meeting, begged me to fire him. He called the entire situation "ridiculous."

Timlen was fired—only for the Lawrenceville tournament.

No anthrax hoax. It was for the failure to report all of the scores in a high school hockey tournament.

Timlen didn't leave with a bang however.

First, he destroyed all of the computer files with hockey school hockey statistics and phone numbers of the coaches.

Second, in the parking lot, he called Bonfield "a fucking asshole."

Editorial employees raced to the window to witness the possibility of Timlen belting Bonfield.

Instead, calling the publisher "a fucking asshole" was good enough for Timlen.

He left.

I was shaken. Bonfield knew it.

He called me later that night saying the corporations is upbeat about the direction of the paper. They have noticed the gains in circulation and believe the product is better.

I finally felt somewhat appreciated—even though I was forced to fire the first employee I hired. Maybe firing Timlen would get Jelenic off our back for a while.

Timlen's firing created numerous immediate problems. We run a weekly feature page on high school hockey in Wednesday's paper. This page features all-time stats, current leaders, state rankings and columns on high school teams.

It was a comprehensive page.

Timlen deleted all of the information out of the system.

We had to track down all of the statistics from scratch—and we had only 24 hours to get it done.

I had to appoint a high school hockey writer immediately.

Scott Frost got the call.

A full-time employee, Frost worked part of the time covering swimming and the remainder on night cops. Frost was a lazy, horrible night cops reporter.

One time he didn't want to check out cop activity across the street from the paper.

"It's too cold," he whined.

A guy with the last name of Frost wouldn't go out on an assignment because it was too cold. Sommers, the most versatile reporter in the paper, became the night cops reporter.

Frost, however, had a passion for local sports. He treated high school swimming like it was professional sports.

He might have been a disaster of a night cop reporter—but he was a solid swimming writer with a great deal of potential.

If he put the same passion into high school hockey as he did swimming, the section will be all right.

Frost accepted the beat.

Frost, Ladley and I came up with a plan to get the high school hockey page together. The part-time clerks would type in the statistics, Frost would cover a game and Esposito, who didn't want any part of high school hockey, agreed to work on a feature about a Lawrenceville coach who played with the Trenton Titans.

We seemingly had everything covered.

◆ ◆ ◆

Another result in the budget meeting was that Jelenic ordered me to have a permanent residence in the area by Dec. 31.

Jelenic was apparently convinced that I wasn't connected enough in the community to know much about local sports. Usually, an editor should live in the market because of being closer to news happenings.

Not here where "sports is the franchise."

I felt leery about moving to the region—ever since Pukanecz made a reference about me losing my job in September.

I was living in a Red Roof in during the week and would commute from Lebanon (at hour and 45 minute one-way trip) on the weekends.

But I wasn't in touch with the local sports scene.

Job stability wasn't glorious at The Trentonian—people were getting canned for poorly covering high school hockey tournaments and missing golf agate.

In my mind, the corporation loved the final product—that's what Bonfield told me after Timlen's firing.

I would get an apartment.

◆ ◆ ◆

On December 18, 2001, I took a day off—my first in three weeks.

Ladley and Frost knew what to do with the high school hockey page. But another problem developed, the high school hockey coaches found out about Timlen's firing, and some were refusing to report their results.

They were boycotting the paper.

Most of them were aware of the Jelenic situation, and this was a way for the coaches to fight back.

Things started falling apart.

On December 19, 2001, it became clear my second tour of duty as The Trentonian editor was near an end.

◆ ◆ ◆

The firing of Rich Timlen left a void in the sports operations. Timlen was fired and Jelenic seeming expected us to not miss a beat.

We missed big time.

The clerk who typed in the agate fucked up. She messed up the all-time statistics.

The high school page was filled with errors.

But one caught Jelenic's eyes.

Under the list of all-time CVC scoring leaders, Lee Jelenic was credited with 213 points.

Actually, Lee Jelenic had 228.

In the Trentonian, the No. 228 is like 715 in baseball.

The number should be etched in everybody's memory.

Also, the Times had the all-state high school girls soccer team. We didn't.

Pukanecz rushed to the Trentonian offices when I arrived.

He screamed at me.

"You and Eric Ladley could go back to Lebanon for all I care," Pukanecz said.

His tirade was right in front of Bonfield.

Bonfield was silent.

He didn't defend his editor—even as the vice president of news for the Journal Register Company was urging me to leave.

After Pukanecz stormed out of the office, Bonfield could only muster "I never seen Chuck like this."

Bonfield left me high and dry.

Then Bonfield slammed Ladley, "Eric might be over his head on this."

A week ago, Ladley was a shining star.

Two days ago, I was being hailed as a hero who boosted circulation. Now, we're dirt.

◆ ◆ ◆

The next couple of days it was nightmarish.

In my opinion, Jelenic was convinced somebody was out to get him—the saboteur who hadn't been nabbed in the last nine years still lurked.

He found transactions errors: New Haven is a UHL team, why does it say it's an AHL team in the transactions.

Everybody knows New Haven has an UHL team, right?

AP made the mistake. Maybe JRC should discontinue that service.

Mistakes in the ski report, latest lines and Little League stories.

Jelenic buried us daily.

We didn't run a story on former Camden graduate and Memphis standout Dajuan Wagner when he played Temple.

Jelenic ripped us.

Bonfield told Jelenic he saw the game on TV and assumed the sports department knew about it.

We didn't.

In my opinion, Bonfield was only interested in self-preservation, and he was more than willing to throw his staff in the line of fire.

I wasn't going to get an apartment.

I wasn't going to stay with the paper.

◆ ◆ ◆

On December 26, 2001, I walked into The Trentonian. Bonfield told me to call Pukanecz because there were problems in the sports section.

The Dec. 26 front page was A CHRISTMAS STOLEN—a tale about a family who had their gifts stolen. The day before, we led with THREE DIE IN HOLIDAY CRASH. Two solid front pages for the newspaper. The paper was on more solid circulation ground. We were retaining some of the readers gained from the attacks.

However, it didn't matter, the sports section was fucked up—again. I did the section myself on Christmas night.

The Trentonian was so shorthanded because of terminations and an unfilled vacancies, the editor had to put out the entire sports section.

I worked on the front and back pages and produced the entire sports section.

Bonfield decided he wanted to talk to me before I called Pukanecz.

"We don't think Frost should be covering high school hockey himself," Bonfield said, "especially this Lawrence tournament. Chuck thinks Espo should help out."

Bonfield had a pile of pages of the paper—markups of what Jelenic and Pukanecz considered mistakes. Those mistakes, in their view, were killing the circulation numbers.

I was furious. They had a week to second-guess the Frost move. Esposito was in Connecticut visiting his family.

The Lawrence tournament was already under way. They could have first-guessed me the week before.

The silence indicated to me that they were satisfied with Frost.

I was fed up.

"That's it," I said. "I'm not getting my apartment."

That was basically telling Bonfield: I quit.

I needed to have an apartment in the circulation area or else.

"You guys are not committed to me," I said. "You are not committed to winning."

I removed the key to the building and my office from the key holder. It was in my right hand.

Bonfield was faced losing an editor—a damn good one. He had to try to keep me.

All he could muster was "call Chuck."

"I'm not going to call Chuck."

I dropped the key on his desk.

I walked out of the office.

Never to return again.

◆ ◆ ◆

Eric Ladley resigned as associate sports editor a couple of days later, and returned to work for the Lebanon Daily News.

Pukanecz got his wish: Ladley and I were living in Lebanon again.

For Bonfield, Pukanecz and Jelenic, the "sun will rise again."

Epilogue

The Trentonian went from a must-read publication with a healthy circulation to dull, lifeless publication with little or no future.

In my opinion, David Bonfield takes the primary blame.

Ironically, most newspaper industry gurus might consider Bonfield a hero for trying to clean up a sleazy publication.

That sleazy publication was liked by the Trenton readers.

That's all it matters.

In my opinion, Bonfield didn't want those blue-collar readers—they weren't the ideal type for advertisers.

Those blue-collar readers were tossed aside—in favor of a more "intellectual, community-minded crowd." He wanted a paper that was classy.

Newspaper editors and publishers push stories telling readers what they should read. They should let the readers dictate what's in the paper. But some editors and publishers put personal interest in front of the readers.

For example, I hate NASCAR, and don't even consider it a sport. It's more technology than sport.

Would I consider even pulling out NASCAR out of the sports pages?

Hell, no. It's too popular with readers.

Somehow, it's OK for editors and publishers put their personal preferences in the news section. They devalue crime and place emphasis on issues they personally want to read.

That's what Bonfield did in 1998. He ignored the core readership and got so wrapped in making the paper "respectable" in his world.

What he got was an irrelevant piece of trash.

A relevant paper is read. An irrelevant paper is not read.

The Trentonian was irrelevant under Bonfield.

A newspaper must run what the readers consider newsworthy. The Trenton reader relished hard-hitting crime stories and sexy articles about celebrities.

They liked those stories that made them say, "holy shit." They like stories about sex in a mortuary.

They liked those stories that made them laugh, cry and got them enraged.

They like an editorial page with an active, strong, subjective voice.

They enjoyed the geek of the week.

They liked local Page 6 girls—not some glamour babe from Los Angeles or Russia or Florida.

They wanted girls from the Greater Trenton Area.

The Trentonian in early 1998 connected with the readership. It lived up to its slogan, "No.1 in the hearts of the people."

Bonfield wanted to be "No. 1 in the hearts of *important* people."

The average Joe could go to hell.

The Trentonian had carved out an amazing niche in a small market that miraculously has two newspapers.

As the circulation slid, Bonfield realized he had a loser. Excuses starting coming up why the circulation dropped.

The recession. Chronic mistakes in the sports section. The people will realize this is a clean product now, they will return.

They didn't.

The readers hold the key to a newspaper.

Readers determine what is newsworthy. They know what they want. But this industry is filled with Bonfield-types who are preaching what readers should be in interested in.

Readers know what they want.

"I'm very happy to be back in the Trenton area," Bonfield said in the story on The Trentonian business page about his appointment.

"After I reacquaint myself with the area. I'm going to be getting actively involved in the community.

"I hope to work with business and community leaders to make Greater Trenton a better place to live. I'll be reaching out to community groups, asking them to help me get involved."

In my opinion, he reached out the community's elite—not the average reader.

Bonfield in 1998 rammed his philosophy down readers' throats—claiming the community leaders wanted it this way. He wanted the paper to makes lives' better—instead of simply reporting the news.

More leads with state politics—less crime. More business and local sports stories led the paper.

All feeble attempts to gain readers. All failed.

The readers are the ultimate judges, and they overwhelming rejected Bonfield's product.

Instead of focusing of rebuilding the news product—they harassed the sports section.

By their actions, they thought most of the sales problems stemmed from local sports.

In their world, it seemed that only local sports could save the circulation. It will determine The Trentonian's fate. The sports department is making too many mistakes in Jelenic's view. Those mistakes are driving away the readers.

Wrong.

Under those conditions, The Trentonian will die.

Even though circulation figures totally contradicted the claims. Whenever we had a special section for high school sports, there wasn't a jump in sales.

There was a bounce in sales for NFL preview section.

There was a remarkable increase for a college football section.

Put high school sports to lead the front page, the sales slumped.

Those are the facts.

But those facts are ignored.

Box scores on the Web site, in their view, hurt sales. Forget about the front page headline that doesn't make sense or a lead with state politics.

Jelenic's ranting made the work atmosphere impossible to grow. The paper will stagnate if he continues to get involved in the day-to-day operations of the product.

The sports section lacked stability—and the talent pool decreased because of knee-jerk firings.

After Ladley and I left the paper, a part-timer was elevated to full-time status and replaced Frost as the high school hockey writer.

Frost was too busy whining about his low salary to take advantage of the opportunity. Instead of covering only hockey, Frost felt obligated to also covering swimming.

Frost stretched himself too thin. He melted to the pressure.

Another part-timer filling a vacancy in desperation. A trademark for the Trentonian over the past three years.

The Trentonian lost its compass in the news department—thanks to Bonfield's attempt to push his own philosophy in 1998.

The Trentonian downfall is typical of that of the industry. Preaching editors and publishers telling what the readers what they should read.

Lecturing them that they should care about issue stories like wastewater and political finance reform. Selling newspapers isn't rocket science. You find out what the readers really want by studying the circulation figures. Unfortunately, intellectual egos get in the way at most papers—preventing any true sales growth.

In a 1995 letter in the American Society of Newspaper Editors (ASNE) Bulletin, Sandy Schwartz stressed the importance of "a paper that shouts from the rack, the counter or the porch: 'Pick me up and read me!'"

"Sadly, what comes through is that today's editors, well-meaning, intelligent, sincere thought they may be are utterly devoid of the passionate love of real news that makes a newspaper great," he wrote.

The Trentonian once had a special link with its readers—and its solid news judgment carried the day.

The link shattered in 1998.

The newspaper industry is filled with tales like The Trentonian. Editors and publisher totally disconnected from the readers really want. This disconnect leads to slumping sales.

"You want to make newspapers relevant?" Schwartz once wrote. "They way you do it is to put out free-wheeling, hard-hitting, strongly opinionated newspapers. In other words, go back to the basics of 'Print the news and raise hell!'"

One of The Trentonian's slogans used to be "Love us. Hate us. Read us."

In 1997-98, the readers enjoyed the paper that raised hell.

Now, they don't care.

Afterword

After leaving the Trentonian, I started to work on this book.

The Trentonian was trying to pick up the pieces of its never-ending mess.

In February 2002, they actually named a sports editor.

Dave Larviere, a copy editor at the New York Post, accepted the offer. It's Larviere's first managerial job.

On paper, it's a dream job.

In reality, it's a nightmare.

It will be a tough test for Larviere.

In his first week, Larviere had a personnel crisis. On March 1, 2002, Scott Esposito resigned after getting into trouble after an altercation with another employee.

Esposito was fed up in dealing with the pressure of working three hockey beats and working the desk three nights a week.

In my opinion, Esposito had been in the crosshairs for nearly five years. He survived. But the pressure was too much.

Esposito is a passionate worker and will succeed in any endeavor he enters because of his work ethic.

A tireless worker, Esposito will rebound.

The Trentonian won't.

Esposito exceptionally covered high school hockey, Princeton hockey and the Titans. The next hockey writer will never be able to even come close to Esposito's level.

The Trentonian desperately looked for a replacement. Pukanecz and Bonfield won't be able to leave such an important beat open too long.

It will likely take a couple of days before Jelenic complains about a box score that doesn't add up correctly. Esposito's departure will decimate not just the sports section—the entire paper.

Bonfield and company told Larviere not to worry about the night operation and step back and look at the big picture.

That's what they told Schiele.

Months later, Schiele had to work nights, and eventually was canned. I had to work nights because of the alleged sports woes, and after a four months, I got fed up with getting pressure about sports when the emphasis for the paper's growth should have been on the struggling news department. I left.

Larviere will go through that period. Bonfield will make him work nights and put intense pressure on him to solve the problem.

Pukanecz is seemingly under fire for the Trentonian woes. The vice president of news for the Journal Register Company had to work nights to design and edit Trentonian sports pages. He was being held accountable because there were no bodies left.

"I get it worse (than everybody)," Pukanecz allegedly told a staffer. "I get it every day."

Ironically, Bonfield says that all the time.

Nobody will have a pity party for both of them. A manager must effective guard his staff from outrageous attacks. Must stand up for his workers. The workers are the ones who deal with the firings and the shortage of staff. They are the ones who have to add the box scores of every sport in the paper—and make deadline the same time.

Schwartz received the same heat. Most of it never trickled down the staff.

For some reason, Bonfield has been unable to even put up any defense for his team.

Because of this, jaded staff members who aren't fortunate enough to leave The Trentonian started a pool in how long Lavantier will last.

Bets ranged from 10 days to nine months.

There's a very good chance that when this book is finally published, he will no longer be with The Trentonian.

◆　◆　◆

For all purposes, The Trentonian is dead.
Finished.
Through.
Newspapers don't experience quick, painless deaths. That's too easy.
Readers don't all of a sudden decide to abandon a newspaper, forcing the publication to pull the plug and put it out of its misery.
Newspapers slowly die. It's systematic. Slow. Painful.
The Trentonian—under its current inept leadership—is methodically dying.
Soon, it won't be around.
When the obituary of The Trentonian is written, look back to July 13, 1998 as the official date of decline.
That is when David Bonfield took over the paper.
In 1996, The Trentonian increased its price from 25 cents to 35 cents. In a short period of time, the paper plummeted from 74,000 to 60,000.
In 1997, Sandy Schwartz, a hard-working staff and I stopped the bleeding.
The patient was stabilized.
In 1998, Bonfield arrived with grandiose plans. He thought the paper was sleazy. He thought the patient was still dying.
He made a tragic misdiagnosis.
His moves in 1998 immediately put the paper on its fatal course—a course that will lead to The Trentonian's demise.
Another date in Trentonian history to remember is March 24, 2002.
It was the day of the worst news decision in the history of the paper.
This decision is symbolic of the Trentonian's fall.

O.J. Simpson, one of the most controversial figures in the last 100 years, partied in Trenton. Simpson, the football great whose trial was the center of the universe for nearly a year.

He's in Trenton—having a good time.

What did The Trentonian lead with the next day?

The paper led with a preview of the high school girls state basketball final between Trenton and Willingboro.

Linda Lisanti, who is developing into a solid reporter despite the lack of guidance in at the paper, interviewed Simpson.

It wasn't enough though.

In the views of the honchos at the paper, an advance of a high school basketball game is a more significant story than the visit by one of the most notorious and colorful figures in U.S. history.

Two months earlier, the paper led with the finals of the Trentonian Cup high school hockey tournament. This isn't a state final—no it's the final of a regular season tournament. OH, WHAT A KNIGHT! screamed the front page depicting West Windsor-Plainsboro North's victory in the final.

But Bonfield, Pukanecz and Jelenic decided it was the biggest news story of the day. A regular-season high school hockey game was selected over a drug kingpin on the loose in the city.

Once again, it stems from the warped view that local sports coverage is the future of the paper.

The readers are losing—big time.

The pathetic news judgment and lackluster leadership of the newspaper is gradually eroding the paper. Take a ride on Route 1—the highway that cuts through Trenton.

Years ago, the highway was filled with billboards for The Trentonian.

"Love us. Hate us. Read us," the billboards read.

The paper was a fixture in the city; it was a paper that connected with its readers.

Now, the paper chooses girls basketball over O.J. Simpson visiting the circulation area.

One by one, the readers are drifting away.

Today, those billboards are gone. The Trentonian's presence on the highway was cut because of budget woes.

These cutbacks are the result of failure.

First, it's the billboards.

Then it's the paper itself.

The end is near.

◆ ◆ ◆

Word of this book began to spread like wildfire. When the publishing company ran the entire edition of it on the Web, the buzz dominated the paper.

Workers hit my promotional Web site in droves.

After a couple of days and thousands of hits on the site, the company's bigwigs decided to block the site from the workers.

◆ ◆ ◆

I served as editor of the Trentonian for about two years, working for the glory days under Schwartz and the dark ages with Bonfield.

That's more than 600 front pages (and back pages) I had to conceive. All of those papers had one purpose: To sell the maximum amount of newspapers.

We had some clear-cut winners and some world-class clunkers. Here are some of the best and worst headlines that led the front page (headlines are in **bold CAPS**):

THE WINNERS

KIDS MUG CORPSE: This headline was significant because it showed how our readers loved basic crime stories. We took a city slaying that most newspapers would scoff as not newsworthy and turned it into a hard-hitting story. On slow news day, Trentonian City Editor Paul Mickle would frequently say "what we need right now is a story like freakin' 'KIDS MUG CORPSE.'" It was the standard.

Under the headline, we ran this deck:

"Pack led by 11-year-old swipes guns, ammo, cash and drugs from shootout scene."

With the inside headline, "YOUNG JACKELLS," Venezia rewrote the lead:

"A mob of looters led by an 11-year-old boy swarmed over a city murder scene in the minutes before cops arrived, stealing guns, cash and even bullets right from the dead man's pocket, police said."

It doesn't get better than this.

SEX IN THE MORTUARY: Linda Dougherty, the Trentonian's fireball of a horse racing writer, said when she saw this front page she was energized by it. There was going to be nothing that would stop her from buying that issue.

It was one of the best sellers in 1997.

Venezia's lead was a work of art:

"A prominent funeral director turned his mortuary into a cadaver-packed bordello—making love with an intern on the embalming room floor, cavorting around in a towel and demanding sex sessions inside a coffin, the woman is charging in a lawsuit."

A great newspaper will scream at the reader from the newsstand, "please read this."

SEX IN THE MORTUARY flew off the newsstands.

SEX KITTENS IN THE CLASSROOM: This was an enterprise package people would like to read. Teachers are vulnerable to sexy sirens who lure them into a tangled web.

This package beats most issue-related crap most newspapers will produce today like hard-hitting packages on wastewater or HOV lanes.

I'll take the sex kittens every time.

MOM TURNS TRICKS AS TOTS BURN: You cannot get more dramatic than that. It was Blackwell's first story with The Trentonian.

Under the inside headline written by copy editor Mary Mooney, "MOM-STROSITY," Blackwell wrote this lead—his first with The Trentonian:

"A heroin-addicted hooker turned tricks on the city streets as her three children perished in the flames of Sunday night's Chambersburg house fire, cops said."

SLEEPING BEAUTY: It was the first of what we called the "powder blue" series. For tragic stories with a significant human interest, we would use a classy, serif font with a power blue background (like the heavens) with a picture of the victim. This victim in this case was an attractive coed who collapsed and went into a coma after a workout.

Powder blue stories became well known in the office. They focused on the human-element of stories. Usually, the front page will have dramatic paragraph for a deck.

The SLEEPING BEAUTY deck read:

"Two weeks ago, Tanya Tewfik was a vibrant, athletic college freshman. Than a workout on a treadmill changed all that. The exertion drove her into cardiac arrest, and eventually, into a coma.

"Now, doctors are baffled as a beautiful teenager continues to hover between life and death, waiting with family by her side for a miracle that may never come."

The "powder blue" effect produced stunning results at the newsstand.

One time a Chambersburg man who aspired to be a chef died suddenly.

We led Page 1 with the headline "A Dream Cut Short" with a titled photo of the chef in his outfit holding a pan.

Underneath the headline, we ran the following:

"Beloved Chambersburg chef Joseph Correia would have been named valedictorian today at the Restaurant School of Philadelphia's Class of 1997.

"But the culinary king's promising career was cut short Thursday by a deadly heart attack just minutes after a young thug blasted his home with a BB gun.

"Now, as cops search for the gunman, Correia's grieving friends and family are demanding justice for his tragic death."

A month later, we ran a similar "power blue" front page on a family who won a lawsuit after their son died in a worksite accident.

We led Page 1 with the headline "A Hollow Victory" next to a photo of the victim.

Underneath, we ran the following paragraph:

"It's been three years since landscaper David Weissman was killed in a tragic accident, when a wall of shoddy soil collapsed and turned this promising 21-year-old's worksite into a dirt-filled tomb.

"Now after winning a lengthy legal battle, his heartbroken relatives are piecing their lives back together."

A classy touch.

SEX DUNGEON BUSTED: The dominatrix bought numerous classified ads in the paper.

We pulled out one of those ads and ran it on page 1.

Todd Venezia came up with brilliant bullet points that appeared under the headline on the cover.

"IN RAID COPS FIND:

- WHIPS AND CHAINS

- HANDCUFFS

- SUSPENSION RACK

- BONDAGE TABLE

- SPAKING BENCH

- SYRINGES AND ENEMAS

- AND LOTS MORE!"

Venezia knew the importance of framing the story correctly on Page 1. Most "mainstream" newspapers probably would have written a dull headline like "Cops arrest woman on morals charges."

A fat dominatrix helped us honor Valentine's day with style.

Nancy Houtz—with Venezia's help—put together this lead:

"MIDDLETOWN TWP., Pa. —Valentine's Day was ruined this year for a host of local perverts after police raided a suburban sex dungeon and arrested an obese 43-year-old dominatrix."

INTERNUTS: Bob Shields, who was truly a tabloid genius, came up with this one for the story about the 39 members of the cult that committed suicide in order to hop on a comet.

JOKE JAIL: Under the bold face type we had three bullet points: "No Fence, No Guards, No Locks."

The lead read: "A private prison housing 300 criminals in Trenton has less security than a convenience store—the only thing standing between these prisoners and freedom is a piece of paper."

We credited this information to a Trentonian probe. This was an inside joke in the newsroom—ridiculing the pompous nature of our business. This probe lasted all of two days. It started on Friday night when Paul Mickle found out about it and ended Saturday when Nancy Houtz did the story. The Times did absolutely nothing. It took Mickle, an old-fashioned news hound with a great nose, and Venezia to dig it up. Everyone else would have just run this story as brief.

Some guy just wanders out of a prison and most people wouldn't have cared. Mickle and Venezia turned this story into a legitimate, comprehensive piece.

BRAIN DEAD AFTER SUCKER PUNCH

TV HUNK CRUISES CITY FOR STRIPPERS: George Clooney will likely never visit Trenton again after we depicted his night at a local nightclub. A gossip legend was born.

Reporter Chris Wilson rode his success on this story to a gig with Star magazine. He now works for Page Six—for the New York Post.

MINISTER WANTED ME TO DRESS LIKE HOOKER: Now who wouldn't read that story?

GRANNY ON LAM: Any story about bad grandmas will sell.

STATE BIG IS SPEED DEMON: This headline didn't sell that well, but Erik Lukens showed how crafty he was during his time with the Trentonian. Lukens, while driving home on Route 1 in Princeton, noticed a state vehicle whiz by him. Lukens estimated he was going about 80 mph.

Lukens got the license plate number and tracked it down to the Human Services Commissioner of New Jersey. The spokesperson actually confirmed the commissioner was speeding. That spokesperson probably was shopping his resume the next day.

Lukens produced this clever lead:

"If the wheels of state government turned half as fast as the ones on Department of Human Services Commissioner William Waldman's car, we'd all get our tax refunds by April 20."

TEACH, TEEN HAD SEX IN SCHOOL: This sparked our hard-hitting SEX KITTENS IN THE CLASSROOM enterprise package. A week later we had the story STUDENT BRAGGED ABOUT SEX WITH TEACH. We unlocked details from the girl's diary.

Those were the good ole days.

CRYBABY KILLER LOSES COOL: The Pitbulls were a knuckle-headed, mob wannabe gang, which killed a man because they thought he was a rat. Brus Post, a leader of the gang, whined in court because he wasn't allowed to wear his dress suit. He wanted to look like a mobster—not a punk in an orange jump suit.

MEGAN ASKED FOR IT: People were wondering what was up with the Trentonian for not leading with the Jesse Timmendequas trial. We did and immediately became the center of a firestorm.

PITBULL CALLS JUDGE SLUT: How many times will you be able to use the word "SLUT" in a 200-point headline?

The word slut sells newspapers.

A couple of weeks later, the Pitbull involved wrote a letter to us.

He said the judge should shut up and "get back into the kitchen."

GET BACK IN THE KITCHEN turned into another lead in this ongoing feud.

Nothing is better than getting mail from inmates. Usually, they want the address of the Page 6 model. Sometimes they want us to give the model the letter.

"Right now, I'm in jail," one letter read. "But I will be out in a couple of months, and you can ride my Camaro."

TRAILER BARK: More than 40 dogs were found in a trailer; what else can you say?

COP'S LECTURE STUNS NUNS: A cop made a sexual remark about his nightstick in front of a group of nuns.

MICE INFEST WAL-MART: Sometimes, this is what you get when you don't advertise with the paper.

MICE DROPPINGS IN SAM'S CLUB EASTER CANDY: Ditto.

$700G GROPE: The Republican Party chairman was sued for sexual harassment and the state made a $700,000 settlement. Schwartz wanted the headline to read "$1M GROPE. But we achieved what we wanted: Getting the word grope in a headline.

STRIP-CLUB BLOODBATH: A man was shot dead outside a well-known strip club; we ran the picture of the corpse—uncovered—on Page 1.

STABBED FOR BEING LATE TO LUNCH: An oldster stabs another because he got sick of waiting for him.

TEEN FORCED TO MAKE SEX TAPES: This front page is a favorite of mine because the story wasn't as good as the headline. This was a teen boy, but we made no mention of it on page 1. Readers immediately think the victim is a girl, which makes the story more compelling. Readers get squeamish with stories about boys have sex with men. It sold well—because we never mentioned the gender of the victim. Readers assumed it was a girl.

CITY TEACHERS CAUGHT RUNNING DRUGS

HERO DOG BAGS BURGLAR: Heroic animals sell. We need more "Lassies" in the world.

DOUG LOST COOL: Trenton Mayor Doug Palmer got into a shouting match with a prominent restaurant owner over parking.

"I know Mike Raffaele, and he would never run a story like this," Palmer told reporter Dom Yanchunas.

I did.

Yanchunas wrote this lead:

"A city restaurateur has accused Mayor Doug Palmer of shouting profanity and intimidating him after Hizzoner waded into a parking dispute last week between the Chambersburg eatery and a nearby rival."

JAILHOUSE SEX KITTEN: A 18-year-old girl was jailed for being an accomplice in the slaying of a businessman. According to a Trenton legend, she was extremely sexy.

Mickle once wrote a story on her telling readers in incredible how sexy this girl was—but he never got the photo.

She became Mickle's obsession.

Mickle constantly wrote her name on his notes. Even though we didn't have a picture of her, we were able to run a story how she had "improper contact" with guards in the pokey. Great stuff.

Two years later, The Trentonian took her picture in court—she wasn't that hot.

PRISON GUARD'S TALE OF TERROR: A guard gives details on a wild prison riot in Trenton.

COPS NAB DRUG DEALER—HE'S 81.

DEAD MAN'S HAND: Todd Venezia proved why he's a tabloid genius. This was a scumbag murder: A man was shot to death over a card game. Tremendous. But Venezia gave me an idea that was brilliant. We ran the headshot of the victim with a collage of cards—aces and eights.

A wonderful touch.

GROUNDHOG ATE MY DIAMOND: A pet masterpiece that most papers ignored or turned into a brief. The next day we ran a tease, "GROUNDHOG 'RELEASES' DIAMOND."

ARE THEY IN HEAVEN?: This is often mocked as one of my worst front pages. No way. We covered a funeral for nearly 40 pets that died in a fire. We gave it the "powder blue" treatment.

Most newspaper executives would frown on this—especially in light of us picking the pet funeral over a story about Trenton schools avoiding a teachers' strike.

Pet funerals were more relevant to our readers.

SCARED JESSE HIDES IN CELL: A story how Jesse Timmendequas is bullied by "Mudman" Simon in death row. Simon ironically was beaten to death by another death-row inmate, Ambrose Harris, a year later.

Unfortunately for The Trentonian, Simon's death wasn't good enough to lead the paper.

NABBED FOR 152 CAR ROBS: A simple crime that was hot with our readers. It was one of the top 25 selling papers in 1997.

This story didn't run in any other paper—none of those publications apparently did consider it newsworthy.

MERCER MAN HAS…EINSTEIN'S BRAIN IN JAR: This is a true story, but it didn't sell as well as it should have. "It seemed too crazy," then-Circulation Director Jim Farrell said. "It looked like something somebody will read in the Weekly World News."

We had a picture with an old man hold a jar with Big Al's brains on Page 1.

MARV LIKES 3-WAY SEX!: A story was about testimony against sportscaster Marv Albert in the sex case against him. The headline made the paper a talker.

HUMAN TORCH RUNS TO FIREHOUSE: On this day, Paul Mickle attended a seminar sponsored by Mercer County on how to cover suicides and how to be tasteful. Meanwhile, a man sets himself on fire in a suicide attempt. Apparently, he had second thoughts and ran nearly a mile to the firehouse for help.

The lead of the story read like this: "A man distraught over his wife's infidelity, soaked himself with lighter fluid and set himself on fire yesterday, then ran flaming down the street as scores of lookers watched in horror."

We didn't care about tastes. We wanted sales, and this story was red hot.

'CANDY BOY' WAS STRANGLED
LONELY GEEK, 15, KILLED CANDY BOY
EDDIE'S KILLER MOLESTS BOYS IN JAIL
TALK SHOW SPARKED LOCAL RIOT: Two guests from the Jerry Springer show got in a fight that sparked a wild melee at a local bar. Any story involving Springer is a winner in Trenton. That issue, which also had a poster girl, was the best-selling paper in 1998.

Here's the lead:

"Two women and their lovelorn mates still hot from a recent appearance on the wild, sleazy and often seedy Jerry Springer talk show erupted into a riot involving 200 people yesterday afternoon."

JULIA'S GREAT ADVENTURE: Julia Roberts tried to celebrate her birthday in our circulation area; she obviously didn't learn from Clooney's experience.

KING OF THIEVES: This was the legendary Bob Shields' final front page with The Trentonian.

The story was about the "Bank Bomber," a man who robbed banks by making tellers believe he had a bomb. He robbed nearly 20 banks in three months. Reporter Dom Yanchunas ran a story—writing that the "Bank Bomber" was one of the most prolific robbers in history. He was more prolific than Dillinger.

We ran a big photo of the suspect at large and in two days he was nabbed—thanks to the Trentonian front page.

GANGSTA RAPPERS BUSTED: A couple of rappers were caught with firearms after being pulled over by cops. It's a favorite of mine—despite Schwartz proclaiming the "story sucked."

TERROR IN PRINCETON: A shooting and a wild bank robbery with a chase in Princeton. If a story happens in Princeton, all the media outlets care. If it occurs in Trenton, it's not news.

This was easily the best-selling paper that week—routing the issue with Gov. Whitman's razor-thin victory over Democrat Jim McGreevey.

HOSTAGE DATED SLAIN GUNMAN: This was the headline for the fourth day of coverage of the Princeton bank robbery. Other favorites from this saga included: MOM WAS OFFERED SLAIN ROBBER'S CUT and PARTY ENDS FOR LAST BANK BANDIT.

DISGRACED!: A story about Trenton's Public Safety Director who allegedly bilked $270Gs from two elderly widows. An editor must not be afraid to use a headline like this—it made this front page more powerful.

BABY DIES IN MALL MISHAP: Officials at the Quaker Bridge Mall told David Bonfield the paper "was irrelevant." Bonfield, of course, believed them. This is one of those "irrelevant" stories.

5-FOOT GATOR ON CITY STREET: This led the Thanksgiving edition of the Trentonian.

TEMPEST IN A D-CUP: A story how one town in Bucks County wanted to get rid of visiting Hooters girls. Lukens dazzled us with this headline. The story gave us a perfect excuse to run a large picture of a shapely Hooters girl.

LAST FLING IN HAWAII FOR POLS: The story depicts how several Jersey politicians who were leaving office took a junket to Hawaii. This is one the few political stories to make the list. Sam Guerrero made a collage of Hawaiian sights and we ran the mugshots of two politicians in a postcard that said "Greetings from Hawaii."

The overline of the front page read: LAME DUCK LUAU.

The pols were burned by Blackwell's lead, not the Hawaiian sun:

"Two lame-duck legislators went on a sun-splashed junket in Hawaii this week, charging taxpayers for their stay in a beachfront luxury hotel replete with waterfalls, cruise ships and a nightclub where singer Don Ho croons his tropical tunes to appreciative fans."

SMOKING GOWN: The story about Monica Lewinsky's famous dress. We ran the headline, BILL ZIPS HIS LIPS the next day.

BOY SETS TEACHER'S HAIR ON FIRE

HERO TEEN SLAIN AT KEG PARTY: A simple human-interest story brought in a lot of readers. A typical example of how reporters shouldn't simply write from the police report. The emotional element of the story was done—thanks to persistent reporting by Yanchunas.

PSYCHO HUBBY KILLS ANOTHER WIFE: The headline tells the story.

WILD TEENS RUN AMOK: It was a slow news day but we strung together four instances of teen mischief for the front page. The next day, Trenton Mayor Doug Palmer called an emergency press conference to address the "issue." And it helped us get another front page "SAVAGE TEENS."

We made something out of nothing and at the same time, made our community better. Most newspapers work in vain for years to achieve that goal.

BEAUTY-SHOP BANDIT: We kicked off 1998 with this issue. Reporters' Dom Yanchunas and Ralph Tasgal double-teamed this story about a crowbar-wielding thug who was robbing area beauty shops.

Most newspapers would have made this a brief with a composite picture on Page 8B. Not this paper

You can't go wrong with hard-hitting story with good-looking hairdressers and a composite picture of the evil bandit on the cover.

Yanchunas wrote this lead: "A money-grubbing thug terrorized women hairstylists with a tire iron in three Burlington County salons this week, making off with the day's take and even swiping the gals' tips out of their jars, cops said yesterday."

How cruel.

Most newspapers led with a story telling readers that "today is the first day of the new year."

Some actually consider it news.

BEAUTY-SHOP BANDIT helped bring in the new year—Trentonian style.

PRINCIPAL BANS STUDENTS FROM LIBRARY: Jon Blackwell received a bizarre tip from a teacher.

Nate Jones, an elementary school principal who was also an aspiring politician had locked down the library—using it for his campaign for City Council. Blackwell had to sneak into the school to find out if the strong accusation was true.

There was no other way.

Blackwell found out it was true, but Jones had him arrested.

We ran a package—including a story about Blackwell's arrest.

Here's an except from that story:

"Trentonian Executive Editor Michael Raffaele reacted with dismay to Jones' heavy-handed treatment of the press on tax-payer funded property.

"'These charges are an outrage,' he said. 'We will fight this.'

"Raffaele also said: 'A teacher from this school pleaded with us to come over and investigate this situation. How else is the public going to find out about the library being closed to the students.'"

Blackwell had to pay a fine.

From then on, Jones became known as the "Nightmare Principal."

KILL YOUR DOG—OR ELSE: Kim Haban—with the help from Venezia—had this lead:

"WALL—A major insurance company has ordered a family to put their 8-year-old dog to sleep or forfeit their homeowner's insurance—all because the protective pooch bit a visitor's hand."

Thanks to the front page, the insurance company backed off.

A suspect's dad charges…FAMILY COVERUP IN CISSY'S MURDER: The mysterious 1989 murder of beloved Princeton socialite Emily "Cissy" Stuart became an obsession of Schwartz.

Each year in the first week in April, The Trentonian would roll out an anniversary package. In 1992, HER KILLER WALKS AMONG US is one of the most famous Trentonian covers.

In 1997, we had the front page, NO JUSTICE FOR CISSY—and there hadn't been any new leads in nearly six years.

Jon Blackwell, a history buff, was able to kick it up a notch in 1998 with a fresh angle.

"On the ninth anniversary of this town's most mysterious murder," Blackwell wrote, "a suspect's father has leveled a explosive new charge at the sons of stabbing victim Emily 'Cissy' Stuart—claiming they know who the killer is, but won't tell police."

Schwartz beamed over the story.

COED KILLED BY MOSQUITO: One of the toughest decision I've made at the Trentonian. What do you lead with: A sexy coed who dies of encephalitis during a trip to Tanzania or an arm with the name "Steve" on it being found in a Dumpster.

I couldn't lose with that choice.

COPS SEEK REST OF 'STEVE': I didn't want to neglect good old "Steve" —so we made him the lead a day after COED KILLED BY A MOSQUITO.

'STEVE' WAS A MOB HITMAN

TEEN DIES CAR SURFING: Trentonian reporter Chris Dolmetsch insists the victim wasn't car surfing.

I don't know what you call it when a kid tries to stand up on the front of a moving car. This story had a strong human element with the death of a beloved high school wrestler.

BUGS IN THE BOOZE AT KATMANDU: In Trenton, bugs in somebody's booze may be the downfall of your bar. It's a step below actually watering down drinks. Somehow, KatManDu survived after this.

PRINCIPAL REFUSED TO FEED STUDENTS

SEX PILL FRENZY IN JERSEY: Viagra was booming, and we wouldn't be doing our jobs if we didn't address it.

BARON'S CASINO RAKED IN MILLIONS
SHED BOY NEEDED TOUGH LOVE
NEWBORN DEAD IN GAS STATION TIOLET
Nobody's laughing at…COUNCIL CLOWNS: Jon Blackwell profiles the bumbling Trenton City Council.

KING OF 'JACKS NABBED: A serial carjacker was captured; we put his headshot on a jack of diamonds card.

RAPE SUSPECT NABBED—HE'S 84!: Even though the Associated Press broke the story, Bonfield thought we made it up.

MIKE GOES BERSERK AT HEARING: We went bonkers over covering Mike Tyson's hearing in Trenton.

FATAL WRECK ON PIKE: This front page was like "Action News" in print. We had teases of a woman who jumped off a bridge because she thought she was too ugly.

The tease read: BRIDGE JUMPER CRIES: I WANT A NEW FACE

Another tease read: GIRL CRUSHED AT CARNIVAL.

COP SHOOTS SLEEPING BABY: A cop accidentally shot a baby who was sleeping on a couch during a drug raid. When the officers were breaking into the house, the piece of the door landed on the trigger. This headline sold well—even though it didn't seem true.

Houtz wrote: "A city cop armed with an assault rifle accidentally shot a sleeping 16-month-old baby yesterday as a squad of fellow officers launched a pre-dawn crack raid, Police Chief Earnest Williams said."

This was a tough period for Trenton cops because they shot and killed 14-year-old Jenny Hightower during a police chase just weeks earlier.

Hightower was a passenger with Hubert Moore, who was driving a stolen vehicle. Moore tried to run over the officers, and in an attempt to save themselves, the officers open fire—killing Hightower. Moore was arrested.

ICE CREAM MAN DIES IN CRASH: "Everybody knows who the ice cream man is," Todd Venezia told a skeptical Bonfield. "This is a tragedy."

It was. And a rarity: It was the good seller. Good-selling papers were rare in August 1998.

SON BEATS UP MOM, 85: The overline of this front page is one of my best: "HE'S ONE TOUGH GUY."

This story broke a streak of ridiculous Sunday political leads. This Sunday paper boosted sales for a change.

DRUG QUEENPINS: We were desperate for a Sunday line. Usually, Sunday lines must be planned in advance—usually a hard-hitting news feature story. Something we would have available for the Sunday paper—just in case nothing newsworthy occurs on Saturday.

We were scratching on the bottom of the barrel. I had reporter David Hoffman working on a package on these high school girls who were busted with running a narcotics ring.

Good stuff, but we needed a picture of the girls.

Artwork in most cases is more important the story itself. Photos add drama to the piece, puts a face to the incident.

Hoffman, who would leave the newspaper a month later for the Morris County Daily Record in Parsippany, N.J., was able to dig up the pictures of the two girls from one of their friends.

They were blondes.

They were stunning.

They were hotties.

They looked like the girls next door.

Girls that any red-blooded, testosterone driven teen-aged male would love to nail. Hell, men of all ages love to nail them.

They will sell papers.

We ran the two pictures large on page 1 with an introduction deck:

An all-American family has a dirty secret…the daughters are charged with running an exotic narcotics ring. Cops say they're…DRUG QUEENPINS

Schwartz loved any headline or deck that had "dirty secret" in it.

And who is going to argue with that. We obviously exploited the "dirty little secret" angle in the story.

Todd Venezia rewrote Hoffman's and reporter Mark O'Reilly's story.

"EAST WINDSOR—Life inside the VanKirk home seemed like a Norman Rockwell dead.

"Mom vacuum and dusted and made dinner for dad, who spent his busy day working at a major aerospace company.

"Their daughters, too, seemed blessed. They were beautiful and smart and, until recently, spent many a Sunday morning innocently sitting in church.

"But behind the thin façade, the VanKirks were hiding a dark secret.

"The suburban family was mired in a pill-packed underworld of dope dealing and pot growing—peddling all manner of deadly exotic drugs to the teenage population of this sleepy, well-to-do town, cops said.

"This drug-selling free for all was allegedly led by 18-year-old Krystal, a fetching blonde whom cops described as the candy lady of Hightstown High School for her extensive inventory of rare narcotics, including ecstasy, LSD, magic mushrooms and marijuana.

"The troubled teen's sister, Gretchen, was implicated in the recent sting when cops found ecstasy and an empty bottle of the so-called 'date rape pill" in the 19-year-old's bedroom.

"The girls' 'pot head' parents, Robert and Linda, were also roped into their teen daughters' trouble when cops found a forest of marijuana growing inside the family's Cape Cod home, cops said."

The dirty, little secret wasn't one anymore.

'POTATOE' KID GROWS UP: Trenton was the center of Vice President Dan Quayle's biggest faux pas. In 1992, Quayle visited Trenton's Luis Rivera Munoz Elementary School to promote President Bush's "Weed and Seed" program, which aimed to give kids alternatives to drugs.

Paul Mickle, the paper's night cop reporter, urged the editors to cover the event. He said that Quayle is always vulnerable to a gaffe or "goofyisms."

Mickle wanted to be there just in case.

Quayle came through. During his visit, kids were stepping to the blackboard to spell words.

Twelve-year-old William Figueroa spelled "potato."

Quayle promptly added an "e" to the end of the word, insisting potato is spelled "potatoe." A world-class mistake.

Mickle was there and so were the television cameras.

Mickle raced back to the newsroom and barged into the news meeting.

"You won't believe this," he said, huffing and puffing.

Next thing, the Trentonian had a front page, "DAN QUAYLE CAN'T SPELL POTATO."

In 1997, I wanted to commemorate the five-year anniversary of the Quayle blunder with an update story Figueroa, who in 1992 had his 15 minutes of fame that included an appearance on the David Letterman show.

Figueroa was a father, a high school dropout and worked at a car dealership. Jon Blackwell provided us with a memorable anniversary line.

GRANNY IS A STALKER: Underneath this headline, we ran the following bullet points:

- Caught following grandson she once kidnapped

- Seized with loaded .38

- Tried for murder in '78

Now, who wouldn't read that story?

BURGLAR RAPES ELDERLY WOMAN: This was another simple, breaking news front page that was the best sale in the first week of March 1998. All of the stories were hard-hitting breaking news. No issues. No canned stories. A front page featured the best news of the day. It was like TV. Those front pages sell the best.

The deck with the read story said "Cops search for thug after attack on 75-year-old."

That means the thug is still trolling the streets in the market area. Fear will help boost the sales in the next couple of days.

Another tease featured the headline CRUSHED BY TRASH TRUCK with the deck, "45-year-old man killed in collision with 18-wheeler." We had a dramatic picture of the driver's seat of the accident. We could tell the man was smoking Marlboro's before his death. Very dramatic.

Another tease read "HIT & RUN TRAGEDY" with the deck "Pedestrian struck & killed on Route 33 in East Windsor. We ran a picture of a covered corpse on the road.

Three dramatic stories hit the front page of The Trentonian. No issues. No features. Just good old fashioned rock 'em, sock 'em breaking news.

All newspapers must strive for covers like this.

CYCLIST, 15, KILLED IN RIDE FOR CHARITY: A dramatic story about how a 15-year-old boy has struck and killed by a van. He died in his father's arms.

TRENTON ANTHRAX STRIKES AGAIN: This is my favorite front page in my second tour of duty as editor.

This anthrax was *our* anthrax. And like "Candy Boy" and "Shed Boy" we used "Trenton Anthrax."

So when the New York Post received an anthrax letter from Trenton, Andy Hussie came up with TRENTON ANTRAX STRIKES AGAIN headline.

THE LOSERS

SOUR NOTES: A front page depicting how the 1997 gubernatorial candidates are "Johnny One-Notes."

To make matters worse, every newspaper in the nation led with Tiger Woods' record-breaking victory at the Masters. We chose "Sour Notes." A horrible headline combined with bad news judgment will kill a newspaper.

GOV'S WEB OF VANITY: This story was about Gov. Whitman's Web site that featured nothing but "grip-n-grin" photos. We obviously didn't have much doing on.

DEMOCRATS' TOP GUNS: We actually tried to appeal to the average reader here. Political writer Sherry Sylvester ranked the 10 most powerful Democrats in New Jersey. On the cover, we ran a collage of the politicians with fighter planes in the background. We were desperately hoping the planes will salvage a mediocre story.

BIZARRE SLAYING IN YARDLEY: This was a crime story that had it all, but a good headline. Schwartz loved headlines with "BIZARRE, SHOCKING OR STRANGE NEW TWIST" in them. This story was about a corpse found in a trunk. I took this day off, and Schwartz knew I hated these headlines. We should have ran CORPSE FOUND IN TRUNK.

It fact, it turned out not to be a murder. The man died of natural causes. Then the caretaker of the home panicked and placed the body in a trunk.

LAUTENBERG: LORD OR LOSER: This is the worst front page during my tenure. Staffers will mock this for years. This paper came out just 48 hours after Mike Tyson's infamous ear-biting episode with Evander Holyfield. The back page HE"S NUTS would have been a much better lead.

Funny thing, most newspaper journalists would consider this a tremendous piece of journalism written by Sherry Sylvester.

That front page left a black mark on my career.

ALL THE GOV'S MEN: This profiled the inner circle of the Whitman administration. It was a snoozer for most readers.

MUDSLINGERS FOR HIRE: Another snoozer of a political story on Sunday.

PRIVATIZATION: IT WORKS: No it didn't.

FALL STREET: Wall Street is forced to close after the Dow dropped more than 500 points. The circulation soon followed after we printed this.

DOW-N WE GO: David Bonfield never figured it out. Average Trentonian readers don't give a fuck about Wall Street. This paper sold only 55,000, newspaper low—at the time.

THE SPOILER: A story about how a Libertarian candidate could thwart Gov. Whitman's chances of re-election. She won.

THE FAVORITE: This told our readers that billionaire businessman Steve Forbes was the front-runner for the GOP nomination in 2000. Oops. We were wrong. The readers knew it was bullshit.

WHAT A NIGHT!: Bob Jelenic wanted us to play the Red Sox coming to Trenton big: We had nearly 20 pages of coverage. It's big news when a Major League team visits your town, but this is Yankee country. The Red Sox aren't welcomed here. Not a good sale.

MERCER'S FINEST & PARTY'S OVER: Jelenic believed local sports sold newspapers; he was wrong in this instance. We led with the Steinert High School boys basketball team in the state finals, and we had the two non-holiday worst sales during the time period of January 1998 to July 1998 (when Bonfield arrived).

IT STINKS: It was a story about auto emissions. The sales matched the content of the front-page headline. Bonfield actually used this front page as part of an advertisement for the paper.

SAVE OUR KIDS: An education story about the floundering Trenton schools. Bonfield wanted to make education an issue. Issue stories in Trenton suck.

THE DIRT ON BILL: We led with an advance on the Starr Report over a story about a State Trooper accused of stealing $2,100 from a crash victim.

DEATH OF A LEGEND: We decided to lead with a death of a community leader instead of an outbreak of a brutal biker war in the heart of our readership. It marked the decline of the Trentonian.

Ironically, most newspaper editors today would have made the same decision. Maybe that's why the industry is dying.

◆ ◆ ◆

Fellow members of the newspaper fraternity often complain to me that nothing ever happens in their town.

"It seems everything happens in Trenton," they would say.

The occurrences aren't rare. It happens every day. It requires the newsroom personnel to dig deeper into the police press releases. Work the neighborhoods and scour every angle possible.

Don't mock any crime story.

Unfortunately, most newspapers just rewrite the police press release—as did The Trentonian did from October 1998 to September 2001.

Don't just mindlessly throw materials into the police blotter. Check it out. Question oddities.

Have solid news judgment and don't pass on any story that may make people say "holy shit."

In our market, we had people killed over a card game, a bottle of rum, a dollar and parking tickets. All of those stories ran in our rivals' briefs or police blotters. They didn't deem it newsworthy.

This is happening across the country. In Lebanon, Pa., we had men put on fire, pervert pastors, naked men running around communities and animal attacks.

Great stories—all in the small city of Lebanon, Pa.

If an editor complains, his market is boring, you have found yourself a bad editor.

Just go the extra mile to find an interesting element to a crime story.

The stories are out there.

Get them.

Get it done.

About the Author

Mike Raffaele has served as editor of *The Trentonian* (Trenton, N.J.), and the *Lebanon (Pa.) Daily News*. He also worked for the *Philadelphia Daily News*, *New York Post* and *Times Herald-Record* in Middletown, N.Y.

0-595-22792-9